Mexico Unexplained

The Magic, Mysteries and Miracles of Mexico

Robert Bitto

www.mexicounexplained.com

This book is dedicated to the people of Mexico.

Este libro está dedicado a la gente de México.

AUTHOR'S NOTE

In the early days of my arts-and-crafts imports business it seemed I was flying down to Latin American countries quite a bit. I made more frequent trips to Mexico because it was more familiar, closer and easier to get to. It must have been on a flight from Guadalajara to Phoenix in about 2002 when I had my "aha" moment for the whole Mexico Unexplained project. I was settling into my seat with my favorite Mexican magazine, *Muy Interesante*, and really got into an article on crop circles. I had some knowledge of the phenomenon, but the magazine showed photos I had never seen before and analysis by Mexican scientists I had never been exposed to. It was then when I realized that there was a lot of material out there about the paranormal and other "fringe" topics having to do with Mexico that never made it out of the Spanish language and into English. On that flight I also began thinking about the stories and bits of pieces of stories I had been exposed to over the course of doing business in Mexico that I had never seen or heard about while living in the United States. I cannot adequately describe the variety of places that I have gone to in order to find the goods to delight my customers who shopped my brick-and-mortar store and now frequent my online stores. I chuckled when I read a Yelp review from a customer that stated I was "the Indiana Jones of arts and crafts" because I would go to the obscure and remote places to find the really unique merchandise that no one else had.   It was only natural that interesting and unusual stories would come from interesting and unusual places, but what to do with all of these stories and bits of pieces of stories?

Long before I started my business back in 1999, I had already been predisposed to ancient "lost" civilizations, the paranormal and so-called "fringe" theories. As a child growing up in Albuquerque, New Mexico, one of the highlights of my week was going to garage sales with my mom on Saturday mornings. As an elementary school kid I wasn't interested in gently used Hot Wheels cars or finding that perfectly worn-in baseball glove; I was on a mission to find books, specifically, those dealing with archaeology, "ancient astronauts,"

Bigfoot and so on. Paperbacks were a quarter and hardbacks were fifty cents. I still have all of those books and have even used some of them here as reference material to write this book. It's really true what they say about your childhood passions. Even if you are not fully engaged in what interested you as a kid throughout most of your adulthood, it all eventually sneaks up on you and you realize what you were meant to do all along. Besides being a dealer in arts and crafts for nearly 20 years, Mexico Unexplained is part of what I was meant to do all along. There are so many wonderful things to investigate and share with the rest of the world. I am very grateful for having the time and energy to indulge in my passions. I have a feeling that this book will be one of many, and that makes me so incredibly happy.
Adelante.

Table of Contents

PART ONE: MYTHS AND LEGENDS

THE SEVEN CITIES OF GOLD

An African slave named Estevanico was brought before the Viceroy of New Spain and kneeled in supplication. The viceroy, Antonio de Mendoza, was the king's first official representative in this part of the New World. He had come to the newly conquered lands from the comfort of his station as a minor noble in Spain to seek his personal fortune and on this day in 1536 Mendoza felt as if he could become richer than the king of Spain himself. The kneeling slave before him recounted a tale of an odyssey lasting nearly nine years that went from the coast of Florida, through Texas and the present-day American Southwest and through most of northern Mexico. A key component of this tale was a rumor. The rumor told of seven cities in the north whose buildings were covered in gold and whose rulers were some of the wealthiest people on earth. As the second son of a wealthy Spanish count who had no right to inherit himself, Mendoza listened with wide eyes at the stories of what would henceforth be known as the Seven Cities of Gold. His course of action was clear: he would sponsor a massive expedition north to find these cities and to conquer them for the Spanish Crown, thus becoming wealthy in the process and making a name for himself in the New World.

The story of the Seven Cities of Gold begins in 1522 when the aforementioned slave Estevanico was sold in a Morocco slave market to a minor Spanish nobleman named Andres Dorantes de Carranza. Dorantes took him to the New World in 1526 as part of an expedition led by Pánfilo de Narváez that set out to colonize the west coast of Florida, with aims of solidifying Spain's claim on the peninsula. As soon as the Narváez expedition left the island Hispaniola in June of 1527, it was fraught with difficulty. The fleet encountered a very bad storm south of Cuba which caused them to lose 2 ships. The remaining tattered ships and demoralized the crew finally made it to the coast of Florida over 9 months later and many men deserted the expedition when they made landfall. After they landed near Tampa

Bay they immediately pressed into the northern interior of Florida. What had originally started out as a 600-man expedition was reduced to 300 at the time of the encounter with the powerful Apalachee Indians in late 1528. At this point Narváez had a plan to build 4 large rafts, sail them down a river and skirt the Gulf Coast until he reached the Spanish outpost in the newly formed province of Pánuco located in the modern Mexican states of Veracruz and Tamaulipas. Once the rafts made it to the open ocean, two of the four were lost in a storm, with the leader of the group, Pánfilo de Narváez, on one of the lost rafts. The remaining two rafts made landfall somewhere near Galveston Island in September of 1528. By then there were only 86 men left and their de facto commander was a man named Álvar Núñez Cabeza de Vaca who was the expedition's marshal and treasurer. The disastrous Narváez expedition did not end on Galveston Island. The remaining survivors were taken into captivity by local natives and stayed on the Gulf Coast until 1532 when the last 4 of the expedition who were still alive made their escape. Over the next 4 years the 4 men – Cabeza de Vaca, Dorantes, the slave Estevanico and a man named Maldonado – traveled among the native tribes of the American Southwest and northern Mexico as traders and faith healers. The entire time the band of 4 was accompanied by various people of the different tribes they encountered. The group made it to the Pacific coast of Mexico in 1536 and soon met up with Spanish soldiers at an outpost near modern-day Culiacán, Sinaloa. From there it was an easy journey back to Mexico City and the court of the viceroy.

At court, the 4 men recounted the tales of their long journey and among those tales, as previously mentioned, was the rumor of the Seven Cities of Gold, also known as the Seven Cities of Cíbola. In their years of traveling in the northern reaches of New Spain they had never visited the seven cities themselves but only heard talk of them. This was enough to energize Viceroy Mendoza who immediately set up an expedition to the north. He wanted to make Dorantes a commander, but Dorantes wanted to return to Spain. As a result, Dorantes sold his slave Estevanico to the viceroy while he returned to Spain along with Cabeza de Vaca. The remaining man from the Narváez expedition, Maldonado, decided to stay in Mexico, but did not want part of the new expedition. The viceroy decided to send a Franciscan priest,

Marcos de Niza up north to investigate this legend with a small contingent of men, among them the African Estevanico as a scout. Estevanico was the only one on the new expedition with any experience in the northern territories.

The de Niza expedition got underway in 1539. Because Estevanico had experience in the northern lands, he traveled ahead of the main expedition as a scout, along with several indigenous guides. Estevanico had heard of the exact location of the Seven Cities and sent word back to de Niza that he was headed in the direction of the cities. Upon reaching the Zuni village of Hawikuh, the first of the supposed seven cities, Estevanico was rumored to have been killed. Scholars have argued that Estevanico may have escaped with the help of the Zunis preferring to live among the Indians than return to Mexico City as a slave. One thing is certain: when rumors of Estevanico's death reached de Niza who was in visual range of Hawikuh, de Niza turned the small expedition around and did not want to suffer the same fate as the African.

In the summer of 1539 the de Niza expedition returned to Mexico City and the Franciscan related his story to Viceroy Mendoza. He claimed that he saw one of the seven cities from a distance and it glimmered in the sunlight, shiny from the gold and jewel-encrusted buildings. Later, scholars would claim that what de Niza saw was either reflections of minerals in the adobe bricks of the Zuni buildings, or corn drying on the rooftops of homes. De Niza told the viceroy that he only saw one city but was told by natives of the area that this one was the least wealthy of all of the seven cities and that there were richer kingdoms nearby, some with cities larger than Mexico City itself. Whether de Niza made this all up to please the viceroy is unknown.

After the priest's return, the time to put all the rumors to rest was at hand. In late 1539 Viceroy Mendoza asked the then-governor of the province of Nueva Galicia, Francisco Vázquez de Coronado, to lead a much larger expedition to find and subjugate the seven cities and to strip them of their gold and jewels. In February of 1540, Coronado soldiered north with 350 Spaniards, over 1,000 indigenous allies and the supporting wagons, firepower and livestock. On July 7, 1540 the first of Coronado's men reached Hawikuh and were greeted by hundreds of Zunis firing arrows at them. Coronado ordered an attack on the village and all fighting stopped in an hour's time. The starving and worn-down Spaniards were disappointed in not finding any gold or anything of great material value at Hawikuh or any of the other pueblo villages. Side expeditions went as far as the Colorado River, the Hopi mesas and the northern Rio Grande Valley. All side excursions found nothing of consequence and came up short. Distraught, Coronado headed east and spent the winter of 1540-1541 in the area of modern-day Albuquerque at a Tiwa pueblo village called Coohfor wondering what his next move will be.

While wintering in the Rio Grande valley, Coronado heard another rumor from an indigenous man nicknamed "The Turk" about a fabulously wealthy city to the east, across the Great Plains called Quivira. Coronado, who was thinking of what would happen to him if he had returned to Mexico City empty-handed, decided to take the expedition east in hopes of finding this other city. In April of 1541 Coronado set off for Quivira. It is unknown whether the Indian named "The Turk" told Coronado of this fabled city to get the Spanish out of New Mexico and lost in the Great Plains, or whether the story was based on what The Turk thought to be true. In any case, Coronado felt he had nothing to lose and spent months crossing the harrowing Great Plains often getting disoriented due to the lack of landmarks to help guide him. In July of 1541 the Coronado expedition arrived at the agriculturally prosperous villages of the Wichita in central Kansas which was a welcome change from the endless plains. Here, too, there was no gold or anything else of material value for the Spaniards to take back to Mexico City with them. No one even knows if these villages Coronado encountered were the fabled Quivira. Coronado, knew, though, that he could not press onward and needed to return to face the viceroy. In August of 1541, after spending 25 days in central Kansas, Coronado turned back and had the Indian informant, "The Turk," strangled to death.

About 1,000 years before the Europeans arrived, what has later been called the Mississippian people had large urban centers in modern-day Missouri, Illinois, Arkansas and Kentucky, with one notable city, Cahokia, having over 40,000 inhabitants at its height. With its pyramids and ceremonial sites, perhaps Cahokia is the Quivira of legend, the wealthy city to the east, but scholars debate this.

When Coronado returned, the viceroy put the Seven Cities of Gold legend to rest. There would be no more expeditions in spite of persistent rumors. The last attempt to find the fabulous cities of gold happened as late as 1601, when the Spanish governor of New Mexico Juan de Oñate sent a small expedition to the area of Kansas and came up with nothing. It took nearly 75 years for the Spaniards to give up on the fantasy of the Seven Cities of Gold.

LA LLORONA: MEXICO'S DITCH WITCH

She's one of the most powerful and enduring pieces of Mexican folklore. She haunts the canals, creek beds, rivers, arroyos and *acequias* of Mexico and the American Southwest. If you are a child growing up in any of these areas the story of La Llorona is more terrifying than any other ghost story and this story is older than anyone can remember.

So, what is the phenomenon called La Llorona?

The story always begins in a small village a long time ago and usually far away. The story is usually set in "Spanish times." There was a beautiful young girl named Maria who caught the attention of many men from all over the territory. She was married off to an older nobleman when she was just a teenager. Her husband was handsome and wealthy and was away from home a lot. Once while he was away Maria heard a story that her husband was going to leave her for a younger woman from a better family. In a fit of jealousy, Maria took her two kids down to the river to drown them. When she threw them in the rushing water, they cried out to her as they were drowning and she had second thoughts. She tried to reach out to save them, but it was too late. They were swept away by the current never to be seen again. It is said that to this day, Maria still roams the arroyos and riverbeds, as an old hag, looking for her children and crying out for them, and will snatch up children who are alone or careless. The story has minor variations depending on the storyteller, but the basic message is always the same. People have claimed to have actually seen the Llorona which further solidifies the legend.

Some people tie the story of La Llorona to the story of La Malinche, the interpreter and guide who accompanied Cortés to the Aztec capital of Tenochtitlán. She is remembered as both a traitor or as the mother of a new race of meztizos, as she bore children with Cortez. Some connect the Malinche with La Llorona because according to some accounts, the historical Malinche killed her kids when she found out that Cortez was betrothed to a noblewoman from Spain.

One could argue that the whole reason for the La Llorona story is to keep kids away from potentially dangerous flash-flood situations. As with many legends, the story of La Llorona is a cautionary tale to keep kids in line while parents are not there. In the United States, even the City of Albuquerque used the Llorona story in their "Ditches are deadly, stay away" campaign to warn children away from playing in the arroyos. This occurred in the 1980s and even came with signs featuring the "ditch witch" to scare off the kiddies. La Llorona to this day remains a powerful legend.

THE 8 OMENS OF MONTEZUMA AND THE END OF THE AZTEC EMPIRE

The Spanish encountered the Aztec Empire not as a bunch of lost cities in the jungle but as a living, breathing civilization. When the conquistadors were welcomed into the Aztec capital of Tenochtitlán by the Emperor Montezuma in 1519, the Aztecs had controlled most of central Mexico by outright subjugation and through various systems of tribute. The Aztec Empire's influence was felt as far away as Central America and the American Southwest. Many living under Aztec control wanted the empire out of their lives, and when the Spanish arrived they welcomed the Europeans who would help them overthrow the empire. Before the arrival of the Spanish the Aztecs knew their control over central Mexico was somewhat tenuous and were always aware of the possibility of internal strife causing a political and social collapse. In the days of Montezuma's reign, at the beginning of the 16th Century and starting some ten years before the arrival of Cortés and his men, Emperor Montezuma was witness to 8 omens which supposedly foretold the end of the empire and his own death. Because of these omens there was an underlying feeling that the Aztecs were doomed, and when the Spanish arrived those who remembered the omens saw their fates as sealed. Whether or not these omens actually occurred is a question for historians and folklorists alike. We first see them mentioned in The Florentine Codex, a massive 3-volume illustrated ethnographic compilation put together by the Spanish Franciscan friar Bernardino de Sahagún. The codex has over 2,000 illustrations in its 2,400 pages and in Book 12 of the Codex we find the 8 signs that supposedly predicted the doom to befall the Aztecs. Scholars are divided as to whether or not these omens were made up after the fact to justify the Spanish Conquest in the eyes of the conquered natives and to the rest of the world, or if they really happened. Myth or real, here are the 8 omens of Montezuma in the order they occurred.

The first omen reportedly occurred a full 10 years before the arrival of the Spaniards, which would put it happening around 1509. One day what has been described as a "fire plume" appeared in the sky. According to the legends, this is commonly referred to as "the sky omen". A great streak of light appeared in the night sky for almost a year, described as narrow at the tip and wide at its base, and so bright that it seemed like daybreak in the middle of the night. This "fire plume" was most likely a comet and is verified by an Aztec source called The Codex Telleriano–Remensis which chronicles natural disasters and cosmic events that happened in central Mexico from the 14th Century to the 16th Century. There is an illustration in this codex showing Emperor Montezuma with a comet overhead and the Aztec calendar date corresponds to the European year of 1509. So, this may be an omen that has an actual historical basis. In any event, the sky "fire plume" omen caused great distress among the people of ancient Mexico. According to one source, "As soon as it appeared, men cried out, slapping their mouths with the palms of their hands. Everybody was afraid, everybody wailed." Comets throughout history have been seen as bringers of good luck or bad luck, and in this case, the comet was seen as a bad omen.

The second omen had to do with the Aztec god Huitzilopochtli and it also involved a fire, but a more terrestrial kind. Huitzilopochtli was not only the god of war, of human sacrifice and of the sun, he was the patron and protector of the Aztec capital at Tenochtitlán and was seen as sort of a national god of the Aztecs. According to Aztec legends it was this god who was with them as a protector from Day One. From their wanderings in the desert through their conquest of most of Mexico, Huitzilopochtli was always there watching over and guiding the Aztec people. It was a national catastrophe when the temple dedicated to this god caught fire in the central ceremonial complex of the Aztec capital. First, the wooden pillars of the temple caught fire suddenly and then the fire spread to the rest of the structure. It seemed that whenever water was poured on the fire, the fire increased. When the fire was finally extinguished with most of Huitzilopochtli's temple gone, the Aztec priests and astrologers declared what the citizens of the great city had already felt: this was a very bad omen.

The third omen occurred at another sacred place, a building used as both a temple and a monastery called Tzommolco-calmecac, also located in the central part of the Aztec capital of Tenochtitlán . The temple-monastery complex was dedicated to the god Xiuhtecuhtli. This god was symbolized by the North Star and was seen as the lord of fire, patron and keeper of the Mexican volcanoes and god of the daytime and of heat. Xiuhtecuhtli was also the god of food during famine, warmth during cold and of life after death. He lived in an impenetrable enclosure made of turquoise located somewhere underneath the earth so that no harm would come to him. The temple at Tzommolco was not as strong as this turquoise enclosure. On a day of misty drizzle, a bolt of lightning came down and struck the temple and its thatched roof caught fire immediately. Witnesses claimed that there was no sound of thunder accompanying the lightning strike and that the storm was not a severe one. It seemed to occur for no reason, other than to be a "bad sign."

The fourth omen of Montezuma happened much like the first, overhead in the skies. Thousands of people throughout central Mexico looked to the heavens bewildered and afraid when they saw three large balls of fire emitting sparks streak across the sky from west to east. Some reported a terrible sound accompanying this spectacle, like a deep roar of a wild animal. Later it was determined that these were most likely meteors entering the earth's atmosphere and heading for somewhere in the Gulf of Mexico. Nevertheless, this heavenly phenomenon was interpreted by all who saw it as a bad sign.

The fifth omen had to do with the lifeblood and the highway of the Aztecs, the very lake on which their capital sat, Lake Texcoco. Fishing boats were out on the water normally one day in calm weather when suddenly the lake welled up. Swirling eddies tossed about the boats and caused a mini tidal wave to hit the settlements on the shore, including the capital city which was on the island in the middle of the lake. Many buildings flooded and some structures crumbled. While not too disastrous, this event had a more devastating psychological effect. No one could explain why the water in the lake would do that and it was another one to put on the list of the bad omens that were foretelling the great disaster that was to come. Modern day scientists and researchers theorize that seismic or underground volcanic activity could have been responsible for the strange behavior of Lake Texcoco that day.

The sixth omen concerns the sounds of a weeping woman which some say may be the basis of the legend of La Llorona. For several nights the citizens of the Aztec capital city had heard the cries of a woman. Some believed that it was the snake-skirted goddess Coatlicue, the mother deity of all the Aztecs, warning her children of the disasters yet to come. On some evenings the female voice was heard to be saying, "My children, it is already too late," and "My children, where can I take you?" The haunting voice filled all who heard it with a deep sense of dread and news of what was happening quickly spread from the capital city to all the corners of the Aztec Empire. What was behind this wailing woman's message of foreboding? What did it mean?

The seventh omen had to do with a strange bird found by fisherman on Lake Texcoco. When the men saw this unusual gray-colored bird, they captured it in their nets and brought it directly to the imperial palace to present it to Emperor Montezuma, who had an impressive private zoo and collected strange and interesting creatures. In his vast collection of animals, the Aztec emperor had never seen such an unusual bird. It appeared to be some sort of crane, but it had a flat, round, black reflective surface on its forehead, almost like a mirror. When he looked at the mirror-like fixture on the bird's head, Montezuma could see the sky and the constellations and then people came into view. He saw a great army with men riding gigantic deer and carrying weapons unknown to him. When Montezuma called the court priests and astrologers over to see the images in the mirror, the images vanished and the bird died.

The last omen occurred just weeks before the Spanish arrived at the Aztec capital. A two-headed man appeared in the streets of Tenochtitlán . Witnesses were alarmed at the sight and people knew that the emperor had a human section of his zoo where he housed people with various deformities, so the two-headed man was brought directly to Montezuma. According to the legend, when the emperor laid eyes on him, the two-headed man just disappeared. Another variation of this omen has a number of two-headed men showing up in the streets of the Aztec capital and all of them vanishing when brought to the imperial palace. As it was known that Montezuma took a keen interest in such people, this omen may have some basis in historical fact.

According to the legends, Montezuma did not dismiss the omens but meditated on them and took them very seriously. In spite of having the best astrological and priestly counsel in the Aztec Empire, the emperor had no idea of what the omens meant or what fate would befall him or his realm. As news of the omens spread throughout the empire, perhaps some people were psychologically prepared for what was to come. Given the brutality experienced by some of the peoples subjugated by the Aztecs, perhaps each omen represented hope instead of doom. Whether good or bad, all who had heard of these omens had a feeling that big changes were on the horizon and they were right.

THE LEGENDS OF THE SANTA PAULA CEMETERY

The date was May 24, 1882. A big storm was about to hit the city of Guadalajara, the capital and center of commerce of Mexico's state of Jalisco. A young couple was putting their son to bed, a boy who was not even 10 years old. His name was Ignacio Torres Altimirano. His parents and grandparents lovingly called the young boy "Nachito." As Nachito was afraid of the dark, he always had to sleep with two lit torches outside his bedroom window and slept with the windows open. On this night in May when the storm hit Guadalajara, the torches blew out. In the morning the next day Nachito's mother entered his room and could immediately tell something was very wrong as the room was extremely cold. She ran to her son's bed to find Nachito motionless and as cold as the room. It was later determined that Nachito had died of a heart attack that night because of his intense, almost pathological, fear of the dark. Rumors began to spread that the young boy's heart had exploded inside his chest and Nachito's horrible death was the result of a curse or was the work of demons. Nachito was quickly interred at the nearby cemetery – called by locals, El Panteón de Belén – and the strangeness that began with his death did not end quickly. The next morning, the boy's coffin was found disinterred and lying peacefully on the ground next to the hole that was Nachito's grave. The parents and the locals alike were alarmed and the cemetery caretaker reburied the boy's coffin. The next morning, the same thing happened, and it happened again for 9 consecutive days. Nachito's parents concluded that because the boy was so afraid of the dark, he did not want to be kept in the ground away from the light. The solution was to create a stone coffin to stand on 4 short pillars above the ground, so Nachito's tomb could always see sunlight. Since the time of Nachito's death many people visiting the cemetery have claimed to have either seen or heard a young boy matching Nachito's description, or have seen mysterious balloons floating evenly about 3 to 4 feet over the cemetery as if being carried by a small child. Strangely, Nachito's tomb draws the curious from all parts of Mexico, some of whom leave him a toy and ask him for a favor. On Children's Day – April 30th – and Christmas Day especially, the area surrounding Nachito's final resting place can become covered in small toys and plush animals. The caretakers of the cemetery always donate the offerings to local hospitals and the items end up in the hands of terminally ill children. From beyond the grave little Nachito continues to have an impact on the living world from his permanent home in this cemetery.

The Santa Paula Cemetery – also known locally as the Panteón de Belén – is located north of the Metropolitan Cathedral of Guadalajara in the heart of Mexico's third largest city. The cemetery was built in 1848, and was located next to the old civic hospital in a former orchard called San Miguel Belén from where it gets is locally-known name. The name Cementerio de Santa Paula, or in English, the Saint Paula Cemetery, comes from the fact that there is a chapel dedicated to Saint Paula on the cemetery grounds. The cemetery was designed by the famous Mexican architect, Manuel Gómez Ibarra, who, 30 years earlier, redesigned the spires of the Guadalajara cathedral that were destroyed in an earthquake. Santa Paula was initially divided into two sections: one for the wealthy citizens of Guadalajara and one for the not-so wealthy. The cemetery design is mostly neo-classical with great influence from French architecture, as that was the style in mid-19th Century Mexico. As the cemetery was open for almost 50 years there are other architectural influences present, including neo-Gothic and Baroque. In the center of the cemetery is a small chapel that is topped with a high, pointy roof that shows Egyptian influence. This building was supposed to serve as a mausoleum to house the "Illustrious Citizens of Guadalajara" but the "Illustrious" got their own separate monument closer to the cathedral. Santa Paula's largest building is the main mausoleum which contains 900 niches and is fringed by a colonnade of pink cantera-stone columns with classical ionic finishes. The main cemetery is full of tombstones and monuments reflecting an eclectic style. Large trees throughout provide ample shade. The Cemetery of Santa Paula draws many thousands of tourists annually who not only come to view the architectural beauty or to enjoy the adjacent museum, but come for the nighttime ghost tours and are fascinated by Santa Paula's many legends. As far as places in Mexico with alleged paranormal activity go, this cemetery may be the one location in the whole country with more ghostly shenanigans than any other, and a bulk of this activity is based on the many legends that emanate from here. Among these legends we find stories involving a pirate, a sick boy who lost his faith and a vampire. These are only a few.

The legend of the pirate goes something like this: A swashbuckling man once sailed the Pacific during his youth and attacked many ships laden with the riches of the Orient. As a middle-aged man, the pirate decided to settle and make a life for himself in Guadalajara. He had only one son, but the son did not know of his father's former life as a buccaneer on the high seas. The man had stashed somewhere in the Guadalajara area a massive treasure comprised mostly of gold and precious stones. A few months after hiding his pirate treasure, the man died and was buried in the Santa Paula Cemetery. According to the legend, if a devout person visits the pirate's grave at midnight and prays the rosary for the man's tormented soul, the ghost of the pirate will reveal the exact location of the treasure. As people have been trying this for years, it is said that the ghost has not yet found the proper devout person.

Another Santa Paula legend involving a child is connected to the former hospital next door. A young boy named Santiago was suffering from a terminal stomach ailment. In some stories it is an aggressive type of cancer. During one of her visits, Santiago's mother brought the boy one of his favorite saint statues from home, to help give her son comfort through his illness. While he was sleeping, the mother placed the small statue in the boy's hands. When Santiago awoke, he threw the statue up against the wall, cursing God for giving him such a terrible disease. He yelled to anyone who would hear his wish that God himself would contract the horrible illness that he was suffering from. Santiago ended his rant by saying smugly, "If God gets this disease, let's see who will cure *Him*." That night, the boy's pain was more intense than ever and he wandered outside the hospital and into the cemetery. The next morning the boy's body was found hanging from a tree, the hospital bed sheets used as a noose. Sometimes at night people claim to see the young Santiago hanging from a tree inside the Santa Paula Cemetery. The story is told to children so that they will not lose their faith in God.

One of the most interesting stories connected with this cemetery has to do with a vampire. In the mid-1800s, so the story goes, scores of small animals were found throughout Guadalajara dead and with all their blood gone. After months of this strange animal exsanguination, the same phenomenon started to happen to human infants. The alarmed citizenry then formed a vigilante group to hunt down the supposed vampire who was responsible for this. The mob rounded up a few suspects and singled out the palest and most vampiric-looking man of the group. As is customary according to the rules in vampire lore, they drove a stake through the man's heart to kill him. The group then took the man's body to Santa Paula, placing it under a large stone slab. The townsfolk rejoiced when the vampire attacks ceased, thus proving that they had killed the right man. A tree started to grow over the slab covering the vampire's grave and now the tree is quite large. It is said that if you break a branch off of this tree, it will spurt blood, and even the leaves of the tree will leave a strange red residue in your hands if you handle them for an extended period. The tree is now rather large with a huge root system that grabs the slab like the tentacles of an octopus. It is said that when the tree's root system eventually breaks the slab or causes a gap between the slab and the rest of the tomb, the vampire will escape and seek revenge on the modern citizens of a cosmopolitan Guadalajara.

While the dozens of legends abound and tourists flock to the Santa Paula Cemetery for the thrill of the nighttime ghost tours, the graveyard has attracted the attention of many serious paranormal researchers. Of special interest is Nachito, as many caretakers and passersby have had unexplained experiences connected with the boy or his grave. In 2015 an investigative ghost hunting team went to the Santa Paula Cemetery armed with cameras and an EVP recorder. EVP stands for "Electronic Voice Phenomenon" and the EVP recorder supposedly can record the sounds made by ghosts and other non-corporeal beings. In this instance, the EVP recorder was set up near Nachito's grave and along with the cameras was left running all night during one of the nights of the investigation. Later, the recording was dissected and analyzed and the researchers discovered what appeared to be the voice of a little boy once all ambient noises were taken away. The voice said, *"Oye, encontraste mi tumba, me das un chocolatito."* In English, this translates to, "Hey, you found my grave, now give me a little piece of chocolate." Whether or not this was little Nachito making demands from the Great Beyond or someone playing a trick may never be known. The one thing we know for certain is that the Santa Paula Cemetery will continue to generate the fascinating stuff of legends for many years to come.

LA TLANCHANA AND OTHER MEXICAN MERMAIDS

In August of 2014, early visitors to Pajapan Beach in the Mexican state of Veracruz stumbled upon a strange scene. Tangled among strands of seaweed was what appeared to be a dead humanoid. The top half looked like a human female with long hair and translucent skin. The bottom half was scaly and ended in a large flipper. Before authorities arrived to take away what people immediately identified as the remains of a real mermaid, the curious snapped photos of the creature and by the end of the day these pictures had been liked, shared and commented on by millions in every part of the internet's social media sphere. Days went by and speculation turned into certainty. Yes, this was exactly what it appeared to be, a mermaid. However it was not a flesh and bone creature, it was made of silicone. The silicone Veracruz mermaid turned out to be a prop from the movie, "Pirates of the Caribbean, On Stranger Tides," starring Johnny Depp and Orlando Bloom which had been filming nearby back in 2011. Some alleged that the mermaid prop was released as a promotional stunt for the next "Pirates of the Caribbean" installment, but of the many mermaid models that were made for this movie, the Veracruz mermaid was simply, "The one that got away."

Mexico has its history of mermaid legends, but never coming from the seacoasts. The heart of Mexican mermaid territory is the lake regions of the *altiplano*, the highland region of central Mexico spanning from Puebla all the way to Guadalajara, with special emphasis on the small lakes and other water sources found in the state of Mexico, just west of Mexico City. Stories about half-woman and half-aquatic-serpent creatures date back thousands of years. The Tlanchana is the most famous of these mermaid creatures and she hails specifically from the small lakes and rivers around the modern-day towns of Metepec, Toluca and Lerma. There is a sculpture of the Tlanchana in the central square of Metepec and she is the subject of an annual arts and culture fair in that town.

The freshwater mermaid stories are said to go back a few thousand years and were first noted among the Otomi people, an indigenous group which pre-dated the Aztec Empire in central Mexico.

Around 1000 AD the Otomis were the primary cultural force in the lake region of central Mexico and were comprised of several groups with somewhat related dialects and a similar belief system. At the time of the Aztec arrival, the primary Otomi city was called Xaltocan named after the island on which it was founded and named after the lake in which the island was located. Lake Xaltocan was really just the extreme northern branch of Lake Texcoco separated by the main lake by a narrow neck and marshes. In the Aztec language, Nahuatl, Xaltocan means "sandy ground of spiders." The Otomi band that lived in Xaltocan was called Xaltocameca and the Xaltocameca believed in the supremacy of the moon goddess, which was worshipped as their primary deity. One of the aspects or manifestations of the moon goddess was called Acapaxapo. In the Otomi dialect of Xaltocan, the word Acapaxapo loosely translates to "water weed mirror." The Acapaxapo appeared out of the lake and was seen as the goddess of intuition and of the future. The Xaltocamecas would call upon her to deliver messages and omens and to impart predictions. She was often "felt" and assumed a spirit form, but sometimes Acapaxapo took on a physical body. She was often described as having the upper body of a woman with long hair and pale skin. She had light eyes. She wore jewels covering her neck and breasts that were illuminated by moonlight. Her lower body was that of a black water serpent. The Acapaxapo could be seen or summoned at Lake Xaltocan, but could appear in any body of fresh water including streams and rivers and smaller lakes and ponds in the Otomi homeland.

When the Aztecs swept across the *altiplano* from the north and decided to settle the Lake Texcoco area around the 1300s, their growing empire absorbed the surrounding cultures, and like most empires, integrated those cultures into their own. The Aztecs respected the older gods and belief systems that existed in the region before they came. So, the Otomi aspect of the moon goddess called Acapaxapo became *"Altonan Chane,"* which is a combination of the words *atl*, meaning "water;" *tonan*, meaning "mother" and *chane* which means "magical being or spirit." By the time of the Spanish Conquest, Altonan Chane had turned into the word "Tlanchana."

The Tlanchana was somewhat syncretic in that it was based on the older Otomi Acapaxapo but was combined with a slightly different spiritual view of the world of the Aztecs. For one, the Tlanchana was no longer a 100% benevolent being. While her older version was seen as a helpful spirit and associated with the moon who was the female deity who created all life, the Aztec version could be good or evil and was mostly malicious. In this aspect she was closer to the European version of a mermaid, that of the temptress who causes the downfall of men and who acts of out jealousy or has selfish intentions. While the Otomi built altars to their half-female, half-snake water spirit, the Aztecs looked upon the Tlanchana with a certain degree of cautious respect. The Tlanchana was more of a whimsical dark sorceress, an enchantress, often lonely and often envious of humans. She only appeared at night and her appearance was almost always a bad omen. According to Aztec legends, she would also sing or cry for help to lure men to their dooms, much like the European mermaid. If she wished, the Tlanchana could also grow legs, so that she could more easily move about the human population, but this was rare. At the time of the Spanish Conquest, men who worked on the lakes, either catching fish or hunting waterfowl, would give offerings to the Tlanchana for safe boating or for a good bounty. A Spanish priest who, right after the Conquest, lived in the small indigenous community of Almoloya del Río on the shores of Lake Chicnahuapan just north of Toluca, wrote that the Tlanchana was a demon and the practice of her worship should be eradicated. The Spanish then did what the Aztecs had done before them: they took the previous belief system and modified it. The Tlanchana idea transformed once again and the post-Conquest female water spirit turned into a very European-looking mermaid, complete with a dolphin-like flipper, often blonde, and joyfully playing a guitar. The guitar-playing mermaid can be seen today throughout the crafts of central and southern Mexico, especially in and around Metepec. The Tlanchana can sometimes even be found as a character in hand-crafted nativity sets, attending the Baby Jesus along with the Three Wise Men, the angels and the shepherd boys.

Many legends and myths often find themselves based on reality. Some people believe that the Tlanchana could be a real creature or based on something real that is experienced at the lakes and other bodies of water, especially at night. There are several modern-day stories of Mexican lake mermaids and many people in central Mexico believe that the stories are indeed real. Here are three of them.

On the shores of the small lake called Laguna de Huamuxtitlan in the Mexican state of Guerrero there is a story of a Tlanchana emerging from the water and calling a young man from the lake. The *laguna* has been seen as a sacred and spiritual place for centuries. It was so important to the Aztecs that they built 14 small pyramids on its shores. There is a small intermittent spring coming out of a rock wall on the shores of the lake and the Aztecs once believed that the spring was a portal to another world. In this modern Mexican tale, the young man's impulse was to run away from the noise which grew increasingly louder as he ran. When he got back to his village he told the townsfolk of his experience and dozens of men returned to the lake with machetes and torches to get to the bottom of things, but found nothing.

Overlooking the town of Toluca, the capital of the Mexican state of Mexico, is a huge dormant volcano called Nevado de Toluca. The mountain is often snow-capped and in the more temperate seasons there is a small lake which forms in the center of the caldera. According to legend once there was a man who went to the mountain with his daughter to gather snow. The little girl was drawn to the lake and went to the water's edge to wash her face. While washing, she fell in the lake and was pulled by an unseen force to the depths of the icy waters. When the man realized that his little girl was missing he became frantic and called out to her. The voice of the girl replied and told the man that she had fallen into the lake and that she was safe but under a spell of the spirit of the lake and could not leave. She also told her father that she had been transformed into something half fish. Distraught and able to do nothing, the father left his daughter at the top of the mountain. Thus, the little girl became probably the only mermaid in the world to be living at 15,300 feet.

Yet another legend comes from a small lake near Puebla called Laguna de Aljojuca. There, the Tlanchana is an evil and jealous spirit who guards the lake. It is said that women who enter the lake or accidentally fall into the lake survive, but men never do. If you are a man and you wish to cross the lake in a boat, the Tlanchana will capsize your boat and will drown you. The same goes if you try to swim or go knee-deep around the edges. According to the locals, if a man ventures into the *laguna* a woman will appear with the tail of a snake and the blue-eyed face of an angel, and that is the last face you will see. This more severe tale of the Tlanchana could have been invented to make sure children stay away from the water, or to punish unruly children, much like the story of La Llorona. In the comments section of an online article about the legends from this lake there were many comments coming from local residents. Those who chimed in and wrote claimed that the Tlanchana living in that lake is 100% positively real and is a cryptid or unknown creature much like Bigfoot or the Loch Ness Monster. A young man in the same comments section noted that he participated in a triathlon which had its swimming portion in that lake and all the male triathletes miraculously survived. As commenting on the internet is prone to play out, the triathlete was ridiculed and called a liar or a troll by those who claimed to have actually seen or heard the evil mermaid in Lake Aljojuca. The whole story and reactions to it just illustrate the sheer power of belief in myths and legends, even in the age of the internet.

THE LOST MISSION OF SANTA ISABEL

The year was 1534. The scraggly band of what remained of the crew from the Spanish ship *Concepción* entered Mexico City asking to meet with Hernán Cortés, the famous conquistador who had become ennobled by the Spanish king and had been granted complete authority over New Spain. Cortés met with the men immediately. As soon as the conquistador entered the room, a member of the crew opened up a small cloth bag and poured out its contents: black pearls as big as grapes. The crew had many stories to tell, starting with the departure of the *Concepción* from the port of Manzanillo on November 30, 1533.

Cortés had dispatched the ship, under command of Diego de Becerra, to head up the Pacific coast of modern-day Mexico to look for a group of ships sent north the previous year. The previous year's expedition, which was declared lost, was looking for two rumored pieces of geography. One was the Strait of Anián, the western Pacific outlet of the Northwest Passage that would connect the Atlantic with the Pacific. The other was the fabled Island of California, a rich land ruled by black women first talked about in the 1510 book *Las sergas de Esplandián* – "The Adventures of Esplandián" – by Garci Rodriguez de Montalvo, a romance novelist popular in Spain. While plying the waters of the Gulf of California – also known as the Sea of Cortez – the pilot of the *Concepción*, Fortún Ximénez, took over the ship, killed the captain, and landed near present day La Paz, Baja California. Ximénez is credited as being the first European to ever land on the Baja Peninsula and he named it California because he was certain he had made it to the fabled island in the Montalvo book. His time there was short lived. While trying to subjugate the Indians, Ximénez was killed, and the remaining crew decided to return to Mexico City.

Perhaps partly influenced by the romance novels of Montalvo but more curious about the large black pearls before him, the powerful Cortés decided to lead an expedition to the fabled Island of California himself, and to do there what he knew how to do best: conquer the kingdom of the black queen, subjugate her people and extract the riches in the name of the Crown. Cortés' expedition never found the Amazon Queen Calafia's Kingdom of California, and besides starting a few pearl fisheries at the tip of the peninsula, the aging conquistador found little of commercial value in Baja. He named what he still thought was an island Santa Cruz. Interest in the region declined thereafter and it became a remote colonial backwater of the Spanish Empire.

The first post-Cortés attempt to colonize Baja was made almost 150 years later in 1683. The Spanish government sent a group of 200 men to settle an area near Cortés failed pearl fisheries at La Paz on the southern tip of the peninsula. The settlement could not resist the attacks of the natives and was abandoned. Europeans would return permanently near the end of the next decade. In October of 1697 Jesuit priest Juan María de Salvatierra established the Mission of Nuestra Señora de Loreto Conchó and the settlement became the administrative center of the territory known as Las Californias. In the beginning, because of the harsh desert climate and inhospitable terrain of most of the peninsula, the early years required help from across the Gulf of California. Over the course of the next 70 years the

Jesuits established 17 missions and several sub-missions called *visitas* up and down the Peninsula of Baja California which all eventually became self-sustaining. The central authority in Mexico City was very far away and for seven decades the Jesuits were left to their own devices, effectively ruling the region as a separate Jesuit political entity.

The rumors of wealth in this faraway place started up again during the time of the Jesuits. Because the Jesuits controlled nearly every aspect of life in Baja, no outsider was permitted to verify the extent of the Jesuits' wealth. Stories began to circulate about secret gold and silver mines that went back to pre-Hispanic times. Some say that even some of the gold from the Aztec Empire came from this region of Mexico. By the 1700s Russian and English fur traders and whalers had been harboring in the coves of Baja and trading with the missions. For basic foodstuffs such as beef, fresh vegetables and fruits, the Jesuits obtained items from the rich cargoes of the ships, including gold coin. In addition to regular commercial vessels, Baja's quiet waters and secluded bays saw pirate ships. The English and Dutch buccaneers traded pirate booty for the essentials, thus increasing the wealth of the Jesuits. People outside the region began questioning whether or not the main reason for the Jesuits being in Baja was not to save souls but to get rich.

A validation to the rumors happened sometime in the late 1750s. A ship whose cargo holds were full of gold, silver, precious stones, pearls and coral landed in the port of Cadiz, Spain. The cargo had come from the Jesuits of Baja and was delivered to a Venetian merchant. Word reached the royal court in Spain and later a representative of King Charles III, a man named José de Gálvez who was not a fan of the Jesuit Order, went to the missions of Baja to investigate. Coffers were empty and his conclusion was that the Jesuit fathers were living a meager existence in a very harsh land.

Gálvez didn't find any evidence of extreme wealth because a confidential communication was sent from Rome to the mission at Loreto to warn the fathers of the coming examination by royal authorities. The fathers did their best to hide what they could and destroyed certain records that would incriminate them. After the royal visit, the Jesuits also must have felt their days were numbered in New Spain. They prepared themselves accordingly.

Ferdinand Konščak was a young Jesuit who was born in a small town in Croatia which was then part of the Austro-Hungarian Empire. He was educated in a variety of places and was well-versed in many subjects. The bright young Father Ferdinand was assigned to Baja California in 1732. He became the head of Mission San Ignacio in 1748 and the chief inspector of all the missions in 1758. Konščak's many abilities included linguistics and cartography, and he conducted 3 expeditions to explore Baja in the years 1746, 1751 and 1753. He was able to communicate with all Indian groups on the peninsula and he was the first European to explore certain regions of Baja. Konščak proved once and for all that Baja California was not an island. His maps were so detailed and his knowledge of the region so complete that legends say that when word came from Rome of the impending expulsion of the Jesuits, he was in charge of the construction of the secret Mission of Santa Isabel in order to hide the order's massive accumulation of wealth.

Santa Isabel, it is said, arose in a desert box canyon, on the Gulf of California side of the San Pedro Martir Mountains about halfway down the peninsula. It was made on the site of a mission that the Jesuits started building a decade before but was abandoned. Construction continued in secret over a few years. 270 burros laden with gold, silver, pearls, jewels and other valuables supposedly arrived at the secret mission and the precious items were stored underground or in caves near Mission Santa Isabel. There is also a legend from across the Gulf in the State of Sonora called *"El Maldición de Isabel"*, or "Isabel's Curse," that tells of missionaries who gathered up their gold from the western part of Mexico and with the help of 50 Yaqui Indians had it loaded all onto ships that set sail for the eastern shores of Baja. When the ship landed, 2 priests supervised the unloading of the treasure and accompanied it as it was taken overland to its final destination, an adobe structure near a steep cliff on the side of a canyon. One of the supervising priests put a curse on the Indians, telling them that if the story got out and people came looking for the treasure, they would die. Could this legend from Sonora be talking about the same secret Jesuit mission called Santa Isabel?

The axe finally fell on February 2, 1768 when King Charles III of Spain issued the Order of Expulsion that closed down all Jesuit operations in the New World. The Jesuits were prepared and when the order came, they caused a landslide in the front of the small canyon in which the secret mission was located, thus sealing it off from the outside world. They planted cacti in the trail leading to the canyon and destroyed all documents relating to Santa Isabel. As most treasure stories go, the Jesuits vowed to return, but they never did, and generations passed with only vague stories and pieces of stories to go by.

Interest in the lost Mission of Santa Isabel was rekindled in the 20th Century. Many adventurers have scoured the inhospitable terrain of the Baja Peninsula with this bit of information or that bit of information, hunting for the Jesuit riches. A mapmaker named Venegas created a chart of Baja in 1757 which shows a few references to Santa Isabel that have kept treasure-hunters hopeful. On the Venegas map there is a "Santa Isabel Water Hole" that is located near the coast about one third down the peninsula. The "Santa Isabel Mountains" are located near modern-day San Felipe. Some legends connected with the lost mission mention certain geographical markers and so far all of the clues have led to wild goose chases. Gold mining operations are in full force in parts of Baja to this day, so it is not implausible that the Indians and the Jesuits both had very productive mines a few hundred years ago. We are left with an open-ended story. Of the many expeditions to find the Lost Mission of Santa Isabel, not one has come up with anything. Has the treasure already been extracted secretly? Did the Jesuit Order return to recover its massive wealth? Or is this just another gold-fever-inspiring tall tale to make foolish people wander in a desert?

THE VAMPIRE WITCHES OF CENTRAL MEXICO

In the early 1950s, an astute government worker assigned to the vital records department in the central Mexican state of Tlaxcala kept noticing a strange phrase on the line marked "cause of death" on many death certificates, especially among those of infants in the more rural areas of the state. The phrase was *"chupado por la bruja,"* or "sucked by the witch." This resulted in an investigation into the rural areas by the state authorities from the capital in Tlaxcala City, and eventually led to a law passed in 1954 by the state legislature requiring municipal presidents to report all causes of death marked *chupado por la bruja* to the medical authorities in the state capital for further investigation.   This strange cause of death was ascribed to the deaths of hundreds of infants over the years exhibiting the same symptoms and conditions: severe bruising and discoloration of the upper body with time of death usually at night. The state authorities had no idea exactly what they were dealing with and after the 1954 law was passed the rural town authorities stopped listing witchcraft as the cause of death on the formal certificates, perhaps to keep the meddling government out of their affairs or perhaps to cover up something larger.

Tlaxcala is a small state in central Mexico, just east of Mexico City, and was the site of a pre-Conquest kingdom called Tlaxcala which resisted incorporation into the Aztec Empire. The Kingdom of Tlaxcala was culturally similar to the Aztecs; its people spoke the Nahuatl language and had shared most of the same religious beliefs with their counterparts in the mighty empire that surrounded them. There was one pre-Hispanic legend, though, that was not shared with other peoples of the region and remained localized even to the modern day, the belief in the Tlahuelpuchi, a shape-shifting female vampire which feeds on the life of young infants. The Tlahuelpuchi phenomenon is so endemic to the rural areas of this small state that many people in Mexico have never even heard of it.

So, what exactly is a Tlahuelpuchi? The idea of the vampire women of this region dates back hundreds if not thousands of years. They are human women and part of families during the day, but at night they transform themselves in a variety of ways to go about their evil deeds. A tlahuelpuchi is born and not made. Once you are born a tlahuelpuchi, you remain that way and it has been said that it is a curse that neither god nor the devil can erase. One cannot distinguish a baby destined to become a tlahuelpuchi from a normal baby at birth or even through most of its childhood. A young woman usually becomes one of these vampire-witches around puberty and the realization is sudden. After the realization, a woman's soul is lost for 3 days after which time she becomes infused with special powers, which do not grow or diminish over time.   One cannot transfer this condition or any of its powers to another person, so, unlike the traditional European vampire, there is no transformation of the vampire's victim into another tlahuelpuchi. There is no recruitment, and there is no master-apprentice relationship. The woman just becomes a tlahuelpuchi out of simple bad luck. Family members may know of it, but they keep it quiet because there is nothing they can do about it. These vampire-women are not group oriented in the slightest and may even fight amongst themselves over territory. They act alone and are independent agents of evil, but sometimes they do the bidding of other more powerful evil entities, such as the devil. A tlahuulpuchi may interact with humans on behalf of the devil, as an intermediary to make deals or to issue warnings, but that is not her primary function.

Much like the European vampire, the tlahuelpuchi needs human blood to survive, but specifically the blood of infants, preferably those aged between 3 and 10 months, because that is the most invigorating to them. They have been known to attack older children and adults but this is rare and usually out of desperation because if they cannot kill a baby for its blood at least once a month, the tlahuelpuchi will die. The killings usually occur during the night and are more prevalent in the colder and wetter times of the year. The tlahuelpuchi does not need to lurk around looking for prey every night but only for a few days a month.

One of the main powers of these vampire-witches is their ability to shapeshift into a variety of different creatures to fit whatever situation they are in. 75% of the time they change themselves into a turkey, but other times they can turn into a wide variety of animals, all the way down to ticks and fleas. When the tlahuelpuchi transforms herself into an animal she gives off a luminescence or phosphorescence. This is one way to identify an animal which is really a tlahuelpuchi and makes it easier to track and kill it. The glowing nature of the creature is so inherent that part of the name tlahuelpuchi comes from the Aztec word *tlahuia* "to illuminate."

The whole transformation process is an interesting one. On the last Saturday of the month the tlahuelpuchi, while still in human form, gathers together ingredients to build a small fire on the floor of her kitchen. The ingredients, each with its own supernatural property include: capulin wood, copal, agave roots and dry zoapotl leaves. She begins to chant and walks over the fire 3 times in north-south and east-west directions. She sits on the fire and that's when the vampire-woman detaches her own legs so as to shed symbolically a part of her that makes her very human, that which enables her to walk upright. The legs are left in the tlaheulpuchi's human home while she is off stalking prey or causing havoc in her animal form.

If the tlaheulpuchi needs to travel far, she will transform herself into a crow or buzzard. If she is local, she may transform herself into a dog, cat or coyote. When she approaches the home of an intended victim, she usually shapeshifts into a turkey and then flies over the house in a cross pattern, before landing. If she cannot enter the house in turkey form, the tlahuelpuchi will turn herself into an insect or rodent to get into the house through a crack or small gap. Once inside, she becomes a turkey again and then hunts her prey. Before she kills the infant, she must immobilize the other humans in the home. She does this by emitting a glowing mist that serves as a sort of knock-out gas. When the tlahuelpuchi approaches her infant victim, she transforms back into a human to go about her nefarious deed. Very few people can resist the paralyzing mist but some humans who have limited supernatural powers of their own, shamans, for example, are immune to the mist and may fight off the tlahuelpuchi. In the rare cases when the tlahuelpuchi has been thwarted, she usually returns to the house, often in daylight, to cause some other mischief as a form of revenge. For example, the tlahuelpuchi may come back in the form of a coyote to eat the person's livestock or take the form of a donkey to mess up a newly planted field. She may also try to put a spell on a person to cause that person to do harm to himself or even kill himself. There have been reports of tlahuelpuchis causing people to walk off cliffs.

There are several ways to ward off a potential tlahuelpuchi visit to your home. In a possible blending of European and native beliefs, garlic is often cited as a good way to ward off these vampire-witches. The tlahuelpuchi is afraid of mirrors and metal. Sometimes parents of infants may put a small mirror in the baby's crib or may attach religious medals to the baby's clothes. One reference stated that a surefire way to ward off the tlahuelpuchi was to put an open scissors underneath the baby's crib. A combination of a sharp instrument and the metal is a certain repellant.

The small innocent victims of these vampire-witches are afforded special treatment in death. The body of the baby is cleansed, usually by a local folk healer who is well-versed in dealing with curses and the demonic. There is no music during the wake or the funeral procession. While the coffin is open for viewing a cross made of pine ashes is laid out on the floor under the table supporting the coffin.

Can a tlahuelpuchi be killed? The answer is "yes." It is a complicated "yes," though, and has a somewhat ritualistic component. In what may be another blending of European and native beliefs, the easiest way to kill one of these vampire-witches is to drive a wooden stake into her heart. The second "easy way" to kill a tlahuelpuchi is decapitation. Another way is to go to her human home, find her detached legs and throw them into a blazing fire. Traditionally, though, an ordinary person could kill one of these creatures after first immobilizing her. There are three ways to immobilize a tlahuelpuchi. One, you can take off your pants, turn one leg inside out and throw your pants at her. Two, you can take a white handkerchief, put a rock inside of it, tie up the corners and throw it at the creature. Third, you can take off your hat, put the hat upside down on the ground and drive a knife or machete through it. Once you have the tlahuelpuchi immobilized, you can kill it any way you want. Much like Europeans and even early American colonists have killed women accused as practicing witches, many women in Tlaxcala have been killed for being suspected tlahuelpuchis. The last known execution of a tlahuelpuchi occurred in 1973.

Can tlahuelpuchis be real? What explains the rash of infant deaths in rural Tlaxcala state, the supposed sightings, and the detailed descriptions of rituals and transformations? Why is this phenomenon relegated to only one part of a small state in Mexico? Is this just a community's way of explaining away high infant mortality in their area? For thousands of years, many people in Tlaxcala have asked these questions with no resolutions.

PART TWO: RELIGIOUS CURIOSITIES

THE VIRGIN OF GUADALUPE: MOTHER TO US ALL

She has many names: Queen of Mexico, Empress of the Americas, Protectoress of the Unborn, *La Virgen Morena* and Mother to us All. She is known formally as the Virgin of Guadalupe, a uniquely Mexican apparition of the Virgin Mary.

Just twelve years after the Spanish arrived in Mexico, on December 9, 1531, a recently baptized Indian man named Juan Diego was walking near Tepeyac Hill right outside Mexico City when he heard beautiful music that sounded like the singing of birds. A cloud appeared and then an image of the sun formed around what appeared to be a young woman dressed like an Aztec princess wearing a cloak full of stars. The woman spoke to Juan Diego in his own language, Nahuatl, and told him not to be afraid. She also requested that a chapel in her honor be built on the top of the hill. Juan Diego went down into Mexico City to tell the Bishop of Mexico, Juan de Zumárraga, of what he saw and heard, which would be later referred to as the First Apparition.

The Second Apparition occurred later that day when Juan Diego returned to the hill. He told Virgin that he had failed with the bishop but she told him to persist. The Virgin was emphatic that a temple devoted to her must be built on that hill and that he could not fail again. Juan Diego promised to try again and then retired to his home.

The next day Juan Diego returned to the bishop's residence to plead with him again to do as the Lady on the hill requested. Zumárraga told Juan Diego that he needed a sign from this mysterious woman, something that would prove to him that this was Mary, the mother of Jesus Christ. When Juan Diego left, the bishop had him followed but the people following him lost track of him when he crossed a ravine and returned to the bishop with no information about the hill or the mysterious woman. When Juan Diego returned to Tepeyac, the Virgin was waiting for him there. This is known as the Third Apparition. Juan Diego expressed his regret in not being able to convince the bishop for the second time and told the shimmering woman that the bishop requested some sort of sign to prove that what he was saying was true. The Virgin then told Juan Diego to return in the morning and she would provide him with what was needed.

Juan Diego did not return in the morning. His uncle, Juan Bernardino, was very sick and Juan Diego tended to him and even arranged for a doctor's visit. The visit to the lady on the hill was on his mind, but he couldn't tear himself away from his family responsibilities. The following morning, Juan Bernardino was not feeling better and asked Juan Diego to go into town and get a priest to make his last confession and to absolve him of all of his sins before he died. Juan Diego did as his uncle wished, but in order to go into town, he had to pass by the hill at Tepeyac. He was a little reluctant to do so because he missed his meeting time with the lady on the hill the previous morning. When Juan Diego skirted the hill the woman appeared again, behind the rays of the sun and in a cloudburst as she had done the other times. This encounter Is known as the Fourth Apparition. The Virgin consoled Juan Diego and told him that there was no need for him to get a priest or any more doctors because his uncle had already been healed. On to the matter of the sign to present to the bishop, the lady told Juan Diego to climb to the top of the hill and to gather the flowers at its crest. Juan Diego ascended Tepeyac Hill and was surprised to see vibrantly colored Castilian roses in full bloom at the top of the hill. This was strange because it was December and the frosts had already come and the area was desolate and devoid of flowers. Juan Diego gathered some of the beautiful dew-covered roses in his cactus-fiber cloak, known as a *tilma*, and went down to the heart of Mexico City to deliver this celestial sign to Bishop Zumárraga. When he got to the bishop's palace to request an audience, the people there knew him as "the pestering Indian," and refused to acknowledge him. When one of the guards saw that Juan Diego was carrying something bunched up in his cloak, he went towards him and saw the beautiful flowers. The guard reached in to take one, but couldn't. The rose he tried to grab looked more like an illustration than a real flower. Convinced that Juan Diego had something of importance, the guard granted him access to the bishop.

When Zumárraga asked Juan Diego what he had for him, the humble Indian unfurled his cloak and a variety of beautiful roses cascaded to the ground. The bishop and those present dropped to their knees, not just because of the flowers but because of the image that appeared on the front of Juan Diego's cloak: the image of Our Lady of Guadalupe, the one known to reverent Catholics to this day. The church authorities removed Juan Diego's cloak, and that same piece of cactus cloth, which should have lasted no more than 20 years, hangs now in the Basilica of the Virgin of Guadalupe which now stands on the top of that hill at Tepeyac where the apparitions appeared.

Soon after a small church was built on Tepeyac in 1532, masses of Indians converted to Christianity and word spread throughout New Spain of the miraculous apparitions, the curing of Juan Diego's uncle, and the beautiful roses that served as the sign from Heaven. Critics claim that the whole story was made up and that the image is a fake. The fact that the "lady on the hill" appeared in a place that been connected to a former Aztec goddess, that the woman supposedly spoke the Indian language and looked like a Native has some people wondering if this wasn't an elaborate trick to make the process of conquest easier. To the world's billion or so Catholics, there is no doubt that the Mother of God, the "mother of us all" appeared to a humble servant that day on a hill in Mexico.

THE MIRACLE OF MILAGROS

It's a warm and sunny day in San Juan de los Lagos. The town is home to one of Mexico's major religious shrines devoted to the Virgin who shares its name. Pilgrims come to the shrine asking for help or to fulfill promises made to the Virgin who dwells there. Many people come from miles around, often making the long journey on foot. To those from the countryside, the skinny twin spires of the basilica are taller and more impressive than anything they have ever seen in their lives. Outside the imposing building are dozens of vendors. Some sell food such as *elotes* and *paletas*. Others sell cheap plastic dollar store merchandise. The bulk of the vendors, though, sell religious wares and play an important role in the cycle of ritual at the shrine. Many items being sold are for the pilgrims to take home as mementoes – the keychains, the images of the Virgin of San Juan in ornate plastic frames – but other items are sold for use in the shrine, items of devotion for the visitors to buy and leave there. Chief among these items are the little metal charms called milagros.

How are milagros used? The traditional way to use Milagros goes back centuries. If a faithful person has something in his or her life that seems insurmountable, he or she may "make a deal" with a saint or a virgin and ask for help.   If the miracle is granted, the faithful person will follow through on his or her end of the bargain, and that may include a trip to a shrine to leave something there as a physical representation of thanks. People who have a little more money may commission a painting called an ex voto, which is usually on wood or tin, which illustrates the miracle that occurred or the favor granted. Those who can afford to part with only a few pesos will buy the metal charms that come in the shape of body parts, people, animals, plants and a wide array of inanimate objects. The milagros usually come in shapes specific to the miracle. For example, if someone wishes to give thanks for the healing of a broken arm, the devotee will purchase an arm milagro and leave it in the shrine. For a cow that recovered from illness, a cow milagro is used, and so on. The milagros are pretty literal and there are no special meanings for the individual pieces other than what is visually evident. Inside the shrine the milagros are usually left in a designated sacred space. This could either be a room off to the side, a wall or separate chapel. Often times these sacred spaces need to be "cleaned out" and the contents are usually sold by the parish to raise money for the poor. Many works of devotional art, and older or more interesting milagros end up in secondary craft markets because of this practice. Many of the little milagros for sale in the stalls outside the shrines have been used multiple times. People believe the multiple uses of these objects only give them more power.

This traditional use of votive offerings similar to milagros dates back thousands of years to Ancient Greece. When the Roman Empire took over the Greek world, the Romans adopted the practice of leaving small gifts of thanks for the gods made out of clay, wood or metal in a symbolic form appropriate to the miracle that occurred. The Roman practice of votive offerings continued after Christianity was adopted throughout the Roman World and continued to live on in Catholic Europe for many centuries after the fall of the Roman Empire (today they are still used in parts of Spain, Portugal, France, Italy and southern Germany). As Christianity spread to the New World, milagros found new territory on which to flourish and in modern-day Latin America they are used most widely in Mexico. Today, many of the traditional shapes – arms, legs, eyes – share religious store shelf space with more modern milagros such as airplanes, cars and even computers. There is a milagro for pretty much everything, except for money, because it's frowned upon to pray for increased wealth. To get around this, many people in Mexico use the corn milagro to symbolize abundance and prosperity and use the charm accordingly.

In an era of international trade and increased ethnic awareness in the States, milagros have become popular among Americans. Many people in the US use these small devotional objects as good luck charms much like a rabbit's foot or a four-leaf clover. Milagros adorn charm bracelets and other pieces of folk art jewelry. Milagros are often found nailed on to crosses or covering other wooden objects like saint statues or shoes, in a purely decorative fashion. Many people who have some degree of belief that the milagros may help them, carry them or have them in their homes in *anticipation* of a miracle or to hope for something and not to offer thanks. They are used to focus intention or even to draw on positive energies. To traditionalists, this may seem like the opposite of the milagros' intended use, but cultural elements always seem to adapt to new conditions when integrated into a new culture. Artists and jewelry makers have popped up on sites like etsy.com with creations like "healing charm necklaces" incorporating Mexican milagros. Creations are often elaborate and can sell for hundreds of dollars even though the cost of milagros at their manufacturing source in Mexico is often less than a nickel per piece. It's amazing how something so small can mean so much to people who value its use.

THE SANTA MUERTE: DEATH RESPECTED

She has many names including *La flaca* ("the skinny girl"), La *hermana blanca* or *la niña blanca* ("the white sister" or "white girl"), *La huesuda* ("the bony one"), *La madrina* ("the godmother") and *La niña bonita* ("the pretty girl"). Often times she is referred to in the superlative and is called *La Santisima Muerte*, or "The most holy death." With tens of millions of followers, the reach of the Santa Muerte extends across the border and the number of her believers has increased in the United States over the years. So who is this hideous-looking saint?

La Santa Muerte – or in English, Saint Death or Holy Death – is personified as a hooded and robed skeleton figure holding a scythe and a globe. She is often holding an old fashioned scale or balance and is sometimes accompanied by an owl. She also may hold an hourglass. Many of her depictions look like an illustration off of a heavy metal band t-shirt, as her imagery closely parallels that of the Grim Reaper. She is dressed in different colors for different occasions and serves multiple purposes. Her veneration is looked down upon by the Catholic Church and has been called "demonic" and "anti-Christian," yet she is followed by millions, mostly the marginalized, the dispossessed and those who have given up all hope.

Anthropologists have called this type of veneration a "cult of crisis" in that it comes out of times of dire social and economic hardship. As economic times have worsened in Mexico and while violence has intensified, people putting their faith in the skeleton saint has dramatically increased.

No one knows exactly where this saint came from, although the imagery suggests that part of this phenomenon came from the Grim Reaper of European legends. The context – Mexico – suggests that part of the phenomenon came from the Aztec goddess Mictecacehuatl, or "Lady Death," the ruler of the underworld. Its modern usage and increase in popularity in these times also stem from modern circumstances. The Santa Muerte phenomenon is what the anthropologists call a syncretic belief system, one that blends two or more beliefs to come up with something altogether new.

The reverence for the Santa Muerte began in the 1960s, but its rapid growth has occurred only in the beginnings of the 21st Century when her veneration became less secret and more overt. The main shrine to this folk saint only appeared in 2001 when a woman from the Tepito area of Mexico City named Enriqueta Romero decided to display publicly the 5-foot-tall statue of the Santa Muerte given to her by her son. Now, there are many similar shrines throughout Mexico, but this is the oldest and most attended. Every first of the month there is a special rosary said at the Romero shrine and people bring their statues and Santa Muerte articles to be blessed. As the Santa Muerte is not an officially recognized Catholic saint, she doesn't have a feast day on the Catholic calendar. Some people celebrate her day on the 15th of August, the 15th of September or November 1. The services performed at the Santa Muerte shrines, including masses and rosaries, are always done by lay people. Behind the Virgin of Guadalupe, the Santa Muerte is the second-most venerated religious icon in Mexico, surpassing St. Jude, the patron saint of the impossible, in the early 2000s.

So, what does the Santa Muerte do and who exactly are her followers? As previously mentioned, she appeals mostly to the marginalized and the dispossessed. People who feel like the Catholic Church has forsaken them have been drawn to this folk saint. This includes the incarcerated, homosexuals, prostitutes, petty criminals, drug dealers and the chronically poor. She has also become the patron of people who work at night and who need protection during the dark hours like taxi drivers, bar workers and so on. She functions much like a regular Catholic saint in that you petition to her for help or give her thanks for favors or miracles granted. As she has wide appeal, the Santa Muerte serves many functions. People pray to her for matters concerning love, health, money, legal issues, and pretty much anything else one can think of. In a major departure from the other Catholic saints, the Santa Muerte is often called upon to work a curse upon an enemy or to exact revenge. Her main function, though, is to provide a smooth transition from this life to the next. Most devotees pray for an "easy death" in the face of an increasingly violent and desperate world. Just as with the Grim Reaper of Europe and the Aztec death goddess Mictecacehuatl, one needs to respect death in order to ensure a pleasant death and this is done by praying, giving offerings, and by lighting candles.

Lighting candles is an important feature of the veneration of the Santa Muerte. Different color candles are lit depending on the different requests of the devotee. Before being lit, the candles must be rubbed all over the person's body to ensure that the energy and intentions of the devotee are transferred to the candle. Blue is used for healing of the sick and also for wisdom. Green is used for legal problems. Yellow or gold is used for money. White is for giving thanks. Red is for love. Multicolored is for everything. Black is for calming, but it is also used to counteract negative magic, for protection against enemies or to invoke a curse. Offerings left for the saint include cigarettes, alcohol, money and fruit, especially apples. Visitors to shrines often blow cigarette smoke in her face for luck.

The Catholic Church has a problem with the Santa Muerte for various reasons. On his last trip to Mexico, Pope Benedict XVI chastised followers of the Santa Muerte and claimed that the whole phenomenon was a cult. Some say that the Church is upset because it doesn't have control over the Santa Muerte movement or that it simply doesn't understand it. The Church however has said that praying to the Santa Muerte is counter to some of the basic teachings of Christianity. Christ came to the Earth to fulfill the promise of eternal life. Death equals sin and therefore praying to Death is in direct opposition to turning to God through Jesus Christ for salvation. Death is a phase of life, not a person, and to have a good death the church says one must have a good life and observe the sacraments. The staunchly religious completely reject the Santa Muerte as the tool of Satan used to trick people into a false devotion. Just in the past 15 years, the Santa Muerte has become one of the most controversial topics in Mexico.

On the American side of the border, unlike other elements of Mexican culture like Day of the Dead and the Virgin of Guadalupe, the Santa Muerte has not generated any sort of cross-cultural appeal with non-Latinos, although some non-devotees may see her image as "cool" or "edgy." Her devotion is mostly restricted to immigrant populations who are recently arrived from Mexico or Central America. The image of the Santa Muerte is popping up in all corners of ethnic

Mexican neighborhoods. In Mexican folk remedy stores called *botanicas,* found in most major US cities, a great deal of space is afforded to Santa Muerte merchandise with some of the biggest sellers being candles and love potions. The merchandise can range from the artful and the thoughtful to the tacky and bizarre.

People will always looking for some semblance of hope and stability in an often violent and chaotic world. Can one be criticized for one's faith, even if it is in a skeleton-faced lady who grants curses? Is this just another example of an object of intention having a desired psychological effect or are there larger forces at work here connecting people in a roundabout way to the Divine? As various crises deepen in Mexico, the devotion to this strange looking folk saint will only increase.

SANTO TORIBIO ROMO: MEXICAN MARTYR AND ANGEL TO MIGRANTS

Somewhere in the deserts of the American Southwest in the early 1980s, a young man from Zacatecas found himself stranded somewhere north of the US-Mexico border near Mexicali. His name was Jesús Buendía Gaytán. A few days of wandering, lost, exhausted from the heat and with no water, a truck approached Jesús when he thought all hope was lost. Out of the truck emerged a blue-eyed Mexican man in his 20s, who offered Jesús water and food and told him of a place to get work. When Jesús asked the stranger what he wanted for payment, the young, man told him that when he had enough money to return to Mexico, to look for him at a small church in the town of Santa Ana de Guadalupe in Jalisco where he served as a parish priest. Years later, Jesús did just that and was amazed to see the portrait of his desert savior hanging over the altar of town's church. The only problem here was that the Good Samaritan who had helped him had died some 50 years before that desert encounter. There are many other stories of a man who fits Toribio Romo's description helping migrants in the desert. Sometimes he appears to offer tangible things like water or money. Sometimes he appears to console the travelers or to encourage them to keep going. Sometimes he has even been known to encourage people to return to Mexico. Sometimes he appears fully frocked as a priest and sometimes wearing the simple clothes of a Mexican cowboy. In all cases, he is there to help with the journey.

No one knows how Toribio Romo became the de facto patron saint of border crossers or those undertaking perilous journeys. While the Catholic Church recognizes him as a saint, they do not recognize him as the patron saint of migrants, a role he has assumed seemingly spontaneously. The Vatican's official saint for migrants, ironically, is the first American citizen to become a saint, Mother Frances Cabrini, an Italian nun who helped Italian immigrants in the US in the late 19th Century. As Mexicans have a hard time identifying with Mother Cabrini, Santo Toribio has filled the void and has been growing in popularity as the patron saint of Mexican migrants ever since his canonization.

So who was Toribio Romo, the man? He was born in the year 1900 in the small farming town of Santa Ana de Guadalupe in Jalisco a little ways off the main road leading from Guadalajara to San Juan de los Lagos. He was from a very poor family, but early on young Toribio stood out from the other children for his intelligent and contemplative nature. From an early age he wanted to go to seminary and become a priest but his family hesitated in sending him away. In 1912 Romo entered the Auxiliary Seminary about 25 miles away in San Juan de los Lagos. Ten years later he became a priest, one of the youngest to be ordained in Mexico which required special permission from the Vatican.

Toribio Romo has been described as a deep thinker and scholar, constantly challenged by matters of faith and always examining his conscience. He was known for having a fine mind and gentle nature. He also loved writing. In an ironic twist, in 1920, while still in seminary, Toribio Romo published a play called "Let's Go North!" a comedy about the perils of crossing the border to find work in the United States and what would happen to a man after spending too much time on the other side of the border. Like many Catholic priests of the time, Romo discouraged people from leaving their small towns to seek work in the United States. His one-act play consists of two characters, the Americanized Mexican Don Rogaciano who returns to his town with money and fancy clothes, and an attitude of superiority and worldliness, and Sancho, a smart-mouthed local who never left Mexico. Don Rogaciano tries to impress the townsfolk with his command of English and his city ways, and denounces village priests as "money-grubbing retrograde obscurantists." In the end Sancho gets the best of Rogaciano by beating him with a cane, but Toribio Romo's main message of the play can be found in some of the final words of the Sancho character when he says this: "Take a good look at what becomes of the Mexican who goes north. He ends up a man without religion, without a country or home… a coward, a feminized man who is incapable of feeling shame for having abandoned his responsibilities to his family. Despite this, the roads are packed with Mexicans headed toward the United States in search of bitter bread. Everywhere you hear the rallying cry: 'Let's go north!'"

Toribio Romo's character was forged partly by the times in which he lived. As a young priest Father Romo found himself in the middle of the Cristero War also known as the Cristero Rebellion or La Cristiada, a brutal internal conflict that lasted between 1926 and 1929 and pitted rural Catholic lay people and clergymen against the forces of the anti-Catholic, anti-clerical central government in Mexico City headed by President Plutarco Calles. Calles sought to enforce the anti-clerical articles of the new Constitution of 1917 produced by the Mexican Revolution and enacted legislation to reduce the power of the Church. This so-called Calles Law was seen as a continuation of the long struggle of Church versus State that dated back to La Reforma of the mid-19th Century. Under this law restrictions were placed on the Catholic clergy and the power of the Church was further limited. Popular religious celebrations were suppressed in local communities along with the number of priests allowed to serve in Mexico as a whole. A few uprisings happened in 1926 and full-scale violence ensued by 1927, most notably in the countryside of the states of Zacatecas, Jalisco and Michoacán. By 1927 all priests were prohibited from celebrating the mass and ordered confined to their residences or to relocate to urban areas. Most clergy did not take part in violence, although many, like Father Toribio, defied the authorities and continued performing Catholic rites. The Church hierarchy in Mexico tacitly supported the grassroots rebellion and the authorities in Rome condemned the Mexican government. Curiously, two groups from the United States involved themselves in this war. The Knights of Columbus, a service arm of the Catholic Church, donated money to the Cristero movement. When the first donation of the Knights was announced, another group of Americans calling themselves knights – the Ku Klux Klan – offered President Calles $10,000 to fight against the Cristeros. By 1928, Dwight Whitney Morrow, the US Ambassador to Mexico at the time became involved and eventually helped broker a truce between government forces and the Cristeros. In the end, approximately a quarter million people died in the fighting, and Toribio Romo was among them. On Friday, February 24, 1928, just a year before the end of the war, soldiers broke into the bedroom of Father Romo who had been taking an afternoon nap. A few tense moments and two bullets later, the humble priest, who never took up arms or antagonized any uprising against the authorities, was dead. He was 27 years old.

Father Toribio Romo later became one of the 25 Mexican Martyrs of the Cristero War honored by the Catholic Church. He was later beatified and then canonized. Since his canonization in the year 2000 great interest has developed in the saint and thousands of people flock to the tiny town of Santa Ana de Guadalupe to visit his shrine and to see where he spent his youth. As with many shrines in Mexico, supporting businesses have grown up alongside the attraction to serve the multitudes of pilgrims who come each year. Where there were no restaurants in Santa Ana, there are now 3, along with an ice cream shop and many other stores to cater to tourists. It was said by one of the locals that Santo Toribio managed to accomplish in death what he couldn't in life: the local population is more permanent now. The people of Santa Ana are not forced to go to the United States looking for work, rather, they now live off the steady income that the tourist trade provides.

The official saint statue of Toribio Romo went on tour to various Mexican-American parishes in California in 2013. The statue includes a relic of the saint, a piece of Romo's ankle bone, encased in glass affixed to the torso of the statue. People flocked to Indio, Hawthorn, Reseda and other cities to catch a glimpse of the saint, to thank him or to ask for a miracle. The traveling saint proved more popular than the

Church could have imagined with thousands of pilgrims showing up at events.

Many migrants who cross the desert - alone, beaten by the sun, dehydrated, running from the authorities and threatened by rattlesnakes - come out of their experience with questions. Who comes to them in the middle of the wasteland when all hope is nearly lost? Is this angelic helper a mere hallucination or a product of wishful thinking, or is this mysterious blue-eyed man sent by the divine to help those unfortunate people along to live a life on earth that for him was cut short? The faithful know the answers to these questions.

EL NIÑO FIDENCIO: MIRACULOUS HEALER OR FAKE?

The date was February 8, 1928. The official presidential train carrying Plutarco Elías Calles, the first popularly elected president of Mexico, slowed down before making its final stop in the dusty desert town of Espinazo, Nuevo Leon. As the train slowed, the Mexican president was taken aback by the massive shantytown that had sprung up on the outskirts of a town of normally a hundred or so people. The shantytown had already gotten a nickname: *El Campo del Dolor*, or in English "The Camp of Pain." People living in these makeshift shelters, some constructed out of twigs gathered from the nearby desert, had come to this inhospitable place for the same reason as the regal-looking President Calles: they were hoping for a miracle, a cure, maybe just some hope, from a notorious local faith healer named El Niño Fidencio. Few people knew that the Mexican president was suffering from a mysterious skin condition, later described as a form of nodular leprosy, and while no doctors in Mexico City could seem to help Calles, the president decided to make an official visit to this small northern town to seek a miracle cure from this young man who had started to become so famous throughout Mexico and the rest of the world. The Niño Fidencio received the most powerful man in the country as he would have received any humble villager who had made the journey in hopes of a cure. After several faith healing sessions with Fidencio, including a 6-hour honey bath, President Calles' skin condition disappeared and he returned in robust health to his life back

in the nation's capital. The Niño Fidencio's fate as a miracle worker
was now sealed.

     Born on November 13, 1898 in Valle de las Cuevas near the town
of Iramuco, Guanajuato, José de Jesús Fidencio Constantino Síntora
would later grow up to be the most famous *curandero*, or folk healer,
in the history of Mexico. At the age of 8 young Fidencio had already
begun to show his knack for healing. When his mother broke her arm,
the young boy set the broken bone with sticks and the healing root of
a night-blooming cactus. When asked how he knew what to do,
Fidencio had no idea where he had learned that technique. Fidencio
was semi-literate as he left school at the age of 10 to work. In 1909, at
the age of 11, he and his older brother Joaquín left for the Yucatán to
work on a maguey plantation. He was away from home for about 2
years. When he returned to Iramuco, he promptly left the town for
the city of Morelia with the family of his friend, Enrique López de la
Fuente. Fidencio, now 13, found work in the home of a wealthy family
as a kitchen boy. Enrique, who was 2 years older than Fidencio, soon
left Morella to fight in the Mexican Revolution up north. Fidencio
would also leave to head up north, but not as a fighter. By 1915 it is
reported that he was living near his sister Antonia who was working
on a hacienda in Nuevo Leon. Also by 1915, after his duties in the
revolution ended, Fidencio's friend Enrique got a job on a sprawling
ranch just outside of the town of Espinazo owned by a wealthy
German named Teodoro von Wernich. When Fidencio heard of his
friend's arrival in the same area, he asked for work at the same ranch
and was immediately put to use in the kitchen and doing household
chores.   By that time, at the very end of his adolescence, is when
Fidencio got the nickname "El Niño" because his voice had not grown
deeper, he was not able to grow a beard and he had a soft-looking
face. The name, El Niño Fidencio, would stay with him until his death
and beyond.

     It was there at the von Wernich ranch where Fidencio honed his
healing abilities. In his spare time he would wander the desert and
commune with nature, observing animals and their interactions with
the plants. He also sat with and learned from a local indigenous
woman, a *curandera*, who taught him more about native plant
remedies. Fidencio was a quick study and soon became known locally

as a healer, practicing his type of folk medicine in his off hours. The owner of the ranch, Teodoro von Wernich, eventually made Fidencio the unofficial medical doctor of his various properties tending to both humans and animals. As Fidencio's regional notoriety grew, his childhood friend, Enrique, tried to control him, seeing Fidencio as a possible money-making machine. Fidencio was never into the money aspect of what he was doing, however, and saw his life on earth as a one of service to God through healing the sick. In his 20s Fidencio claimed to have had several supernatural visions and visitations, sometimes slipping into trancelike states to connect with an unseen spirit world. In one vision he was visited by a bearded man who showed him previously unknown secrets of desert plants that went beyond what the indigenous *curandera* had taught him. It was during this vision, sometime in 1927 that Fidencio believed he was given his mission on earth to heal and perform miracles, using a combination of plant-based remedies and his own techniques involving energies and a special connection to the Holy Spirit. To compound this, locals also believed that Fidencio was the fulfillment of a prophecy of a desert hermit who lived in the mid-1800s, a folk healer named Tatita Santo. Tatita Santo claimed that a great redeemer would arrive in Espinazo and would appear underneath the large pepper tree that grew in the center of town. The event that really propelled the Niño Fidencio's healing career happened in late 1927. His employer, Teodoro von Wernich, was suffering from a sore on his leg that would not heal. He had been to many doctors but no one could cure him. Fidencio made a paste out of desert plants, applied the paste to the affected area, bandaged the leg, and von Wernich's wound miraculously healed. Von Wernich was so impressed that he placed an ad in a major newspaper in Mexico City celebrating the healing powers of his young employee. It was after this ad ran in the capital city's newspaper when the floodgates opened and people began arriving at Espinazo by the thousands. The shantytown around Espinazo grew as multitudes of people – suffering from all kinds of afflictions, from tuberculosis to insanity – waited weeks or even months to be seen by the Niño Fidencio. The town soon got a post office and a telegraph station to accommodate the increase in population. Trains arrived with more frequency. During 1928 and 1929 reporters representing newspapers throughout Mexico came to Espinazo to write stories about this miracle worker. Through all of this, Fidencio maintained his humble demeanor, never demanding money or special treatment, and could be seen walking about the dusty streets of the town barefoot, dressed as a simple pilgrim. To many, Fidencio was a living, breathing saint.

Not all of the attention Fidencio received was positive. As he was not an officially ordained member of the clergy, the Catholic Church had a problem with Fidencio's healing ministry. The fact that tens of thousands of sick people were congregated in the shantytown on the outskirts of town drew concern from governmental health authorities. The possibility of contagion was very high. Indeed, many people did die in the Campo del Dolor as the wait was long for a cure or because they were already in the terminal stages of their ailments when they arrived at Espinazo. Several times Fidencio was called before the health authorities and each time he was allowed to continue with what he was doing with no changes made. A charge of practicing medicine without a license, for example, was dismissed because Fidencio never used packaged medicines, only local plants and his own faith-based techniques.

And what were some of these techniques? Although sometimes it appeared that the Niño Fidencio would go into a trance before curing someone, he always denied that he was part of the spiritist movement that was popular in the late 19th and early 20th Centuries that relied on trance mediumship to connect with the spirit world for healing. To many outsiders and non-believers his healing techniques were more theatrical and shocking than clinically serious. To make the mute talk, for example, sometimes he scared them with a chained-up mountain lion. He often performed healing sessions while swinging on a swing with his patient on his lap because he believed that when one was not connected to the earth, one was also not connected to earthly sin and the mundane. Fidencio performed many operations and he operated on people using no more than a shard of broken glass. All of his operations, from removing tumors to extracting bad teeth, were performed without anesthetic and were reported to be completely painless. Sometimes Fidencio would climb the large pepper tree in the middle of town and throw fruit into the crowd of the faithful that had gathered around him. Anyone who was hit with an apple or an orange was immediately pronounced blessed and was surely on his or her way to recovery. Fidencio once made a paralyzed girl walk by throwing candy at her to encourage her to get up to gather it (and it worked).   It is unknown what his actual success rate was, but the number of people who claimed to have been healed by the Niño Fidencio run into the tens of thousands. He continued to see hundreds of people per week up until his death on October 19, 1938 at the age of 40. It is said that he died of exhaustion and that his charge on earth to heal all the people he could was too much for him in the end.

The legacy of El Niño Fidencio lives on. On his deathbed he predicted that his spirit would live on in other mediums once his physical body passed away. Immediately after his death, people began to channel the spirit of the Niño Fidencio and claimed to heal by using his energies. The most famous among them was a woman named Cipriana Zapata, more commonly known as Panita, who founded the Independent Fidencista Movement which has spread throughout Mexico and to parts of the United States. These Fidencio-inspired mediums are called *materias* and there are several of them who operate in the town of Espinazo to this day, sometimes concurrently, which may seem baffling, as it is a mystery how the spirit of the Niño can occupy several mediums at once.   On and around every October 19, on the anniversary of Fidencio's death, the town of Espinazo has a fiesta which can draw up to 40,000 people. As there are very little accommodations in such a small town, many faithful people just camp out, and the outskirts of the town are reminiscent of the famous shantytown of the sick and hopeful that existed in the 1920s and 1930s. There are many focal points during the annual fiesta. There is the shrine devoted to Fidencio that contains his tomb and personal effects. Dedicated pilgrims crawl on their knees or get down on the floor and roll up to the main altar of the shrine. People often faint in the shrine's presence and slip into trances. It is believed that during the fainting spell the consciousness leaves the body so that the person can be taken over by the spirit of the Niño Fidencio. Outside the shrine is what is called the *charquito*, a pond of sulfurous mud imbued with special healing properties. Those looking for relief from an affliction or malady are dunked three times in the black pond.

Another place in the town of special reverence is the remains of the famous pepper tree found in the prophecy of the desert hermit and used by Fidencio as a place from which to conduct mass healings and blessings. The tree died many years ago from a frost, but the trunk and some of the branches remain, cordoned off by a fence. Another main focal point of the modern-day Fidencio pilgrimage is the Cerro de la Campana, a bell-shaped hill outside of town studded with white crosses and small shrines. Here, mediums channel the Niño Fidencio and other spirits and offer healings, blessings and advice. While the fiesta lasts for days, on the exact date of Fidencio's death, no mediums are allowed to channel Fidencio's spirit, as it is understood that on that day Fidencio's spirit is everywhere.

The Niño Fidencio story has lived on for many decades after the death of this mysterious folk saint, but some people remain unconvinced of this man's power to do anything. Debunkers and disbelievers claim that Fidencio's success rate was really not that large and that many people left Espinazo disappointed and uncured. The death rate in the shantytown was high and the town had to open up two new cemeteries to accommodate the deceased. Some point to a very political motivation for the popularity of this supposedly miraculous healer. Plutarco Calles, the president with the alleged skin condition who visited the Niño Fidencio was a declared atheist who enacted laws to break the power of the Catholic Church. Calles' anticlerical laws were responsible for the Cristero War, a bloody conflict from 1926 to 1929 that claimed over 100,000 lives and pitted government forces against pro-Catholic Church fighters. Was President Calles' visit to the Niño Fidencio, and the massive attention Fidencio received from the press at the time, part of a plan to create an independent spiritual movement to further dilute the power of the Catholic Church in Mexico? Was Calles really in need of a legitimate healing? We may never know. We do know that what happened in that dusty town in the early part of the 20th Century still reverberates to this day and has believers and non-believers completely mystified.

THE CHILD MARTYRS OF TLAXCALA

Pope Francis had made his decision. The date was March 23, 2017. This first Latin American pope, the outgoing and unconventional Jesuit *argentino* decided he would fast-track to sainthood three Mexican indigenous children who died in the early decades of the 1500s. The Christian names of the three who would be known to the world as the "Child Martyrs of Tlaxcala" were Cristobal, Antonio and Juan. The case for sainthood for these three began on January 7, 1982 when Pope John Paul II declared them to be "Servants of God." On his second visit to Mexico in May of 1990, Pope John Paul the Second furthered the cause of the Tlaxcalan martyred children and announced their beatification at the Basilica of the Virgin of Guadalupe in Mexico City. The Congregation for the Causes of Saints met in Vatican City on March 4, 2017 to approve the cause and to continue the children along the path to sainthood. This would require further investigation into their lives and whether or not they were associated with any miracles. The Congregation knew that Pope Francis had taken a special interest in the cause of sainthood for these children and its members were not surprised when the Holy Father bypassed the normal route taken for Catholic saints by issuing a papal decree stating that no customary confirmation of associated miracles would be required. The children had been killed in what is termed *in odium fidei* – in hatred of the faith – and had thus become the first people in the New World to die as martyrs for Christendom.   That, apparently, was enough to warrant such special consideration for sainthood.

To understand the Three Martyred Children of Tlaxcala it is important to examine the world in which they lived. Where did they come from? What was life like in the area known as Tlaxcala? What was it like to be an indigenous child in the early days of colonial New Spain?

At the time of the first Spanish contact in 1519, Tlaxcala was an independent state and had been for about 150 years. It consisted of the cities of Tepetícpac Texcallan – also called Tlaxcala - Ocotelulco and Tizatlán just east of the Valley of Mexico, and the city of Quiahuitzlan which was founded later within the boundaries of the

Valley of Mexico. The surrounding lands were fertile and supported a rather large population. The Tlaxcalan people were originally a conglomeration of 3 different ethnic groups speaking Nahuatl, Otomi and Pinome. Early on, the Nahua people dominated the state of Tlaxcala. This group of Tlaxcalans were closely related to the Aztecs whose empire nearly surrounded them. Tlaxcalan government was a very early example of a republic. As in the Aztec Empire there existed two classes in Tlaxcalan society, the *pilli*, or noble class, and the *macehualli*, or commoners. Whether *pilli* or *macehualli*, Tlaxcalans could be elected to the government council of *teteuctin*, which consisted of anywhere between 50 and 200 men who proved their loyalty through service to the state. The Tlaxcalan council of *teteuctin* made a variety of decisions based on popular vote and is one of the earliest examples of representative government in the Americas. A constant in pre-Hispanic Tlaxcalan society was perpetual war with the Aztecs. Historians theorize that the small state of Tlaxcala could have easily been gobbled up by the Aztecs who had one of the most powerful military forces in the world, but the Aztec Empire preferred the never-ending state of war with their smaller neighbor. One of the captains of Spanish conquistador Hernán Cortés named Andres de Tapia once asked Emperor Montezuma why his empire just didn't defeat this small state and be done with them. The Aztec emperor replied that wars with Tlaxcala provided excellent military training for his soldiers and ample captives for human sacrifices. Anthropologists refer to these series of conflicts between the Aztecs and Tlaxcalans as the "Flower Wars." Both sides would fight according to a set of conventions including predetermined spots for battles and limited use of weapons so that fighters would engage in more hand-to-hand combat. For whatever reasons these wars occurred, the Tlaxcalans were worn down by them and when the Spanish arrived in their territory asking for men to march to the Aztec capital of Tenochtitlán to take on the Aztec Empire, thousands of Tlaxcalans volunteered to join the fight. As history shows, with Tlaxcalan help, the Spanish were the ultimate victors.

Colonial life in Tlaxcala, the context in which we find the three martyred children, was slightly different from most of the rest of New Spain. As a reward for their help during the conquest of the Aztecs, the Spanish king granted the Tlaxcalans special privileges. The old republic of Tlaxcala remained somewhat intact for the next 300 years with the practice of limited self-government within the structure of the *teteuctin* which was allowed to continue. The Spanish had divided the Tlaxcalan homeland into 4 fiefdoms or, in Spanish, *señoríos* based loosely on the administrative regions that already existed in connection to the main cities of the old independent Tlaxcalan state and renamed the capital city of Tepetícpac Texcallan, Nuestra Señora de la Asunción.   The Tlaxcalans were given the highest status among all the indigenous people of New Spain. They had the right to carry guns and to ride horses. They could retain their noble titles and indigenous names. The first archbishopric established in colonial Mexico was in Tlaxcala, and the first archbishop, a 73-year old Dominican from Aragón named Julián Garcés, assumed the post in 1525 when the martyrs Cristobal, Antonio and Juan were still alive. In addition to his primary mission of evangelization, Archbishop Garcés fought for the rights of the indigenous, established welfare services, built a hospital, and started construction of the cathedral at Puebla. Much of what Julián Garcés wrote in his diaries and letters survives to this day. He wrote this general statement about the children found throughout his immediate ministry in Tlaxcala:

"The children of the Indians… learn more rapidly and with greater joy than the Spanish children the articles of faith in their order and the other prayers. They are not chattering or quarrelsome, nor stubborn, nor restless, nor arrogant, nor disapproving, nor ill-tempered, but agreeable, and very obedient to their teachers.
"They are very intelligent, so that they can be easily taught anything. When they are ordered to count, or read or write, paint, perform any type of manual or artisan work or art, they show great clarity, quickness and facility of mind in learning the basic principles.
"No one objects, no one mumbles, nor complains because all of the care and concern of the parents is to make sure that their sons make good progress in teachings of Christianity. They learn perfectly ecclesiastical song, as well as that of the organ and Gregorian chant and harmony to such a degree that foreign musicians are not needed."

It was the Spanish king himself who suggested that the clergy in New Spain start the evangelization process with the children of native noble houses first so that their conversion to Christianity would set an example for others living under Spanish rule who had not yet completely accepted the new faith. Great effort was made by early missionaries to focus on children with two primary objectives in mind: Conversion to Christianity and to transmit useful knowledge and skills. The first thing clerics did was to try to learn the local indigenous languages by day through playing with the children, then compiling dictionaries and grammars at night. There were some 20 major and 100 minor languages in New Spain at the time of the conquest and this was a formidable task for the friars and priests, but as a whole, this group was very well educated and very patient. One of the first of the clergy to arrive was a relative of the king of Spain himself, a Franciscan from Flanders named Pedro de Gante. De Gante came up with a catechism for the Indians done in the style of the old Aztec bark-paper pictographic books called codices.   He also set up the first school to educate indigenous children called San José de Belén in the former Aztec capital of Tenochtitlán. Many native noble families did not follow the Spanish king's orders and instead of sending their sons off to be educated by the Dominicans and Franciscans, they sent young household servant boys in their places. This had the unintended effect of evangelizing the lower classes along with the upper classes. The king of Spain's idea had the intended effect. As Archbishop Garcés said, the youngsters were quick learners and helpful, obedient students. More learned children often instructed other children. Bilingual children often worked closely with the clergy when it came to translation. And so, the children of New Spain adopted their new faith with zeal and spread it to their families. The evangelized became the evangelists. The newfound faith included with it the complete rejection of the old, and this caused strife within indigenous families. Here is where the story of the three Tlaxcalan martyrs begins.

Cristobal was born into a minor Tlaxcalan noble family in about 1514 or 1515, just a few years before the Spanish arrived in Mexico. When he was a young boy, Cristobal's father, Acxotécatl, reluctantly sent him away to a Franciscan school. Acxotécatl didn't concern himself too much with Cristobal's evangelism until the boy started to destroy idols to the old gods that were still being venerated in the family home. At that point, the boy's father told him to stop immediately, but Cristobal continued with his personal crusade to eliminate all physical representations of the Nahua belief systems in the house. Acxotécatl grew more infuriated with his son the more "Spanish" he became and had thoughts of killing him. These thoughts were further encouraged by his second wife, Xochipapalotzin, Cristobal's step mother. After one of Cristobal's idol-smashing tirades, sometime in the year 1527, Acxotécatl took his son by the hair, dragged him through the house and beat him terribly so as to cause many broken bones. In his fury, the father took his son outside and threw him on to a pile of burning wood. Cristobal did not die immediately but suffered with his wounds until the next day. From his deathbed, Cristobal's last words to Acxotécatl were, "Father, I forgive you." Acxotécatl hastily buried Cristobal's body in a room in their house but word quickly spread among the Tlaxcalans about what he had done. The Spanish authorities got involved and then sentenced Cristobal's father to death for his crime.

The martyring of the second and third Tlaxcalan children – Antonio and Juan - happened together two years later. Antonio was the grandson of a prominent Tlaxcalan noble named Xiochténacti, and as the eldest grandson, Antonio was set to inherit his titles and lands. Juan was a servant to Antonio and around the same age; both boys were born in 1516 or 1517. Both also converted to Christianity at the same time and were evangelists for their new faith. They found themselves in a similar situation as Cristobal: The two were destroying indigenous idols in the name of Christianity and they were caught by disapproving adults. An angry mob formed, surrounded the two and clubbed the boys to death. This was 1529. Their bodies were hurled off a high cliff but were later recovered by a Domincan friar known to history only as Bernardino.

In a gathering of cardinals at Vatican City on April 20, 2017, it was announced that Cristobal, Antonio and Juan would be canonized in Rome on October 15, 2017. It was decided by the Pope that they would be the patron saints of Mexican childhood, serving as an example of piety for generations to come.

THE RISE IN MEXICAN EXORCISMS

Soothing mariachi music filled the air as crowds gathered outside the Colegio Miraflores in the city of León in the Mexican state of Guanajuato. It was right after sunset on Sunday, March 25th 2012. The people and music coaxed out of his guest quarters Pope Benedict XVI who was wrapping up his first visit to Mexico. The 84-year-old German-born pontiff made his appearance to the delight of a cheering crowd on his last night visiting the nation of nearly 100,000,000 Roman Catholics. A teenage girl presented His Holiness with a highly ornate sombrero which he wore as he was given a microphone. Benedict stated that in all of his official trips he had never been received with such enthusiasm and love as he had experienced there and, "Now I can say that Mexico will always remain in my heart." The next day the pope was on a plane bound for Havana, Cuba, and while his visit to Mexico was full of much joy and celebration, the pontiff had a lot on his mind with regard to the second largest Catholic country in the world. He had gone to Mexico under troubling circumstances. Chief among the pope's concerns was the rise in the cult of the Holy Death – or in Spanish, "Santa Muerte" – which seemed to be experiencing exponential growth in Mexico along with other religious practices that stray away from the Catholic Church orthodoxy. The stories that Pope Benedict had heard about the increasing power of the Holy Death devotion along with the rise in satanic ritual abuse reported throughout Mexico were some of the real reasons why he visited that country. He was concerned that the Catholic Church was losing its grip on the Mexican people and he wanted to know why. In the wake of the Pope's visit, the Church would come up with a strategy to solidify its base and try to expel the evil forces that it saw as a threat to its hegemony. The following year, in April of 2013, the President of the Pontifical Council for Culture of the Vatican, Italian Cardinal Gianfranco Ravasi, visited Mexico with the intent in conferring the first "Atrium of the Gentiles" outside of Europe. This meeting was intended to bring together believers and non-believers to talk about the spiritual destiny of Mexico. While open to dialogue to try to figure out what was going on, the cardinal reaffirmed the Catholic Church's position on the more "demonic" styles of worship going on in Mexico, calling the increasingly popular adoration of the Santa Muerte, "A dark, hellish cult of denial" and that, "the greatness of culture and of the true religion is just to celebrate life, and this is exactly the opposite."

Indeed, it is very difficult to travel around Mexico these days without seeing the image of the Santa Muerte in various places, from store windows to bus stations. It's estimated that some 10 million people worship the bejeweled, dressed up grim-reaper-looking skeleton known as the Santa Muerte and the phenomenon has nothing to do with the Mexican holiday Day of the Dead, or Día de los Muertos, which is a celebration of those who have passed and is a harmonious blend of Catholicism and ancient pre-Christian traditions. The Santa Muerte "death cult" is only part of what the Catholic Church sees as a larger problem, however, and the increase in the following of this folk saint and others appears to be a symptom of an underlying moral decay in Mexico and an increase in power by unseen, darker forces which have attempted to gain dominion over all of humanity since the beginning of time. To counter this view, others say that threats of drug violence, dire economic conditions and a breakup of the traditional social framework have led to tens of millions of people in Mexico living lives in despair. The seemingly empowering death cults give these marginalized Mexicans hope and fill the needs not being met by either the family, the Catholic Church or the Mexican government.

To combat what it believes to be the growing forces of evil in Mexico, the Catholic Church has either deployed or created a vast number of exorcists to deal with what it sees as an abrupt increase in literal demonic possession throughout the country. In fact there are more exorcists currently in Mexico than in any other country on earth. So, what exactly is an exorcism? According to the Catholic Encyclopedia found at New Advent dot org:

"Exorcism is (1) the act of driving out, or warding off, demons, or evil spirits, from persons, places, or things, which are believed to be possessed or infested by them, or are liable to become victims or instruments of their malice; (2) the means employed for this purpose, especially the solemn and authoritative adjuration of the demon, in the name of God, or any of the higher power in which he is subject."

The Catholic Church regards demonic possession as incredibly rare and before the 1970s when popular media such as movies and television brought demonic possession and exorcism into the mainstream, there were very few members of the clergy who were trained in conducting exorcisms. In 1999, the Vatican issued revised rules for conducting exorcisms as it noticed the increase in interest in the ritual. First, a victim must be examined thoroughly by doctors and psychologists to rule out any mental or physical illnesses or evidence of substance abuse. From paragraph 1673 of the Catechism of the Catholic Church:

"Exorcism is directed at the expulsion of demons or to the liberation from demonic possession through the spiritual authority which Jesus entrusted to his Church. Illness, especially psychological illness, is a very different matter; treating this is the concern of medical science. Therefore, before an exorcism is performed, it is important to ascertain that one is dealing with the presence of the Evil One, and not an illness."

The case is escalated to ecclesiastical authorities if medical or basic spiritual help is not effective. Individuals who are demonically possessed may exhibit the following signs:

1. The loss of personality; for example, flying into tantrums or fits of rage
2. A change in the person's voice
3. Unnatural body postures or contorted facial features
4. Unnatural physical strength
5. Levitation of the person or nearby objects
6. Intense aversion or hatred toward religious objects
7. Coldness in the room
8. Understanding or speaking another language previously unknown to the possessed
9. Biting or cutting of the skin
10. Prediction of future events and knowledge of things unseen
11. Intense bodily pain or other physical ailments not explicable by science
12. The hearing of voices or receipt of other supernatural messages

This is not an exhaustive list.

The exorcist approaches the demon-possessed with a sense of humility. The Church believes that Christ acts through the exorcist to cast out the demon. Standard prayers are used along with oils, incense and candles. The approach an exorcist takes is usually situational. Often, the victim of the possession is physically restrained so as not to cause harm to himself or herself, or to those in his or her surroundings. It may take many attempts for the exorcist to be successful, and sessions may stretch over months or years. Many people in Mexico believe that those who are possessed have a "spiritual inheritance" that gets passed down for 4 generations if the demons are not taken care of and expelled. This is not formal Church dogma, however.

On May 20, 2015 the Archbishop Emeritus of Guadalajara, Cardinal Juan Sandoval Íñiguez, along with the Archbishop Jesús Carlos Cabrero of San Luis Potosí and world-renown Spanish demonologist and exorcist Father José Antonio Fortea, gathered together with several Mexican exorcists from around the country to perform a mass exorcism in the Metropolitan Cathedral of San Luís Potosí. The mass exorcism did not involve a large group of possessed individuals, rather, it was a mass casting out of demons for the entire country of Mexico. Called a Magno Exorcismo the complex ritual was not publicized beforehand so as not to draw attention to the rite. The participants gathered in the cathedral behind locked doors, and began chanting and praying according to a proscribed ritual, including calling on the four directions – north, south, east and west – in the names of specific saints. An important part of the mass exorcism was the call to close The Door of the Abyss. One of the participants hit the floor of the cathedral with a large hammer and called upon the Virgin Mary to close the gates of hell to keep the Devil from escaping. Did the mass exorcism work? Is Mexico now free of demons? As with exorcisms on an individual, the Spanish demonologist who participated in the Magno Exorcismo told reporters that the ritual must be performed many times over the course of several years to make sure it is effective. If the Santa Muerte cult is any indication, the mass exorcism had very little effect, as the numbers of devotees in this folk saint, along with the reported number of exorcisms, have only increased since the event at the San Luís Potosí cathedral.

If the Santa Muerte devotion and satanic rituals are just symptoms of the increase of demonic influences in Mexico, then what do people believe is the cause for the increase in demonic activity in Mexico that would warrant these exorcisms? One of the most seasoned exorcists in Mexico, 80-year-old Father Francisco Lopez Sedano of the Parish of the Holy Cross in Mexico City, who has performed over 6,000 exorcisms in his 40-year career has some explanations. Father Lopez is the National Coordinator Emeritus of Exorcism for the Archdiocese of Mexico and has devoted his life to this subject. He has repeatedly stated that the Devil enters a person's body because the person has allowed him access. In other words, the victim has in some way let his or her spiritual guard down to permit the possession. The Devil's whole objective is to create a barrier between God and the individual human. Many people in Mexico believe that people are more easily possessed nowadays because there are just more demonic entities existing among humans on the earthly plane. The faithful cite the 2007 law that legalized abortion in Mexico City that intensified demonic activity throughout the country. With every baby aborted, so the folk wisdom goes, a new demon gets released upon the earth. The demons look for people to torment and to inhabit, and the same folk wisdom states that there are several ways which a demon can access a possible victim of possession. Many occult practices or even simple good luck rituals are said to make a person vulnerable. A séance, a use of a Ouija Board or other "spirit board" to call on ghosts or spirits, even if used in good fun, may be exposing the participants to potential harm. The use of tarot cards has also been cited as possibly dangerous. There are many games that have popped up in Mexico as a result of the internet that have been causing concern among church officials because they are attractive to children, notable among them are the Charlie Charlie Challenge and the Bellena Azul or Blue Whale game. Children are more susceptible to these bad influences nowadays than in any other time in Mexican history, a church official stated. This is because of the breakdown of the traditional family and the fact that many children now come from a home where the mother is working and thus many children are left with a lot of unsupervised time. Charlie Charlie is a game of divination in which two pencils are put on a piece of paper in the shape of a cross and in each corresponding quadrant created by the pencils are the words "sí" or "no". A ghost called "Charlie" is invoked and participants ask the spirit yes or no questions, watching the pencils for movement. The Blue Whale game consists of a few dozen tasks of increasing complexity agreed to by participants beforehand with the last task usually involving suicide or murder. The very act of engaging in these games, demonologist believe, are incredibly dangerous, and participation in them may even open up portals to Hell. Other things that increase a person's vulnerability to evil forces according to Mexican believers include things as seemingly innocent as the practice of yoga and even the seemingly magic spell that Disney movies have over children. The extremely faithful would caution us to put away the yoga mat and turn off "Beauty and the Beast." In a country so haunted by evil and so overrun by demons, apparently one can't be careful enough.

PART THREE: OTHERWORLDLY PHENOMENA

UFOS OVER MEXICO

The first Mexican documentary on UFOs was not a television show or a movie, but a 33 1/3 12-inch vinyl record titled *"El Enigma de los OVNIs,"* or in English, "The UFO Enigma." It was recorded in the late 1960s by two Mexican UFO researchers, Jorge Raiger and Ramiro Garza. The recording was re-released in 2015 and according to many Latin American UFO buffs and serious investigators alike, the breakthrough audio documentary has stood the test of time.

Theories of ancient astronauts and the extraterrestrial origins of ancient Mexican civilizations began to pop up in the mid- to late-1960s, around the same time as the "Enigma" recording. Books like *Chariots of the Gods?* and *The Outer Space Connection* were published decades ago and propose that Mexico has been visited by off-world intelligences for millennia. The first reported Mexican UFO sighting in modern times came from the Zacatecas Observatory in August of 1883. Astronomer José Bonilla was studying the sun and he recorded and photographed over 300 dark and unknown objects crossing the sun's surface. Other than hot air balloons, there was no form of aircraft around at the time to explain away Doctor Bonilla's observation. The movements of these objects suggested something organic, but as it has not yet been determined what these objects actually were, they remain to this day unidentified flying objects, or UFOs.

The modern UFO phenomenon in Mexico seemed to run a parallel course to its counterpart in the United States. UFOs in the shape of flying saucers, called *platillos volantes* in Spanish, began to appear in Mexican skies in the 1940s and 1950s, much as they did in the skies over the United States. Before the flying saucer epoch, Mexico had very few reports of strange objects in the sky. There were a few stories of mysterious cigar-shaped craft, but they were often dismissed as zeppelin prototypes coming from the US or Germany. The metallic, disc-shaped *platillos* seemed to dominate the Mexican skies for a few decades. It has only been in the last 30 years of the

20th Century that UFOs have taken on other appearances. Everything from blinking lights, to geometrical shapes like cubes and orbs, to squid-like objects, to dark triangles. These mysterious objects have been solo or have been classified as "fleets" when a handful or more have been found flying together in some sort of formation. There have been several "mothership" sightings, as well. A notable one occurred on October 11, 2014 over Mexico City during which observers saw and filmed a massive object in the sky and several smaller ships around it. In May of the previous year, a cigar-shaped mothership also appeared over Mexico's capital and it seemed to "drop" smaller orbs into the sky before taking off.

It is important to note how many sightings have occurred over Mexico City and why. As one of the most populated urban centers on earth with almost 25 million people living there, there are many eyes available to look toward the sky. A "mass sighting" over Mexico's capital city may involve tens of thousands of people, if not more. With more and more people living in the Valley of Mexico and with more and more people equipped with cameras ready-made on their cell phones, it seems like the sightings are ever more frequent. It may be that unknown objects in the skies above Mexico City have always been there and have always been this frequent, but now there are just more eyes and more recording devices. The biggest mass sighting in Mexico City came almost 2 decades before most people had cell phones, in 1991. On July 11, 1991 Mexico City was preparing for what was called "The Eclipse of the Millennium." A total eclipse of the sun lasting 6 minutes and 45 seconds was to occur over the Mexican capital city in early afternoon. With people looking to the sky numbering into the millions, according to some estimates, hundreds of thousands of people noticed a shiny metal object hovering in the near distance a few minutes into the eclipse. It was metallic, disc-shaped and rotated. Guillermo Arreguín, a cameraman for the Mexican television network Televisa, who was filming the eclipse, got footage of the object. It was broadcast on Mexican television later that night. After that broadcast 17 other people came forward with similar videocam footage recorded from various parts of the city. With so many people looking up to observe the eclipse, this July 11, 1991 sighting may be the most observed UFO experience in human history.

A very curious phenomenon with regard to UFOs in Mexico is the strange frequency that UFOs are observed flying in and out of volcanoes. Three volcanoes of note with such sightings are Nevado de Toluca, the Colima volcano and the massive Popcatépetl, which looms in the distance over Mexico City. All of these volcanoes are located in central Mexico. In January of 2014 a glowing orb was filmed rising in and out of the caldera of Nevado de Toluca. The Mexico City volcano, nicknamed "Popó," has had the most UFO sightings connected with it than any other volcano. In the year 2013 alone there were sightings recorded in every month of that year. The Colima volcano and Popó have been further scrutinized by the emergence of a website in 2011 called "Webcams de Mexico." This site provides live footage of these volcanoes and many UFOS have been spotted going in and out of these mountains by the cameras connected with this web site. This web cam site is also responsible for other UFO footage taken throughout Mexico at various other locales. Online there is ample footage of mysterious objects taken from these live webcams.

The most well-known UFO-related incident in Mexico happened in the state of Chihuahua in 1974 when a large metallic disc supposedly crashed into a small private plane. The alleged flying saucer crash at Coyame has been nicknamed "The Mexican Roswell." Another famous Mexican plane-related incident happened in May of 1975. Carlos Antonio de los Santos was flying his small private plane over the town of Tequesquitengo in the state of Morelos when three metallic objects only about 8 feet in diameter – some would call these *platillitos volantes* – took control of his aircraft. One hovered below the fuselage and one over each wing. De los Santos landed without incident and with no harm to his aircraft or his person.

No exploration of UFOs or extraterrestrial visitation would be complete without examining the abduction phenomenon. In this phenomenon abductees, or "experiencers," are taken aboard alien spacecraft and experimented upon, taken for rides or given information or messages for humanity. The first American case of alleged alien abduction happened in New England in 1961 to Betty and Barney Hill. The first major abduction case in the entire world, according to most UFO researchers, occurred in Brazil to a farmer named Antônio Vilas Boas in 1957. However, there was an obscure case that happened in Mexico in 1953, a full 4 years before the Brazilian abduction. In August of that year, so the story goes, a taxi driver named Salvador Villanueva Medina was on his way to the border town of Laredo traveling on an obscure road in northern Mexico. His car broke down and out of the sagebrush appeared a being with long blond hair, light eyes and a sleek body with milky skin. Medina asked if the person was American and the being told him that he was from the planet Venus. He stood there talking to Medina and described his home world. There was one ocean, there was one government. Children were in the care of the government until they reached maturity. There were no wars and the whole world was under one flag. Medina did not believe the blond being, known in the UFO terminology as a "Nordic," so the being invited him to see his spacecraft which was parked over a hill. Medina followed him and over the hill he saw the typical disc-shaped metallic craft resting on metal legs so that the underbelly would not touch the ground. The Venusian asked Medina if he would like to take a trip in the saucer. The humble Mexican taxi driver agreed. The flight through space was quick and Medina stayed on Venus for 5 days, experiencing what the blond being had described to him on that back road in Mexico. Medina then returned home and wrote a book about his trip titled *Estuve en el planeta venus*, in English, *I Was on the Planet Venus*, only available in Spanish. After publication, Medina suffered much derision and ostracism from family and friends. He visited a psychiatrist who did not find him to be delusional. By anyone's measure, this seems like a fanciful story. At the time – the decade of the 1950s – many people believed that Venus was an inhabited world. Many believed that Medina's story was just a made up tale to capitalize on the nascent interest in other planets and the possibility of space travel. In any case, the Medina incident is the first reportedly documented alien abduction ever to be publicized, although it did not make it very far out of Mexico. Was it real? Many have a hard time believing it or anything else connected with extraterrestrials. But what of the objects in the sky? No one seems to have any definitive explanation for what millions of Mexicans see overhead.

THE ZONE OF SILENCE: MEXICO'S BERMUDA TRIANGLE

In April of 2013 a curious diary began appearing on various paranormal-themed internet sites. The diary was written by Héctor Álvarez, a park ranger at the Mapimí Biosphere Reserve, a UNESCO-designated protected area found near the intersections of three northern Mexican states: Durango, Chihuahua and Coahuila. Located in the Chihuahua Desert, the biosphere encompasses over 1,300 square miles of rugged terrain and contains the habitat of many different types of animals ranging from the puma and mule deer to the desert tortoise and the sandhill crane. The latter bird species calls Mapimí home because of the large salt lake found within the biosphere preserve. Additionally, there exist over 400 different types of plant species within the confines of the park. The diary of Héctor Álvarez did not detail anything about the stark but beautiful natural landscape of the author's workplace, however. It was written, presumably, to document what the ranger was experiencing while working the graveyard shift at the reserve. According to the diary, Álvarez reported to his superiors what he had been experiencing and they paid no attention to his reports so he decided to document things in his own handwritten accounts. The diary is full of strange encounters and unexplained occurrences. Álvarez wrote mostly of the unexplained lights he saw in the desert sky. While the park ranger saw his share of glowing orbs, he wrote most details about the flying colorful triangles he saw above the biosphere reserve. They measured about 6 feet across with colorful, prismatic borders that appeared to be on fire. The inside area of the triangles had shifting patterns of color that seemed to him to be an attempt at communication. Sometimes the triangles would appear alone or sometimes in groups of three. Álvarez tried taking photos of these flying triangles but each time he tried, his camera malfunctioned. In addition to the UFOs, the young park ranger also wrote about something bizarre that happened to all of the research station's computers one night. The speakers on the computers blared a strange white noise, even those which did not have their power turned on. Immediately after this incident, the computers were no longer functioning. In the morning when a technician came in to try to fix the computers, he noted that all the motherboards appeared to have been subjected to high amounts of heat or radiation and were not fixable. Other diary entries mentioned paint patches changing colors on the walls of the facility, sometimes in triangle patterns. The diary entries ended on March 15, 2013. This was the last day anyone saw Héctor Álvarez. It was a mystery as to where he went as his car was still in the parking lot of the main facility of the reserve. He was never seen again.

A part of the Mapimí Biosphere Reserve has been christened La Zona del Silencio - or "The Zone of Silence" in English – and has drawn researchers and curiosity seekers for years. The first reports of anomalies and bizarre things happening in this area became public in the 1930s. Famous Mexican aviation pioneer Francisco Sarabia Tinoco claimed that when he flew his plane, nicknamed *Conquistador del Cielo*, over the area of this part of the desert his radio would not work and his instruments would go crazy. Magnetic anomalies and electronic equipment malfunctions have been reported from Sarabia's time to the present day across this Zone of Silence. Some say that the mysterious properties of this region caused a US missile to crash here in July of 1970. The Athena test missile was fired from a US military base near Green River, Utah, with its ultimate destination being White Sands Missile Range in southern New Mexico. The missile never made it to White Sands but went hundreds of miles off course and impacted the earth in the Zone of Silence a few miles from where the biosphere reserve's research station now stands. Although many local ranchers saw the flash of light and heard the noise of the wayward missile, it took the Americans weeks to find it in the desert expanse. In the meantime a group of locals had found it and watched over the crashed remains and when the Americans finally came, they participated in the extraction and clean-up efforts. Supposedly the missile had contained radioactive material and because great fuss had been made in its retrieval and the decontamination of the area that followed, locals got together to see how they could best exploit this incident to try to bring tourists to the region. It was then when the "Zone of Silence" got its official name and the world became aware of the strangeness of the area through local press stories that were picked up by international news media. According to the locals, the strange magnetic anomalies and atmospheric conditions of the *Zona* cause vortexes to be formed that stretch up through the upper atmosphere and out into space, thus drawing in everything from missiles to meteors to extraterrestrial craft. A year before the American missile mishap, what was later known as the Allende Meteorite crashed into an area near the zone. For years locals have claimed that the Zone causes pretty much anything to fall from the sky and cite the many examples of meteorites found on the desert floor throughout the region. The claims of the weird atmospheric and magnetic conditions are also accompanied by local claims of observed mutations in flora and fauna, such as tortoise shells found in the shape of triangles and coyotes that grow to twice their normal sizes. Also, cactus has been found to change into strange colors, which has been substantiated by photographic proof. Could these natural aberrations be the result of radiation leaked from the American missile crash back in 1970?

In the late '70s when the biosphere research center was being built after the reserve had been declared a protected area by the Mexican government, rumors began to surface about the true intentions behind the creation of the reserve and the building of the facilities within the Zone. Locals claimed that NASA had constructed a secret scientific research center there not only to investigate the atmospheric and magnetic anomalies, but to study and communicate with possible extraterrestrials. The water tower near the main building of the park's welcome center, the locals contended, was really a secret observatory. The supposed vortices found within the Zone of Silence, it is claimed, can be used to contact intelligences from other worlds and other dimensions. The alleged alien connection to the area has been supported by dozens of eyewitness observations of strange lights in the sky, like the mysterious triangles of the Álvarez diaries, and by on-the-ground encounters with strange beings in the desert. There have been about a half dozen reports of locals and tourists alike having encounters with tall, humanoid beings with long blonde hair and light blue eyes. In the Zone, these beings – always two men and one woman - have asked local ranchers only for water and speak perfect Spanish. In UFO lore, these beings are commonly referred to "The Nordics" and are generally described as a benign race of enlightened beings hailing from the Pleiades, the same star cluster as the nefarious Greys, the stereotypically big-eyed, skinny and short race of extraterrestrials who abduct humans and conduct medical experiments on them. The trio of Nordics was once spotted by a scientist from the biosphere research center who had gotten lost while conducting research in the field. Tourists have also reported sighting these beings and always in helping or non-threatening situations. A Mexican New-Age paranormal research group called El Centro de Investigación de Antropología Cosmica de la Escuela Filosofica Lu Men – in English, the Reserch Center for Cosmic Anthropology of the Lu Men School of Philosophy – claims that the Nordics may represent members of what has been called the "Yellow Maya", the people of the lost civilization of Tulum-Balaam who live below the Mapimí Biosphere Reserve. The small mountains in the Zone of Silence are really pyramids, the group claims, and other natural geological formations are really very ancient ruins. They have named this subterranean civilization "Magneto Tzen" which loosely translates to "The Land of Magnetism." The Lu Men School of Philosophy people are not the only paranormally inclined individuals to visit the reserve in hopes of experiencing the high strangeness. Since the 1980s various other New Age groups and paranormal researchers from all over the world have held conferences and overnight stays in the Zone in hopes of experiencing something otherworldly. Adding to the overall strangeness, many researchers are quick to point out that the Zone of Silence exists on the same line of latitude on the earth as the Bermuda Triangle, the pyramids of Egypt and the sacred cities of Tibet.

Serious scientific researchers have a hard time pinning down exactly where the boundaries of the Zone of Silence are and the zone seems to shift over time. Many people visiting the area, even for extended periods of time, have experienced no strange activities whatsoever. Claims of increased magnetism, equipment failure and strange atmospheric disturbances have been seemingly difficult to quantify. Most of the serious scientific research in the area has been done in connection to the local flora and fauna and other aspects of preserving the desert environment, at least what has been made public. Locals, for the most part, appreciate the increased tourism and make money off of it, but at the same time the people seeking to experience something supernatural in the Zone of Silence are seen as a bit crazy or somewhat of a nuisance. What is really happening in this area may forever be a mystery or at least remain an open topic for the curious.

THE FLYING SAUCER CRASH AT COYAME: A MEXICAN ROSWELL?

It was a cold February day in suburban Washington DC when UFO investigator Elaine Douglass received a knock on her door. It was the mailman with an oversized envelope with no return address in its upper left-hand corner. The year was 1992. Douglass, who had been investigating UFOs and the UFO abduction experience since 1985 opened the envelope and was immediately enthralled by its contents. The envelope contained a report and pieces of other documents about a mysterious incident that happened in the deserts of the Mexican state of Chihuahua in August of 1974. Apparently, an unidentified flying object collided mid-air with a small private plane and both crafts crashed just outside of the small Mexican town of Coyame about 50 miles from the border with Texas. The documents supposedly came from someone who signed his or her name "J.S." and declared that he or she was part of the "Deneb Team." As the founder of Operation Right to Know, an organization that published information and sponsored public protests against UFO secrecy, Elaine Douglass seemed the perfect person for this information to be given to. Douglass had a master's degree from MIT and she knew she must approach this information with a serious dose of skepticism no matter how excited she felt.

On August 25th 1974 at approximately 10:00 pm a young radar operator at US Air Defense detected an unknown object approaching American airspace from the Gulf of Mexico. When first spotted, the object was flying at over 2,500 miles per hour at an altitude of 75,000 feet. It was due to enter US territory 40 miles southwest of Corpus Christi when the object decelerated, turned and began a slow descent. It entered Mexican airspace about 50 miles south of the US border at Brownsville, Texas. The object continued its descent: 45,000 feet, then to 25,000 feet. Two different US military installations continued to track the object 500 more miles inland until it disappeared from the radar. It was originally assumed that this object was a meteor, but natural celestial objects falling from the sky do not change course and do not have abrupt changes in speed as this object did.

About an hour after the disappearance of this object from radar, chatter occurred on civilian radio: a small plane out of El Paso, bound for Mexico City, had gone down in the same area as the mysterious object's disappearance. In the early morning of August 26th, Mexican authorities began looking for the downed plane, knowing nothing of the other object spotted on US military radar the night before. At around 10:30, a field of wreckage was spotted from the air and ground rescue and recovery operations commenced. Within minutes of *this* discovery, another crash was spotted a few miles away. This crash left no debris field. Instead, it appeared to be a banged up, smoldering metal disk of highly polished steel, about 16 feet across and 5 feet thick. There were no doors or windows or markings of any kind. The damage to the disk was described as one 12-inch hole and a dent about 2 feet across. After the report of this shiny disk-shaped object came over the airwaves, the Mexican authorities issued a complete radio silence on the search and rescue effort.

They had good reason to do this, as the CIA was listening. The CIA had been monitoring the radio transmissions closely and at the time of the report of the discovery of the disk, they were already assembling an extraction team at nearby Fort Bliss just outside of El Paso. The team included about a dozen men, a large Sea Stallion helicopter and 3 smaller helicopters. Researchers marvel at the speed with which this team was assembled, noting that the CIA must have done similar extraction operations in the past. While the CIA scrambled the team, requests were initiated between the American and Mexican governments using high diplomatic channels. All offers of assistance were denied or ignored. Meanwhile satellite data and reconnaissance aircraft flying above the area indicated that the wreckage of the plane and the crashed saucer were already loaded on to flatbed trucks by the Mexican military. Later images showed that the convoy was headed south.

Instead of letting the disk fall into the hands of the Mexican government, at this point the CIA made an "executive decision" and ordered the recovery team to enter sovereign Mexican territory to recover the disk. While readying the team to leave Fort Bliss, intelligence analysists monitoring the situation made an interesting observation: the Mexican convoy had stopped in the middle of a dirt road far away from any populated areas or major roads. Monitors also noticed that all communications from the convoy and its base of operations had ceased. What was going on?

The American recon operation arrived at the site of the stalled trucks later that afternoon. They beheld a grisly sight: all Mexican military personnel were dead, with most of them still in their trucks. There is great speculation as to why the Mexicans all died. Was it the radiation from the possible spacecraft? Was it a biological agent released from a leaky disk? Or, did the pilots of the disk escape and kill their human captors? Over 4 decades later, we do not know exactly what happened. The recon team had no time to ponder reasons for what they saw. They were prepared, however, and were outfitted in Biohazard suits. Immediately after they arrived, the recon team re-lashed the crashed disk and hoisted it out of the flatbed truck with their Sea Stallion helicopter. By all estimation, the object weighed about 1,500 pounds. Conflicting reports tell of what happened to the remains of the Mexican convoy after this. Some say that everything, bodies and all, was incinerated or blown up in the desert to prevent contamination and to cover up any physical evidence of the event. Others say that the bodies and pieces of the wreckage of the plane were taken away for further study. We know this: The helicopters from this clandestine mission landed in a secret rendezvous point in Texas' Davis Mountains just north of the town of Valentine. In the 2:00 hour in the early part of August 27th, he helicopters again took flight and met up with a convoy of trucks near Van Horn, Texas. The saucer was loaded on to the back of another flatbed truck and was carried along back roads and small highways. Its destination remains unknown. Some say it was taken to Atlanta, to the CDC possibly. Others say that it was taken to Fort Bliss. Yet another account says that the craft ended up at Wright-Patterson Airforce Base in Ohio.

Since that envelope arrived at Elaine Douglass' door, there have been several investigations into what happened at Coyame. The seminal book on this incident was written by American UFO investigators Noe Torres and Ruben Uriarte in 2013. In their book, *The Coyame Incident: UFO Crash Near Presidio, Texas,* the two investigators talked to hundreds of people in and around Coyame to get a better idea as to what really happened. They discovered that there were few eyewitnesses to the crash and after 3 decades passing from the incident to the publication of their book, Torres and Uriarte found conflicting stories about related incidents. For example, in September of 1967, a Pershing mid-range missile launched from a base in the United States crashed in the area of the Chihuahua desert near where the 1974 crashed saucer wreckage was supposedly found. In 1980, Mexican military authorities conducted an extensive search of the area north of Coyame to recover drugs and cash scattered across the landscape from a plane crash of a failed drug run. Many people suspect that some residents of the area might be confusing other incidents with the supposed 1974 saucer crash.

While most of the focus of this case has been on the mysterious crashed saucer, little attention has been paid to the small private plane that supposedly collided with it. After several inquiries to the FAA, no documents have turned up regarding the crash of the small plane, perhaps because the crash occurred outside of the United States. One astute observer noted that had the plane filed a flight plan in El Paso then its disappearance would have triggered a search within minutes of loss of contact and we would at least have a name of the pilot of the plane. Also, if the aircraft was a non-jet airplane, Mexican air regulations at the time would have required the plane to land in the city of Chihuahua to clear customs and immigration. As Mexico only accepts air traffic into its airspace on designated routes, the Coyame crash would have been 80 miles outside the accepted air lane at the time. The fact that no tangible records exists of this small plane is particularly troubling to those investigating this seriously but seems to be glossed over by many researchers. Flight plans and investigations of downed airplanes leave verifiable facts behind. Could the lack of verifiable facts for the small airplane in the Coyame case be part of the whole cover-up?

Much time has passed since this incident which occurred back in August of 1974. The memories of local people seem foggy and any sort of official documentation as to what happened out in the Chihuahua desert so long ago seems non-existent. We are left wondering if that envelope given to UFO researcher Elaine Douglass that started this all was part of an elaborate hoax or if it was a piece of a genuine flying saucer mystery.

THE ALIEN ARTIFACTS OF OJUELOS DE JALISCO

In the high desert of the far northeastern corner of the Mexican state of Jalisco, a former Mexican military doctor set up camp after a long day of exploring the country. The man's name was Dr. Pablo Enrique García Sánchez and the year was 1999. Dr. García was near the area known as El Toro in the municipality of Ojuelos de Jalisco, near the confluence of the states of Jalisco, Zacatecas and Aguascalientes. This is a pretty sparsely populated and somewhat barren part of Mexico and the doctor took the camping trip alone to get away from the rigors of modern civilized life. What he found on his trip astounded him: a stone weighing a few pounds and about the size of two hands cupped together. On the surface of the stone were strange markings seemingly done by a craftsman of a forgotten civilization. To García's untrained eye, the carving on stone looked Maya in origin, but that would have been nearly impossible owing to the fact that this part of Mexico is a thousand miles from the ancient Maya heartland. It was somewhat more believable for the artifact to be of the closer and more recent Aztec civilization, as trading routes of the Aztec Empire did go that far north into the desert areas. Had he found an item that had been carried there over a long distance? Were there other carved stones like this one? The camping trip over, Dr. García returned to the town of Ojuelos and showed his find to locals. Some people in the town had recognized the style of the carving immediately and had told the doctor that farmers and ranchers had been stumbling over artifacts like his for 80 years or more. There were even rumors of hundreds of elaborately carved objects being found in a cave near where García had been camping, along with a skull that did not belong to any creature known to man. Others told him of a lost city and of a large temple that few knew of. Some locals even shared with him some of their own finds: stones and pieces of stones with strange carvings on them. A curious man by nature, Dr. García decided that he would dedicate more time to these curious pieces, and together with a few other people interested in studying the stones, he formed a research group called Nahui Ollin, which in the Aztec language Nahuatl, means "Fifth World," or the world in which humanity currently resides according to the old Aztec legends.

So what do these artifacts look like? What are they made of and is there any indication as to how they were fashioned? There are many of these items and they are very visually appealing. Dr. García's Nahui Ollin organization has catalogued over 400 unique items gathered from the hills and desert valleys outside the town of Ojuelos and across the countryside into the Mexican state of Zacatecas. Over 95% of these pieces are made of carved stone while the rest are made of a high-fired clay substance. The artifacts are perhaps the most controversial in Mexico because of what they depict. In a strange fusion of Mesoamerican art styles, the pieces appear to show flying saucers, the typical "Grey aliens" as reported by modern UFO abductees, humans in space suits and allegorical outer space scenes along with fanciful animals and strange bits of writing reminiscent of Maya glyphs. What has been interpreted as star maps have also been found on some of these stones. In the collection under study there are a few representations of the central part of the Aztec calendar or sun stone, with the center face of the sun replaced by a more otherworldly-looking, stylized grey alien face. For many years before García took his camping trip, the artifacts had long been sold to tourists, which have led many skeptics to believe that all of these pieces are fakes, and that selling these items, along with guided tours to the caves and surrounding areas to hunt for artifacts, is just a way for locals to make money off of the gullible. Although the Nahui Ollin group has over 400 of these pieces in its collection for study, researchers believe that there are thousands more of these artifacts in private collections all over the world, and a great many of them in the private homes of local families.

In 2015 Dr. García published a book about the studies conducted by his research group called *Aztlán y los Aztecas: Una historia más completa de la humanidad,* or, in English, "Aztlán and the Aztecs: A

More Complete History of Humanity." The book starts with the premise that the area in which the artifacts were found was part of the mythical point of origin the Aztecs called Aztlán, and that the pieces discovered show a definite off-world influence on the beginnings of Aztec civilization in the Aztlán homeland. García draws fire from skeptics for his assumptions. The biggest criticism comes from people who see García as the center of a money-making venture and that his organization, whose mission is supposedly to have an objective approach to researching the pieces, clearly has an agenda. This agenda fuels conferences, books, tours, a small museum, and an on-again/off-again internet show called *Aztlán, Paraíso Perdido*, or in English, "Aztlán, Lost Paradise." The Nahui Ollin group employs no formally trained archaeologists or those with any academically-based field research experience. A huge criticism of the group is that it does not thoroughly document finds by including information about specific artifact locations, detailed testimony of witnesses or methods used to unearth the pieces. Laboratory tests have been haphazard or do not make sense. In one report, some pieces were claimed to have an age of 16,000 years, but the dating method cited was Carbon 14, which is not used to date objects that are not organic in nature. If testing has been done of organic materials found at dig sites, such as charcoal found in the same strata as artifacts, this has not been made clear. Critics and people who are generally curious about the problems these pieces pose are demanding more scientific research on these finds. This has not been forthcoming, as state and national archaeological and historical groups in Mexico refuse to examine these pieces and dismiss the whole Ojuelos affair as a shoddy hoax.

In 2011 the son of Puerto Rican actor Raúl Julia, a Mexican man going by the name of Raúl Julia-Levy brought the strange artifacts of Ojuelos into the international spotlight. Julia-Levy claimed that through family connections he had to former Mexican president Vicente Fox that he would be part of the Mexican government's plan to release sensitive information confirming Mexico's longstanding relationship with extraterrestrials, beginning with the ancient Maya. The Ojuelos pieces, which Julia-Levy had claimed were inspired by extraterrestrials but were really Maya in origin, were part of the large corpus of evidence to show this ET contact. The finds at Ojuelos would be combined with other artifacts and documentation provided by the highest government sources to be showcased in Julia-Levy's book and documentary called *Revelations of the Mayans: 2012 and Beyond*. This project was not endorsed by Dr. García or his organization, the Nahui Ollin group. The documentary began filming in Mexico in March of 2012 with an expected release date of December of 2012, but a contract dispute between Julia-Levy and the film's executive producer halted production on the project. Raúl Julia-Levy vowed to complete the manuscript connected with the movie titled either *Chronicles of the Mayan Tunnel* or *Secrets of the Mayan Time Machine*, but this never happened. Sometime before the end of the Maya calendar cycle in December of 2012, the man calling himself Raúl Julia-Levy disappeared amid allegations of faking his identity and fraud. The Puerto Rican actor Raúl Julia publicly claimed he did not have a son by that name and that this man was an impostor. Later investigation showed that the man claiming to be Julia's son never attended Harvard or the University of Southern California as stated in his bio. Amateur researchers later discovered that Raúl Julia-Levy was really a man named Salvador Fuentes and has no connection whatsoever to actor Raúl Julia. The story of the Ojuelos artifacts may have a hoax within a hoax.

Since the attention brought to the Ojuelos artifacts by the man calling himself Raúl Julia-Levy, many paranormal, ancient astronaut and UFO-related investigators have come out in support of the finds. Is this just a case of "I want to believe"? Have any other elements of ancient material culture been found in the area besides these carved stones? What of the rumors of a temple and lost city? As of now, they have not been revealed to outsiders, if they ever existed at all. In 2014 a supposed skull of an extraterrestrial was found in a remote cave just outside of Ojuelos de Jalisco. An informal examination of this supposed skull showed it to be a haphazard creation fashioned out of various animal bones. To quote Mexican paranormal researcher Daniel Galarza Santiago, who runs the web site *El Esceptico de Jalisco*, or, in English "The Skeptic of Jalisco": "The supposed extraterrestrial skull of Ojuelos looks a lot like Jar Jar Binks from Star Wars." Besides this skull, no burials have been claimed to have been found, no pottery, no other bones, and no evidence of any other artifacts. All we have are the carved stones that mysteriously seem to appear during walks in the desert. The investigators of the "I want to believe" persuasion have tried for many years to get serious attention focused on Ojuelos from legitimate institutions in Mexico which study ancient artifacts. The ultimate authority for archaeology in the land is Mexico's National Institute of Anthropology and History based in Mexico City with offices and representatives in every state in Mexico. In response to an inquiry about whether or not it was legal for these supposedly extraterrestrial artifacts found at Ojuelos to be sold off to tourists, the National Institute of Anthropology and History actually crafted something in writing in one of the first times it had ever even acknowledged the controversial finds. Archaeologist Dr. Ana María Pelz Marin stated, "That despite the falsity of these pieces are being marketed as real pre-Hispanic items, and although people are deceived, there is no crime to pursue, since for the National Institute of Anthropology and History they are not historical objects, but simple crafts." Dr. Pelz Marin continued stating, "The sale of a nation's heritage is a federal crime. People have to understand that they are not original pieces."

Of course, people will counter what Dr. Pelz Marin wrote and allege that governments have historically covered up evidence of alien visitation and have denied any contact with extraterrestrials, past or present, and that institutions like Mexico's National Institute of Anthropology and History are established merely to aid in such cover ups. While this may be true, perhaps we have an undeniably cut-and-dry example of a hoax coming from a remote corner of Jalisco, or perhaps not.

THE MEXICAN AIR FORCE VS. THE FLYING SAUCERS

April 21, 2004 was an important day for Jaime Maussán, the white-haired and white-bearded host of the Mexican television show *Tercer Milenio*. He had gotten the scoop of his career. Since 1970 Maussán had distinguished himself as one of the leading journalists in Mexico, having worked for many newspapers and broadcasting outlets primarily as an investigative reporter focusing on science and environmental issues. In the early 1990s Maussán's interests turned toward UFOs on a show he co-hosted called *Y usted que opina?* This show was the first step on a long path that would eventually lead him to become known as a top expert in Mexico on unidentified flying objects, or *OVNIs*, in Spanish. As one of the principal ufologists in the country, it was logical for Jaime Maussán to have such an important meeting on that day in April of 2004. It was then when he met with General Gerardo Clemente Vega García, Mexico's Minister of Defense who was appointed to the position by Mexican President Vicente Fox in the year 2000. It was an important day for General Vega, too. The career army officer had served Mexico well as a military attaché abroad in such countries as Poland, West Germany and the Soviet Union. In his very long and distinguished career in service for Mexico the general had never had such a strange task fall in his lap. In the meeting with Maussán, the Defense Minister asked the journalist if he could get his help in analyzing a strange batch of video footage and audio clips. General Vega wanted Señor Maussán's help in investigating the incident behind this footage: On March 5, 2004, just weeks before their meeting, a Mexican Air Force anti-drug trafficking surveillance flight over the coast of the Mexican state of Campeche had a strange encounter with 11 orbs of light that flew around the aircraft. Maussán was honored and a bit astounded that the Mexican government would come to him for help with their investigation. He realized at the time that his meeting with the general was somewhat historic. In all his years of research, Maussán had never known of a case in which a national government of any country went beyond the mere acknowledgement of the existence of UFOs and asked for civilian help in trying to understand the phenomenon. Maussán had a great scoop, and a great burden, and on May 11, 2004 he took part in a press conference announcing to the world the news and the details of the historic partnership.

Soon after the press conference, Maussán released to the public video footage and audio clips provided to him by the Mexican Ministry of Defense. Even those with a Sesame Street level of understanding of Spanish can make out the counting on the tape. Radar operator Lieutenant Germán Marín is counting off the objects on his screen and ends with the number eleven. So, what exactly happened that night over the Gulf of Mexico?

The date was March 5, 2004. The time was between 5:00 and 5:30 pm. The location where the objects begin to appear is marked at 18 degrees, 26 minutes and 60 seconds north latitude, and 90 degrees, 43 minutes and 69 seconds west longitude. The Merlin C26A Bimotor airplane, part of the Mexican Air Force's 501 Aerial Squadron, was flying at 10,500 feet, near Ciudad del Carmen off the coast of the Mexican state of Campeche in the Gulf of Mexico.   The plane was staffed by a captain and two lieutenants, who were responsible for operating the radar and infrared systems onboard the plane. The range of the radar was approximately 50 miles. The range for the infrared system was between -40°C and 1,500°C. Visibility was at 96% and weather conditions were calm, with no storms nearby or in the forecast for the evening. The airplane was only used for surveillance and detection. It was not commissioned for combat or intercept maneuvers. The purpose of flights like these was to identify suspicious and possibly drug-related aircraft, report the activity to the ground base and then Mexican Air Force planes would be scrambled to intercept whatever unauthorized plane was in the area.

At 5:00 the first object appeared on the plane's radar and was confirmed with infrared but was not visible with the naked eye. The captain of the plane radioed the ground to tell the base that they had identified a possible suspect and to maintain interceptor planes at alert status while they flew closer to investigate. As the Air Force plane got closer to the object, the object accelerated. The incident was being recorded by the radar and the infrared device, and the plane was in constant communication with the ground providing detailed descriptions of what they were experiencing. The captain of the plane was perplexed because they still were not able to establish visual contact. The object briefly disappeared from their detection devices when it was joined by another. The pilot maneuvered the plane in a circular direction to get a better view of the two orb-like lights when something unexpected occurred: the two objects they had been tracking were joined by even more objects. Out of nowhere, 9 more flying balls of light appeared, the same size and sharing the same characteristics of the first two, and seemed to fly in formation.

What was even stranger than 9 objects appearing so suddenly was their apparent invisibility to the naked eye. As with the first two, these 9 new objects were only visible on radar and through the infrared detection equipment. The pilot of the plane radioed the base to ask for further instructions. In the meantime he cut out all the lights to his aircraft to try to see if that would make visual contact easier but they still could not see the objects without the instruments. By that time the 11 objects had maneuvered around the aircraft. At around the time interceptor planes were to be scrambled on the ground, the objects flew away, disappearing off the radar and infrared sensors.

When the crew landed the debriefing began. All instrument recordings were turned over to the Mexican Department of Defense and the Campeche case got the attention of the highest levels of military and government in Mexico. After weeks of examining the in-flight recordings, multiple interviews with the flight crew and analysis of the weather-related data from that evening, the Minister of Defense, General Vega, made the decision to seek outside help. Going to television ufologist Jaime Maussán was a giant leap in the UFO field because, as stated before, it was one of the first times in history when a sovereign government of a country not only acknowledged the existence of UFOs, but solicited help from the private sector to aid in an investigation. On Sunday, May 9, 2004, on his show, which was then called, *Los Grandes Misterios del Tercer Milenio*, or in English, "The Big Mysteries of the Third Millennium," Jaime Maussán announced his collaboration with the Mexican military in this case. He also announced that further details would be shared with the public at a press conference to be held on May 11, 2004 at the Sevilla Palace Hotel in Mexico City.

The Campeche incident generated a lot of attention both inside Mexico and abroad, and as with many UFO sightings this case found itself on the receiving end of harsh criticism almost immediately. Many theories arose to try to explain what exactly happened over the Gulf of Mexico in March of 2004. Debunkers were then answered by counter-debunkers who shot holes in supposed air-tight "rational" explanations. The most famous round of debunking came from Americans. Ben McGee, resident skeptic on the National Geographic

Channel's show *Chasing UFOs*, elaborated on a theory proposed by previous researchers and alleged that what the Mexican Air Force personnel had experienced had a more terrestrial explanation. McGee believed that what their instruments were seeing were really fires from the tops of oil rigs on platforms in the Gulf of Mexico and he was determined to prove it. For the National Geographic show, McGee took a plane and similar equipment the Mexicans used and demonstrated how the pilot and the crew had mistaken the distant fires for UFOs, even claiming that the swirling of the clouds that night gave the impression that these stationary fires were moving and that they were higher than what would have expected. What was shown on *Chasing UFOs* and in subsequent lectures by McGee seemed like an open-and-shut case and a thorough analysis which satisfied many people in the skeptic circles. More critical eyes saw flaws in what Ben McGee was saying. How would oil rig fires show up on radar? The experienced flight crew, who had logged thousands of hours in the air, had reported movement of the objects. Wouldn't they know the difference between something stationary and something moving outside the plane? Why were oil fires, which would seemingly be visible at night from a plane, not visible to the flight crew with the naked eye? One investigator noted that the oil rigs were 100 miles away from the plane and would not have shown up on any of their instruments anyway because they were way out of range. And what of other sightings? If these bright objects were really the oil rigs, wouldn't other pilots in the area have reported similar experiences? No such stories exist. In spite of the debunking and the debunking of the debunkers, the Mexican military working with the country's top ufologist, Jaime Maussán, could not come up with an explanation for what happened in the skies off the cost of Campeche in March of 2004 and this was after months of research and the solicitation of help of dozens of experts. So, it seems we are back to square one. Perhaps we are just left with a mystery and no one will ever know who or what was behind those lights in the sky, that is, unless they return.

THE ALIEN ABDUCTION OF SALVADOR VILLANUEVA MEDINA

It was August, 1953. Taxi driver Salvador Villanueva Medina's car had broken down while he was shuttling two Americans to the US-Mexican border at Laredo. Medina's passengers opted to take to the road by foot to flag down help or walk to the nearest town while the seasoned driver assessed his car trouble. While examining the transmission of the 1952 Buick, Medina heard soft footprints on the gravel on the side of the road. He got up to behold a strange sight: A blond man with shoulder-length hair and a slight build was standing beside his car. He was wearing a sort of uniform that appeared to Medina as being made of wool or corduroy fabric. Medina described the stranger as having a face as white as polished ivory and bright green eyes. His teeth were very small and when he spoke, asking about Medina's car, the blond man used flawless Spanish. Medina assumed that the man was a pilot, as he made references to his craft being parked over a hill nearby. The two chatted for a while until it began to get dark. The blond stranger told Medina that he needed to go, and activated a series of lights on his belt. He walked rather rapidly into the desert wilderness and Medina wanted to follow him, but couldn't see where he went. Medina returned to his car and went to sleep for the night.

The next morning the taxi driver awoke to the rapping sound on one of the car's windows. Thinking that help had finally arrived from the day before, Medina got up and out of the car only to find the blond man from the previous day along with a very similar-looking companion. As the temperature outside was cold, Medina invited the two to sit with him in the car. While in the car he asked the two a little bit about themselves. Medina thought that their features were too exotic to be European or American and that the two must have been from somewhere else. One of the strangers began to describe where the two came from. It was a place with no open space like the deserts of northern Mexico, rather, it was more like a continuous city with a dense population and endless roads. Public transportation included vehicles with 10 levels. Farming occurred vertically, as fruits and vegetables were grown inside walls and on top of buildings because of lack of space. Their place of origin had one ocean, which was three times deeper than any ocean on earth. Children were entrusted to the care of the State until they reached maturity. It was at this point when the taxi driver realized that he was speaking with beings from another world. After a brief discussion about their planet and how it differed from earth, the beings asked Medina if he wanted to see their spacecraft. He agreed and they led him over the hills and through some scrub forest until they came upon the oval-shaped metallic craft standing on three legs among the bushes like an egg in a nest. The Mexican taxi driver, so used to shuttling other people around for a living, was then offered a ride, allegedly to the planet Venus.

No exploration of UFOs or extraterrestrial visitation would be complete without examining the abduction phenomenon. In this phenomenon abductees, or "experiencers," are taken aboard alien spacecraft and experimented upon, taken for rides or given information or messages for humanity. The first American case of alleged alien abduction happened in New England in 1961 to Betty and Barney Hill. The first major abduction case in the entire world, according to most UFO researchers, occurred in Brazil to a farmer named Antônio Vilas Boas in 1957. However the case of Salvador Villanueva Medina predates the Brazilian case by about 4 years, thus making it probably the first documented alien abduction in modern history. The Medina case didn't make it out of Mexico until 1973 when a small book was published called *Estuve en el planeta Venus*, or, in Enlgish, *I was on Planet Venus*, which did not generate much international attention. The case was reexamined and an update to the book was released a few years ago by a group out of San Luís Potosí, Mexico called Gnosis Instituto Cultural Quetzalcoatl which specializes in dream research, meditation, the study of the Kabbalah and a handful of other topics which may be considered "fringe." All materials about this alleged abduction case have previously been available only in Spanish. As an aside, if one would like to be technical about this case, Medina's experience would not strictly be classified as an abduction as he did board the craft voluntarily and knew exactly where he was going with these mysterious blond beings.

Return to the humble Mexican taxi driver, somewhere between earth and Venus, the small craft piloted by the two beings Medina met on the side of the road in Mexico docked with another larger ship that was staffed by 8 people. There were two "chiefs" aboard the larger ship who were bigger in stature and wore different uniforms. The larger ship had ample seating and more complicated controls and was made, presumably, to fly longer distances. Medina was welcomed by the crew, who found humans to be curious creatures, and was invited to what appeared to be a mess hall. He was offered food, and remarked that it was quite tasty and aggregable. After the meal he became sleepy and dozed off. When he awoke, he was wearing the same uniforms as the crew. In Medina's own words, he described his new clothing, specifically his pants, as being, "tight as a bullfighter's. I felt it materially attached to the body, but without hindrance." After he awoke, Medina was led to the bridge of the ship and on the three main screens he watched as they approached Venus. They descended vertically to the planet's surface, hovering until the ship extended its "legs" and they landed. To disembark, the crew and their earthling guest entered a hollow column and put their hands and feet on what seemed to be a ladder and descended through the column to the planet's surface. On the slow way down, Medina noticed trees full of fruit. He reached out to touch one and it felt ripe. The trees had no leaves and the trunks had gigantic roots. Medina noticed that the surface of the planet looked wet and somewhat like a sludge. One of the Venusians explained to him that what he was looking at was a kind of chemical mixture that was used as food for the fruit-bearing trees. Besides the trees, Medina noticed a massive building that seemed to go on forever. They explained to him that indeed it did, and it was a continuous structure that ringed the planet and sent out light rays in all directions. It was because of this building which absorbed light from the sun and emitted light continuously, that Venus never experienced the darkness of night or the dim light from thick cloud cover. Medina also noticed the various forms of aerial transport flying nearby. Some ships were cylindrical, others were orb-like. Some were made of a metal similar to the craft he flew in, some were made of crystal. There was a lot of air traffic, but it seemed to be comprised mostly of smaller vehicles. Sometime during this slow descent, Medina became sick. He had trouble breathing and felt feverish. He was given a cigar-sized breathing apparatus that helped him. By the time they got to the main building complex, he was fine.

At the main building complex their first stop was a gigantic cafeteria. It was here where Medina was among other people who seemed to pay little interest in him. He noted that everyone dressed the same and most of the people were no more than a meter tall. All were blond and pale and women were barely distinguishable from men. After their meal, Medina followed his friends from the spacecraft out to the street. He noticed that there was light everywhere and it was hard to pinpoint the source, as it was coming from all the buildings. There were no signs on the buildings and all structures on the planet were identified as to their function by colors. The buildings had no windows and no doors, but people accessed the buildings through open arched entryways. The small vehicles they used on Venus for personal transportation were communal and used by everyone. If someone needed a car, they would grab the closest vehicle, use it, and then leave it for the next person to use. As mentioned before, they had another type of public transport, a *colectivo* - in Medina's Mexican terminology - that was sometimes multiple levels high and traveled to pre-determined destinations. These *colectivos* could go up to 70 kilometers per hour. For those who did not want to take a personal car or a multi-layered public bus, there were sidewalks that moved. Sometimes boats could be seen in the streets of the city. All boats had small rollers on the bottoms of their hulls that allowed for ease of movement on land. Underneath the cities were elaborate networks of pipes that delivered goods to different parts of the city. There were also underground roads for moving larger items, like construction equipment.

In his book, *Estuve en el planeta Venus*, Medina painstakingly describes many of the mundane tasks he witnessed during his 5 days on Venus. One of the rather lengthy explanations had to do with how the people of Venus manufacture tires, for example. As a taxi driver back on earth, anything pertaining to transportation interested him, including how the Venusians got so many aerial craft to fly around their cities. According to what he was told by his hosts, the small aircraft did not use fuel the way we did on earth but harnessed an energy emanating from the planet itself, a kind of magnetism. The larger ships used for actual space travel were equipped with energy weapons that were capable of destroying everything. This destructive power, saddened and troubled the Mexican visitor. Another interesting thing that Medina observed was how the Venusians cultivated and prepared food. Food came from two sources: the sea and the gardens found within the walls and on the rooftops of the buildings inside the city. The bounty of the sea was harvested in massive floating factory-fisheries. Sea creatures approximating sharks, manta rays and salmon were caught, lightly processed and sent to other factories on land to be ground into a flour. This flour was used to create different types of food of various flavors, textures and colors. The fruits and vegetables from the gardens were also processed at the same facilities and made into a similar type of flour. Fruits and vegetables were picked by hand. The trees were rather short, much like the people picking the fruit. All nutrition was balanced in laboratories and food was optimized in such a way that Venus had none of the diseases that earth had that came from having a poor diet. People did get old and die of natural causes related to advanced age, but no one suffered from ailments or died early because of poor eating habits or bad nutrition.

In his final days on the planet, Medina met other earth people. His first encounter was with two twins who had a French father and a Spanish mother and were born somewhere in the eastern Mediterranean. They had been on Venus for 5 years and they had acclimated to the atmosphere just fine but did not fit in well with the culture.   Instead of wearing the skin-tight suits of the Venusians, they wore only what Medina described as a type of underwear. The Mediterranean twins found work in one of the docks for aerial craft and that is where Medina met them while touring the main part of the city with his hosts. There was no indication as to why these two were there or whether they went to Venus voluntarily or if they were abducted for whatever reason. Medina met no other earth people while on Venus.

The aliens eventually returned Medina to his car back on earth and he got the help he needed from a nearby gas station to get on with his life. In parting, the Venusians encouraged Medina to tell his story to everyone and the humble taxi driver said that it would be difficult because he had very little education. With some help, Medina eventually got his book out. After publication, Medina suffered much derision and ostracism from family and friends. He visited a psychiatrist who did not find him to be delusional. By anyone's measure, this seems like a fanciful story. At the time – the decade of the 1950s – many people believed that Venus was an inhabited world. Many believed that Medina's story was just a made up tale to capitalize on the growing interest in other planets and the possibility of space travel. In any case, the Medina incident is the first documented alien abduction ever to be publicized, although it did not make it very far out of Mexico initially. The incredible details and descriptions of what Medina experienced begs the question: Was this story real?

PART FOUR: LITTLE-KNOWN HISTORY

THE MYSTERIOUS DOÑA MARINA, LA MALINCHE

She is known by many names: La Malinche, Doña Marina, Malinalli, Malintzin and disparagingly as La Chingada. Although many of the details of her life have been lost or embellished over time, history casts her alternatively in the role of savior, villain, lover, betrayer, evangelist, helper, and the mother of a new race. So, who exactly was Doña Marina and what role did she play in the history of Mexico?

The woman later known by her Spanish name Doña Marina was born sometime at the end of the 15th Century or the beginning of the 16th Century. Her given name was Malinalli, and she was named for the 12th day of the ancient Mesoamerican calendar. According to firsthand accounts published by Bernal Díaz, one of the Spanish conquistadors who arrived with Cortés and who knew Marina, she was from a minor noble family in the Isthmus of Tehuantepec in south-central Mexico. Marina was most likely not a native speaker of Nahuatl, the language of the Aztec Empire, but knew it fluently because it was the lingua franca of the region and known by many people of non-Aztec groups who were either subjugated by the Aztec Empire or who interacted with the Aztecs through trade. Most of what we know about Marina's early life comes from Díaz's written accounts, recorded almost 40 years after the Conquest in a book titled *La historia verdadera de la conquista de Nueva España*. In English, this translates to "The true history of the conquest of New Spain." When she was a young girl, Marina's father - who was the Cacique of Paynala - died and her mother remarried. With her new husband, Marina's mother had a son. The mother wanted her son to inherit the family's status and wealth and had a plan to send Marina away. When Marina was in her early teens, her mother sold her to traders in the market city of Xicalango and told everyone that Marina had died. In Xicalango Marina was sold off to a Maya lord who ruled Potonchán, a small kingdom located in the present Mexican state of Tabasco. When Marina was brought to Potonchán she served in the household of the noble lord, and after a short time she became fluent in the local Chontal Maya language. At that time, Marina was fluent in at least 3 languages: the native language of her town of birth, the Aztec language Nahuatl, and Chontal Maya.

While Marina served in the house of the Chontal Maya ruler, Spanish conquistador Hernán Cortés was taking part in the conquest of the island of Cuba. While Cortés served the Spanish king in Cuba he heard stories of a mythical land to the west and about a mighty empire whose capital stood on an island in the middle of a lake. Cortés was determined to locate this city and take over the empire and in 1518 he left Cuba with over 500 ambitious Spaniards to undertake this grand scheme. His expedition landed on Mexico's gulf coast and the Spaniards made contact with the local Maya-speaking people. In the course of the expedition's journey down the coast, to their surprise Cortés and his men encountered a 30-year-old Spanish priest named Jeronimo de Aguilar who had been shipwrecked on the Mexican coast in 1511 and had lived among the Maya ever since. As a consequence of living among the coastal Maya for almost 7 years, Aguilar knew their language and proved invaluable to Cortés because he could translate for the expedition, at least in that region. Cortés used Aguilar to help form alliances and make deals with the locals. It was soon after meeting up with Aguilar that Doña Marina comes back into the picture. In March of 1518, the Spanish arrived in the Maya kingdom of Potonchan where Marina served in the royal court. The Maya decided to fight the Spanish and lost. As part of their reparations the Maya gave the Spanish food, turquoise, jade objects and 20 young women, and Marina was among the group. The women were baptized by the two priests on the expedition and this is when Malinalli became Doña Marina. Marina was then given to one of Cortés' friends Alonso Hernández Portocarrero.

Marina showed her worth once the Spanish left the territories of the Maya-speaking people. Emperor Montezuma the Second, having heard of the arrival of the strangers from the east, sent emissaries to try to reason with Cortés and to at least find out his intentions. The emissaries met up with the Spanish expedition on the fringes of the Aztec empire in a town where Cortés set up an encampment. The emissaries only spoke Nahuatl, a native language that Father Aguilar was unfamiliar with. Cortés was discouraged because Aguilar was of no use and there was no way for them to communicate. During the initial meeting with the Aztecs and amid the frustration, according to the firsthand accounts of Bernal Díaz, this is when Marina stepped in, and answered the questions of the emissaries and pointed to Cortés. Cortés was surprised that Marina knew Nahuatl and he devised a way to communicate with the Aztecs: Cortés would communicate in Spanish to Father Aguilar, Father Aguilar would speak to Marina in Chontal Maya, and Marina would speak to the Aztecs in their native language of Nahuatl. When the Aztecs would speak, the process would be reversed. This way, Cortés, through Marina, was able to communicate with many native groups on his march toward the Aztec capital of Tenochtitlán . Along the way they gathered intelligence from these groups and were thus better prepared to face Montezuma and the weight of his empire.

In the fall of 1519 the Spanish arrived at the independent Kingdom of Tlaxcala, just east of the Aztec homeland. The Tlaxcalans had fiercely resisted Aztec incursions into their territories and were some of the few independent kingdoms in central Mexico that held out against the armies of Montezuma. They greeted the Spanish with suspicion but through Marina, Cortés made a deal with the Tlaxcalan king not only to spare his men but to join him on his march to the Aztec capital. To the Tlaxcalans, Cortés represented an opportunity to crush their enemies once and for all and to rid Mesoamerica of the Aztec hegemony. When the expedition left the Tlaxcalan kingdom they had thousands of more soldiers in their ranks. This was a turning point in the Conquest of Mexico. It is unclear what would have happened in this situation without the help of Marina, who, after being with the expedition for over a year and a half, had mastered Spanish and could translate directly the wishes of Cortés.

While in Tlaxcala, Marina acquired one of her other names, "Malintzin", which may translate loosely to "noble captive," a reference to Marina's noble birth and the fact that she was given to the Spanish as tribute in a war. The Spanish on the expedition could not pronounce the Nahuatl "Malintzin" and called Marina "Malinche", sometimes using the definite article in Spanish "la" in front of her name. This is why Doña Marina is often referred to as "La Malinche" or in English texts, "The Malinche."

From Tlaxcala, the Spanish expedition moved to Cholula. Here again Marina's role was pivotal. Cholula was part of the Aztec Empire and didn't trust the Tlaxcalans Cortés was traveling with. Cortés told the Cholulans, however, that he was traveling to Tenochtitlán on an official state visit to see Emperor Montezuma and needed quarter in the town as a favor to their overlord. The Cholulans reluctantly agreed. While there, Marina made friends with local women and soon found out about a plot that the Cholulan army was planning to attack the Spanish unsuspectedly. Marina told Cortés and the Spanish quickly attacked the Cholulans, killing thousands and disabling their army. Their path to the Aztec capital was now clear.

The initial arrival at the Aztec capital was peaceful. On November 8, 1519 Cortés, followed by thousands, marched on the causeway across Lake Texcoco connecting Tenochtitlán to the mainland. In the middle of the causeway, Cortés was met by Montezuma and his entourage. Gifts were exchanged and so were pleasantries, with Marina as the go-between. The emperor invited the Spanish to enter the city, the Tlaxcalan warriors and all other non-Spaniards – with the exception of Marina – were told to stay on the mainland. Marina would serve a vital role in the ensuing two weeks, during which time the Spanish were received as honored guests.

It's important to note how Marina completely broke the standards of behavior of Mesoamerican women at the time. Women in the Aztec Empire were prohibited from speaking in public places, especially at public events. Anyone surrounding the Aztec Emperor was required to look away from him. Marina, however, boldly spoke directly to Montezuma on Cortés' behalf and always conducted herself in a noble way, according to Spanish and native observers. All would agree that she had a powerful, commanding presence which served to enhance her physical beauty. At one point, now a devout Christian, Marina even spoke fearlessly to Montezuma about converting to Christianity, telling him that the gods he worshipped were evil. This was definitely a bold woman.

The weeks of talks and deal-making did not yield what Cortés wanted and he had Montezuma taken prisoner. It was Marina who informed the emperor that he was to be taken captive. For six months Montezuma was in custody, a prisoner in his own land. Many people who were dissatisfied with Montezuma's rule were indifferent to his imprisonment. During that time, however, the relations between the Spanish and the Aztecs slowly deteriorated. When Cortés was away from the city and when he Aztecs were having a nighttime celebration to honor one of their main gods, Huitzilopochtli, Cortés' lieutenant, Pedro de Alvarado, attacked the celebrants, mistaking the fiesta for the beginnings of an armed insurrection against Spanish rule. Hundreds of unarmed nobles were killed and soon after, when Cortés returned to Tenochtitlán , the Aztecs were furious and began their open rebellion against the Spaniards. Some accounts say that Montezuma was hauled out of captivity and stoned to death by his own people, other accounts say that Cortés had Montezuma killed.

Right after Montezuma's death, on the night of June 30, 1520, the Spanish retreated and fled Tenochtitlán . Hundreds of Spaniards and possibly over a thousand Tlaxcalans were killed as a full force of Aztecs attacked the invaders on the causeway and on the mainland. The night in history is known in Spanish as *"La noche triste,"* "the sad night." Marina survived the battles by hiding under a bridge. She regrouped with Cortés and his forces. Nearly a year later, and with more help from surrounding tribes, the Spanish re-entered Tenochtitlán and completely subdued the Aztec capital. Marina was there at the side of Cortés to translate for the formal surrender on August 13, 1521.

During the whole time of the expedition, Marina became closer to Cortés. Remember, Marina was "given" to the man named Portocarrero, but Cortés had sent him back to Spain half way through the expedition. After Portocarrero's departure, Cortés took Marina as his mistress and they remained together for 4 years. After the fall of Tenochtitlán and after the new city of Mexico was built on its ruins, Marina lived with Cortés and gave birth to his first son, Martín, in May of 1522. Martín Cortés was the first publicly acknowledged person of *mestizo*, or mixed-race, heritage in Mexican history. This is the reason why Marina is sometimes referred to as "The Mother of Mexico."

Marina took one last journey with Cortés to the Maya area of Honduras in 1524. Because Cortés had a legal wife in Cuba, Marina was free to marry, and on this 1524 trip she married a man named Juan Xaramillo de Salvatierra. On the journey to Honduras the expedition stopped at Marina's birth town where she was able to visit family members. Instead of staying in this town she opted to continue the journey with the Spaniards to Central America. While there are no records of the rest of the life of Marina, there is a lot of speculation as to what happened to her. It is certain that after the Honduras expedition she never saw Cortés again because he returned to Spain soon after. There are various legends about the rest of her life, including that she died tragically of strangulation or that she died a very old woman. In any event, there are no records of her existence after the Honduras trip, save a brief mentioning of her still being alive in a text dated 1550 recently found in Spain.

Marina's legacy lives on, mixing historical fact with myth, and full of pointed opinions as to her impact. Many people see her as a Judas figure, a traitor to the native peoples of Mesoamerica. There even exists a word in Spanish, *malinchista*, used to describe a disloyal or unfaithful person. Marina's arrival in Tenochtitlán symbolizes the end of great indigenous civilizations of the Americas and she should never be forgiven for her betrayal. On the other hand, some see her as a liberator of the peoples who were living under the Aztec jackboot. With the Spanish arrival came the end of human sacrifice and the brutality of everyday life under the Aztecs. As a devout convert to Christianity, Marina is seen as an evangelist bringing a peaceful religion to a new people. Her closeness to Cortés is seen as a softening influence on the conquistador and many believe that with this influence the Conquest of Mexico was less brutal. As the mother of one of the first mixed-race children in the Americas Marina is seen as the mother of a new race, *La Raza Cosmica*, or the mestizo. Other modern interpretations see her as a scapegoat used to take the fall for whatever opinion one may have about the Conquest. It is generally agreed, though, that The Malinche was a woman caught in the middle, a person who used her intelligence and tact to the best of her ability when faced with difficult choices. We cannot know how she felt, as she left no written diary and no firsthand accounts of her exist outside of those brief passages written by Bernal Díaz. We can only guess what she was feeling as she saw the history of the New World unfold

in front of her, a history that she played more than an active role in
actually creating.

THE ISLE OF PASSION: MEXICO'S FORGOTTEN COLONY IN THE PACIFIC

The year was 1944. Andrews Sisters tunes were heard blaring
over the shady coconut groves on a small Pacific atoll. The boys in
service of America's war effort just completed 3 runways capable of
handling the massive B-29 Superfortresses that would land there and
would help win the war. The clean-cut young American servicemen
building this secret base designated "Island X" were mildly curious of
the ruins that they found on this remote island when they arrived.
None of them knew of the drama that played out there just a quarter
of a century before, or of the people who were born or died there.

Island X has had many other names in its long history. Located
670 miles southeast of the coast of Mexico in the eastern Pacific, this
remote island was discovered in 1526 by a Spanish sea captain named
Álvaro de Saavedra and he named it La Isla de Mídanos. There was no
evidence of any previous habitation, as it was hundreds of miles from
the nearest land. It remained on nautical charts with the name
Mídanos for many years and starting in 1576 was an important marker
on the Manila to Acapulco galleon route linking the colony of New
Spain with the Spanish Philippines. In the 18th Century the island
appeared on Englishmaps as Clipperton Island, named after an English
pirate who visited the island in 1705. Two French ships arrived in 1711
and named the island Ile de la Passion, or Passion Island. In Spanish it
would be known henceforth as Isla de la Pasión although Clipperton
Island would be used interchangeably. Today it is known as
Clipperton.

The many name changes of the island showed the conflicting
claims to Clipperton and various interests that the island was subject
to. In the 1840s in a Pacific offshoot of Manifest Destiny, many
uninhabited islands in the Pacific Ocean were claimed by the United
States or at least had economic activities on them directed by US
companies. Clipperton had attracted the attention of companies

interested in extracting the island's hardened bird droppings, or guano, used in making fertilizer and gunpowder. In 1856 the US enacted the Guano Islands Act and the first part of this act reads:

"Whenever any citizen of the United States discovers a deposit of guano on any island, rock, or key, not within the lawful jurisdiction of any other Government, and not occupied by the citizens of any other Government, and takes peaceable possession thereof, and occupies the same, such island, rock, or key may, at the discretion of the President, be considered as appertaining to the United States."

The French were aware of American activities on the island because of its proximity to French Polynesia, notably the Marquesas Islands and Tahiti, and sought to exercise is claim on Clipperton. On November 17, 1858, a French expedition anchored offshore and read a proclamation that declared the island belonged, "to his Majesty the Emperor Napoleon III, his heirs and successors in perpetuity." A French guano mining operation landed there 2 years later and declared the island not worth anything. A few years later the American Agricultural Chemical Company, with its brand Red Dragon Guano, arrived on the island and started a small operation, but as with other schemes, this one was short-lived. Dreams of guano fortunes would be rekindled in 1893 when a San Francisco company would declare the resources on the island to be worth 50 million dollars. After their declaration, the company raised enough capital and started operations on Clipperton. 100 men, mostly Italian and Japanese immigrants who lived in San Francisco, mined the guano, built a small railroad and constructed a dock. In a few years, with money running out, this venture was bought out by the British Pacific Islands Company which continued to mine the guano.

In Mexico, President Porfirio Díaz had heard about the activities on Clipperton and he and many Mexicans had considered the island part of Mexican territory citing claims going back to the 16th Century. Díaz reasoned that when Mexico gained independence from Spain in 1810 that this territory became part of the new nation of Mexico because it was once Spanish territory in the sphere of New Spain. In December of 1897 Díaz sent a gunboat, *La Democrata*, to occupy and annex the island. In the following year in Mexico City, Mexican Foreign Minister Ignacio Mariscal met with Arthur Hamilton-Gordon, the First Baron Stranmore, an English nobleman who was chairman of the British Pacific Islands Company. They drew up an agreement and Mexico bought the guano rights to the island for 20 years. The Mexican government's plan was to buy the rights, set up a colony and then stake a legitimate territorial claim to Clipperton. No one really knows the motivation behind Porfirio Díaz' desire to possess the island. Was it a political distraction? Was it a way to foster national pride in a greater Mexico? His reasons are not clear to this day.

Mexican officials were dispatched to Clipperton to oversee the guano mining but it wasn't until 1906 when President Porfirio Díaz ordered a permanent Mexican garrison and civilian colony to be established on the island. The first governor of the colony was Ramón Arnaud, a captain in the Mexican army who was born in Orizaba, Veracruz to immigrants from France who went to Mexico during the reign of the Habsburg ruler of Mexico, Emperor Maximilian. Ramón Arnaud was stationed in the Yucatán fighting Maya insurgents during the Caste Wars and after a brief secret mission to Japan he was given the post of governor. Before he embarked on his new post, the 29-year-old dashing military officer married the beautiful Alicia Rovira who was excited to be the consort in this colonial adventure. Alicia's enthusiastic attitude changed soon after arriving on the island.

Conditions on Clipperton were harsh. The skeleton crew of the previous mining operation was still there and there was little for the 21 colonists to do outside of building the lighthouse commissioned by Porfirio Díaz and making other minor improvements to the island. Within a year, the first child was born on the island, the first son of Ramón and Alicia Arnaud. They named him Ramón, or Ramoncito. By 1910 all guano mining operations were abandoned. By then the good deposits had already been mined and it was too labor-intensive to refine the remaining deposits. Most of the miners left, with only one German man, Gustav Shultz, staying behind. During this time the Mexican Revolution was underway back home and Porfirio Díaz was deposed. The supply ships to Clipperton stopped and the colonists were left to their own devices, cut off from the outside world and seemingly forgotten by Mexico which had other concerns. The islanders subsisted on mostly seafood, land crabs, birds and bird eggs. The coconut groves on the islands produced 3 coconuts every six months per tree and this was not enough vitamin C for the islanders. Slowly, the colonists came down with scurvy and a few died. An American ship ran aground in February of 1914 and was so appalled at the conditions they saw at the Clipperton colony, they took their lifeboat to Acapulco and pleaded for assistance from the Mexicans. The provisional revolutionary government denied any help. This is where the US Navy stepped in. The commander of a US Navy ship in Acapulco at the time had heard of the islanders' plight and decided to mount a rescue operation of his own. When the ship arrived at the island, Governor Arnaud refused to give up his post and refused evacuation. The last remaining guano miner, the German named Schultz, was the only one who left on the US Navy ship. The ship left behind 5 months' worth of provisions to keep the colony afloat until the political situation on the Mexican mainland sorted itself out. By then there were 6 children on the island, all born there, 6 women and 15 remaining men, mostly Mexican army. When the colonists waved good-bye to the US ship, they had no idea that the next ship to stop and take notice would be 3 years into the future.

They did see a ship the next year on May 5, 1915. Because some colonists had recently died of scurvy, Arnaud felt that it was time to abandon the colony. All able-bodied men on the island except one got into a small boat to try to go out and flag down the ship. Clipperton's choppy surf and dangerous reefs are often very hard to navigate. The boat never made it out to the passing ship. It capsized and all hands were lost. Ramón Arnaud would be the first and last governor of the colony of La Isla de la Pasión.

This is where the story takes a certain *Lord of the Flies* twist but without Ralph or Piggy. As the sole remaining man on the island, the lighthouse keeper, Victoriano Alvarez, declared himself the King of Passion Island and began issuing proclamations fitting of his title. Notably, Alvarez declared that all the women on the island were his personal property and he could have his way with any one of them as he wished. When he commanded that a 15-year-old girl live with him in his shack at the base of the island's volcano, the girl's mother refused. Alvarez killed them both. The rest of the women and children, now numbering 10, lived in fear of Alvarez who issued a never ending stream of declarations and forced them to do things at will. The high hopes of the young bride of the dashing Mexican colonial governor had turned to secret plots with the other women, and Alicia Arnaud eventually vowed to kill Alvarez. In July of 1917 the lighthouse keeper entered the hut of Família Arnaud and proclaimed that Alicia Arnaud would live with him and she had a few days to prepare. On the morning of July 18, 1917, fellow colonist Tirza Rendon went to Alvarez' home along with Alicia and little Ramoncito who was 9 years old at the time. Alvarez was surprised and told them to leave, at which time Tirza Rendon grabbed a hammer and hit the lighthouse keeper in the head. The blow knocked him down, but he got up and came after Alicia with an axe. Tirza hit him again as Alicia yelled at little Ramón to leave, and to take the guns with him. When little Ramón left the hut, to his surprise he saw a large ship very near to shore. Excited, he ran back into the lighthouse keeper's shack to announce the news. The little boy was met with a grisly scene, the battered body of Victoriano Alvarez dead on the floor. The women left the shack and called the other colonists to the shore to get the attention of the passing ship.

The ship was the USS *Yorktown*. The American naval vessel was on maneuvers as part of its duties connected with World War I, specifically, it was searching the small islands of the Pacific for Germans who were hiding out. The captain of the *Yorktown* described the haggard condition of the colonists: children were wearing clothes made of sailcloth or old flour bags and it was clear that everyone was malnourished and distressed. The *Yorktown* sailed into the port of Acapulco on July 21, 1917, and family members were waiting for the islanders. The news in Mexico had said that the colonists had perished, so the reunion on the Mexican mainland was a joyous one.

After the colonists returned to the mainland sensational stories circulated in the press as to what happened on the island, especially in connection with the death of Captain Arnaud. Stories said that his small boat was attacked by a huge manta ray or octopus. There were also stories of cannibalism that were not true, and plots involving German and French intrigue. In the 1930s there was a movie made in Mexico called *La Isla de la Pasión* in which the main protagonist, played by Mexican film star Pedro Amendáriz, fights off an attack by French gunboats that arrived to take over the Mexican colony. At the same time of the movie's release, the ultimate fate of the island was decided. In Porfirio Díaz' time, the president had asked the king of Italy, Victor Emmanuel the Third to arbitrate the dispute over Clipperton between the Mexicans and the French, with both countries agreeing to be bound by the king's decision. The king decided in 1931 that the island was French territory based on the 1711 "discovery" and the 1858 formal declaration by the French emperor. In 1932 the Mexican Congress ratified the declaration and gave up all territorial claims to Clipperton Island.

The saga of the Mexican colony of Isla de la Pasión has a curious footnote. 6 decades later, little Ramoncito Arnaud, the first person to be born on the island, returned to Clipperton on an expedition led by French oceanographer and adventurer Jacques Cousteau. Most of the evidence of Mexican habitation had long since gone but surprisingly Arnaud's memory was very clear. Besides the brief American presence during World War Two there has been no permanent settlement on the island since the doomed Mexican colony. The island was attached to French Polynesia for many years until 2007 when it reverted to the direct control of the Minister of Overseas France. The French have no current plans for an island that they never really controlled or inhabited. Clipperton has been left to the terns, the crabs and the ghosts of the unfortunate Mexican colonists.

JESUS MALVERDE: ROGUE OR SAINT?

He is known by several nicknames: Mexico's Robin Hood, The Generous Bandit, The Angel of the Poor, The Drug Saint and The King of Sinaloa, but was Jesus Malverde even real? And to whether or not he was real, does it matter? He has a following of hundreds of thousands of people in Mexico and the United States, mostly the dispossessed and the downtrodden, and to them he is very real. Who was this man?

There is very little in the historical record to support Jesus Malverde as a real historical figure. The legend is supposedly based on a man named Jesus Juárez Mazo, who was from a small town outside the city of, the capital of the great state of Sinaloa on the Pacific coast of Mexico. Mazo was born on December 24, 1870 and died on May 3, 1909, killed by the authorities for his banditry. He grew up extremely poor during a time of huge disparities in income in Mexico, and especially in Sinaloa. This was the age of the Porfiriato, the reign of the Mexican dictator Porfirio Díaz, and Sinaloa was ruled by an elite class of wealthy hacienda owners, known as *hacendados* in Spanish. Mazo's parents either died of a curable disease or because they were just poor, according to legend, and instead of struggling to earn a living with his menial labor jobs, the man later known as Malverde turned to a life of robbing from the rich. He is called *El Bandido Generoso*, the Generous Bandit, because he gave away most of what he stole from the wealthy *hacendados*.

In one of the more popular versions of the story, the wealthy governor of Sinaloa, Francisco Cañedo, challenged Jesus Malverde to steal the governor's sword out of his hacienda, and promised to grant him a pardon if he was successful. Malverde slipped in and out of the governor's home and left a note in place of the sword. Incensed, the governor went back on his word and had the police hunt down Malverde to face justice.

According to popular lore, Jesus Malverde met his demise through hanging. He was executed outside the courthouse in Culiacán and was denied a proper burial. He was just left to hang on the makeshift gallows the governor had set up. When his body fell to the ground, people placed stones and pebbles on top of it, in the sort of a fashion of a cairn, to give their popular bandit a more proper burial. Later, a shrine popped up on the spot. An alternate ending to the Jesus Malverde story has him shot by firing squad and left to lie in the dirt. A woman then ran up to his body and dug up some of the dirt that was soaked in his blood. Later that blood-soaked dirt was put into small bottles and shrines throughout northern Mexico grew up around the veneration of these relics.

As previously mentioned, there is little evidence that Jesus Malverde was even real. The dates and incidents of his life loosely coincide with the life of Jesus Juárez Mazo, but there is no confirmation that Mazo ever gave back to the poor or that he had the famous run-in with the Sinaloan governor. Researchers claim that the Jesus Malverde persona is based on an amalgamation of two other bandits from the state of Sinaloa popular around the same time. They were named Heraclio Bernal and Felipe Bachomo. These two were seen as heroes of their time because of their disdain for authority and for their elusiveness. The death of a real man, Mazo, though, seemed to be the starting point of the development of Jesus Malverde as a folk saint.

In the various versions of the legend, a shrine to Malverde sprang up near the courthouse where he was supposedly killed. For most of the 20th Century, this man was seen as a miracle worker of the common person, the poor and the otherwise marginalized. Jesus Malverde was a victim of society's injustices while he was alive, so as a poor person who is also a victim, he will listen to you. He will hear your prayers and deliver miracles to you. People have sought out his help mostly with issues regarding finances, employment, incarceration and other run-ins with the law and business problems. The devotee can petition Jesus Malverde for help, much like one would ask for a miracle from any Catholic saint. The only difference here is that if the devotee fails to uphold his or her end of the bargain, the petition for a miracle will turn into a curse.

What does the Catholic Church think of all of this? Simply put, it doesn't recognize him even though the common people treat Jesus Malverde as they would a Catholic saint on par with Saint Jude or even the Virgin of Guadalupe. He even has a feast day, May 3rd, the day he was supposedly executed by the authorities. There are shrines all over northern Mexico to Jesus Malverde and people go to them as they would any other saint. In his 2012 visit to Mexico, Pope Benedict XVI admonished followers of folk saints like Jesus Malverde likening the phenomenon to a cult. Even with the pope coming to Mexico and shaking his finger at wayward parishioners, the adoration of Jesus Malverde has increased over time and sees no sign of stopping.

Long before the pope's visit, the popularity of this saint got a huge boost from the illegal drug trade. In the 1980s and 1990s the various cartels appropriated the Jesus Malverde phenomenon as part of a calculated PR strategy. See, Malverde was like them, fighting against authority and giving back to the community with their illicit earnings, building hospitals, schools and roads in poor and rural communities and providing employment when the government refused to help. The drug traffickers used their supposed devotion to this folk saint to also show that they, too, are common people, just like you and me. Many Jesus Malverde shrines throughout Mexico have been built by the *narcotraficantes* themselves. The mustachioed image of Jesus Malverde is associated with the drug trade more on the American side of the border than on the Mexican side.

The modern shrine to Jesus Malverde in Culiacán is across the train tracks from the original shrine that sprouted up right after the bandit's supposed 1909 death. The original shrine was demolished in the 1970s to make a parking lot to accommodate the ever expanding government buildings surrounding the original courthouse. No one wanted to be the one to do the actual demolition of the shrine and according to accounts at the time the bulldozer operator was drunk while doing the demo so as to ease the pain of the thoughts of the sin he was committing. Eyewitnesses claim that when the bulldozer got to the cairn that covered the body of Jesus Malverde that the rocks were jumping out like popcorn popping out of a fire. Alas, no film footage exists.

The new shrine is modern and has a main altar with a bust of the saint and ample room for adequate veneration. People come from all over Mexico to make this pilgrimage to ask Jesus Malverde for help. Alms are collected for local charities, and those articles left behind in thanks are given away to the poor. Every May 2nd there is a lively celebration at the shrine in the evening and in the morning of May 3rd - the day of Malverde's supposed execution - the main bust of the saint is taken out of the shrine, cleaned, and paraded around the neighborhood. Vendors sell food and the atmosphere is very festive, much like any Mexican fiesta to celebrate a saint, except the statue doesn't end up at a church and there is no mass. To those people who celebrate him and believe in him, there is no doubt that Jesus Malverde is the real deal.

So what do we make of the miracles ascribed to this folk saint? Are we seeing the power of focused intention in action? Is it mass psychosis? Wishful thinking? The questions are left to the researchers and the faithful.

HILDE KRÜGER: NAZI SPY IN MEXICO

The year was 1941. While it seemed the whole world would explode in a new world war, in one of the many French-Revival mansions in the upscale Colonia Roma neighborhood of Mexico City an elaborate party was about to begin. The gathering included noted industrialists, artists, members of the social and intellectual elite of Mexico and young politicians. On the guest list was Miguel Alemán, the Mexican Secretary of the Interior, who 5 years later would be president of Mexico. Soon after the handsome Interior Minister arrived at the gala, a young woman entered the room accompanied by Ramón Betata, who served as Mexico's Undersecretary for Foreign Relations. The platinum-blonde young woman, who instantly commanded the attention of the entire party, was Hilde Krüger a German-born movie actress who had recently arrived in Mexico via Hollywood. The future president of Mexico, Alemán, whose name in Spanish, ironically, means "German," finally caught the attention of this Teutonic goddess and stole a few moments away to chat with her privately. To Hilde, the man before her was just another person of influence to add to her ever-growing circle and the party was just another lavish event on her social calendar. She smiled, sipped her drink and chatted flirtatiously with the future president.

After many years of research from history buffs and cinematic biographers, Hilde Krüger's life remains somewhat enigmatic. There are two sources with conflicting dates and places of her birth. In one, she is born in Cologne, Gemany in 1912. Another source cites that she was born in Berlin in 1914. She did seem to spend her early childhood in Berlin and as a teenager she became a stage actress. By the early 1930s, on the eve of the Nazis coming to power in Germany, the young Hilde distinguished herself as a budding film star and modeled for fashion magazines and cigarette cards. It was after Hilde's appearance in a 1934 film that she caught the eye of Joseph Goebbels, the Minister of Propaganda for the new Hitler government who also controlled the German film industry. Goebbels cast the buxom, blonde, blue-eyed Krüger in propaganda films to promote the glory of the new Third Reich, but even a powerful man such as Goebbels was not immune to her charms. Goebbels wife, Magda Goebbels, knew of the affair between her husband and the young starlet and not coincidentally Hilde's roles in the German film industry dried up. Goebbels tried passing Hilde off to the Gestapo, the secret state police of National Socialist Germany, but she eventually caught the attention of the Abwehr, Germany's military intelligence agency. Hilde was personally recruited by Admiral Wilhelm Canaris, the head of the Abwehr. Canaris was no fan of the Nazis, but he was a German patriot having distinguished himself in the First World War for saving his ship, the SMS *Dresden*, in a 1914 battle with the British in the South Atlantic called the Battle of the Falklands. Canaris would later be captured and escape his captors after his ship ran aground in Chile's Juan Fernández Islands. Canaris had a deep interest in Latin America having spent most of his seafaring career in South American waters, and knew of the need to gather intelligence from this area of the world to help Germany. He had a plan for the beautiful and alluring Hilde.

In 1940, after a brief sojourn in England, Hilde Krüger arrived in Hollywood. She never became the star that some had expected her to be, but she did burst onto the social scene and moved in influential circles, capturing the attention of swashbuckling actor Errol Flynn and American oil millionaire John Paul Getty, on whose arm she could be seen at parties and movie premieres. She was also associated with Gert von Gontard, the heir to the Budweiser beer fortune, with reports of her traveling between Los Angeles and St. Louis, where the King of Beers is headquartered. There are some reports that Hilde had married a German-American businessman during the brief time she was in the States, but this does not fit the greater narrative of her time in America. At the time the FBI and the OSS had been watching Krüger and had wondered who was paying her bills. The actress did not get many parts in Hollywood and so how could she afford her luxury suite at the Beverly Wilshire Hotel, her beautiful clothes and fashionable jewelry? Who was behind this? The Gestapo? German military intelligence? Joseph Goebbels himself? In an FBI file declassified in 1985 we found that the agency figured it out. Oilman Getty was paying her bills, and after it became clear that the United States would most likely side with the British in the eventual war with Germany, Getty arranged for Hilde's travel documents to get her into Mexico. This was in early 1941.

By the time of Hilde Krüger's arrival in Mexico, German propaganda had been flooding the Mexican media for over half a decade. Arthur Dietrich, the press attaché at the German embassy in Mexico City, fed the two major newspapers, *Excelsior* and *El Universal*, a steady stream of pro-Third-Reich news stories. He even was instrumental in founding a high-culture magazine called *Timon*, to help disseminate the message of the new German Reich among the more educated Mexican readers. By the late 1930s, public opinion in Mexico was being swayed in favor of Germany, much to the regret of the Americans and British. Scholars argue that one of the main reasons for the 1938 nationalization of Mexico's oil industry was due to pressure from Adolf Hitler and fascist Italy's Benito Mussolini. The American and British companies that formerly controlled Mexico's oil production were not selling to the Axis Powers and Hitler had his eyes on Mexico's petroleum to help fuel the Luftwaffe and the rest of the growing German military machine. As soon as the nationalization was complete, oil tankers left the port of Veracruz for refineries in Hamburg. Arthur Dietrich's propaganda machine in Mexico not only helped win sympathy for Germany's cause in that country, it inspired hundreds of Mexicans of German ancestry to return to the Fatherland and help in building Hitler's new society. Others were recruited to help on the Mexican home front. This is when Operation Pastorius was born.

Operation Pastorius, developed by German military intelligence and carried out by two dozen Mexicans of German heritage, had several objectives. Its nexus of operations was in the northern Mexican industrial city of Monterrey and its primary purpose was to assess military capabilities of the United States. Its other purposes included industrial espionage against the Americans and the smuggling of strategic raw materials such as mercury and tungsten out of Mexico. The head of the spies in Monterrey was Georg Nicolaus whose cover was working for Blaupunkt, a small German electronics firm. Another major spy was Otto Guido Moebius whose father founded Mexican megabank Banorte, and who owned several businesses in northern Mexico, including a chemical plant on the top of which was erected a massive radio antenna that would connect him directly with Berlin. In the midst of all of this was Hilde Krüger who was passing along information she received from Nicolaus and Moebius to the head of military intelligence, Wilhelm Canaris. Hilde's time with the Monterrey spies is pretty murky and it is unclear who she was working for at this time. By late 1941 Canaris had grown resentful of the Nazis and began working for the underground resistance to oust Hitler from power. So, we will never know if Hilde was working for the Nazis or indirectly working for the German resistance, or whether or not she even knew who she was working for. One can only wonder what back room deals were made between her and those in power for her own survival. As a footnote, her mentor Canaris would face execution for his involvement in the 1943 Generals Plot, a plan to assassinate Adolf Hitler.

After the United States declared war on the Axis Powers in December of 1941, the Americans put increasing pressure on the Mexicans to give up their neutrality and take sides in the war. In January of 1942 Mexican President Manuel Avila Camacho allowed the US to use Mexico's ports and airfields for the war effort. Also that month, the US pressured Mexico to deal with Nazi spies in its territory and to end the propaganda coming from Arthur Dietrich's office at the German embassy in Mexico City. Dietrich was expelled from the country, and the US government handed over a list of 24 people who were part of Operation Pastorius in Monterrey. All 24 on this black list, except one, were arrested and sent to a hard labor prison in Perote, in the Mexican state of Veracruz. The lone person given clemency was none other than Hilde Krüger.

Mexico declared war on Germany on May 25, 1942. Hilde Krüger remained in Mexico and went on to make 4 feature films: "Casa de Mujeres" – "House of Women"- in 1942 and three films in 1945. Those films were "Adulterio" ("Adultery"), "Él que murió de amor" ("He who Died of Love"), and "Bartolo Toca la flauta" ("Bartolo Plays the Flute"). There were rumors in the press about her secret life and there was some pressure to have her deported in the days after Operation Pastorius. Hilde solved her problems once again by using her associations with the influential. In 1942 she married Nacho de la Torre, a wealthy businessman and grandson of former president of Mexico, Porfirio Díaz. De la Torre suggested she enroll in UNAM, Mexico's largest university, and earn a degree in Mexican history to learn more about her adoptive country and to further legitimize her stay in Mexico. Krüger went on to become quite an accomplished scholar, specializing in the era called the Second Empire in which Hapsburg Emperor Maximilian and the Empress Carlota ruled Mexico. In 1944 Hilde Krüger published her thesis titled *La Malinche o el adiós a los mitos – The Malinche, or Goodbye to the Myths* – about the life and times of Doña Marina, the beautiful and intelligent indigenous woman who served as the translator and lover to Spanish conquistador Hernán Cortés and helped to overthrow the mighty Aztec Empire. Undoubtedly, as a woman in a similar situation and faced with difficult choices in the circles of wealth and power in which she moved, Hilde could identify with The Malinche. As an aside, the artwork for Hilde's book on La Malinche was done by famous Mexican social realist painter José Clemente Orozco. This just shows how well connected she actually was.

In 1956, Hilde Krüger divorced the grandson of Porfirio Díaz and married the richest man in Cuba, the Venezuelan-born Julio Lobo Olavarría. The marriage lasted less than a year and with a hefty divorce settlement Hilde relocated to New York City where she set up house in a luxury apartment in Manhattan. Moving among the wealthy social circles there, she soon married a Russian-born industrialist. Hilde made one more movie in 1958 called *"Zum Goldenen Ochsen"* ("The Golden Ox Inn"), a German-Swiss film shot in France, but little is known of her life after this. Some sources claim she died on a visit to a newly reunified Germany in 1991. Another source claims that she died at the age of 94 in the year 2008 in Manhattan. There are so many discrepancies and missing pieces of Hilde's life we may never know how or where she died or what she was really up to during World War II. To this day, Hilde Krüger remains a somewhat delightful and fascinating enigma.

CAJEMÉ AND THE YAQUI INDIAN REPUBLIC

The fiesta in Bácum was one of the largest the town had ever seen. The year was 1876. After over 340 years of domination from outsiders, the dusty municipality located in the desert of Sonora had a reason to celebrate. The Yaqui leader known as Cajemé had just declared that the 8 Native American villages and their surrounding lands would henceforth be independent from Mexico, thus creating the first self-governing, sovereign, wholly indigenous political entity in the area since the Spanish Conquest. While the town celebrated, the native elders knew that a peace with Mexico would be a long way away, and after three centuries of struggle many had their doubts of the new nation's survivability. Cajemé had years of military experience, a deep knowledge of Mexican politics and culture, and overwhelmingly enthusiastic support from his people that seemed to contradict the feelings of the most cautious of the elders. The leader of the new country in what used to be the northwestern part of Mexico felt invincible on his day of declaration.

Cajemé was born to Yaqui parents in Villa de Pitic, now called Hermosillo, the modern-day capital of the Mexican state of Sonora, in 1835. His Christian name at baptism was José María Bonifacio Leiva Pérez. His Yaqui name of Cajemé, used throughout most of his adult life, means "The one who does not stop to drink water." Before we get into the life and times of this man and the independent republic formed in Sonora in the 1870s, we must first give a little background of the Yaqui people.

For thousands of years the Yaquis – also known as the *Hiaki* or *Yoeme* - and their ancestors occupied parts of the American Southwest and parts of the Mexican states of Sinaloa, Sonora and Durango. The Yaqui adapted to whatever geographical area they found themselves in. Those living on the Sea of Cortez lived a maritime existence and subsisted mostly on fish. Those who lived in the mountains and the northern deserts tended to be hunter-gatherers. The majority of the Yaqui people lived in villages and cultivated corn, beans and squash. The heartland of the Yaqui was along the Yaqui River, a lifeline flowing through one of the harshest deserts in Mexico. The first documented encounter between Yaquis and Europeans was in 1533 when a small expedition led by Diego de Guzmán entered Yaqui territory. In the early 1500s the Yaquis numbered about 30,000 living in almost 80 villages which were mostly located near the Yaqui River. When the first group of Yaquis met the Spanish face to face, a tribal elder literally made a line in the sand for the Spanish not to cross and told Guzmán to leave the area, refusing him food, water and shelter.   A battle ensued and the Spanish retreated. Thirty years later an attempt to set up a Spanish colony in Yaqui territory failed and the settlers were driven back to central Mexico.   In 1608 the Spanish and the Yaquis clashed once again, resulting in two disastrous defeats for the Spanish. A peace agreement was reached in 1610 and the Jesuits arrived seven years later to set up missions in Yaqui territory. The 150-year relationship the Yaquis had with the Jesuits was mutually beneficial and for the most part peaceful. Jesuits saved souls and set up small industry; the Indians got to keep most of their culture, their lands and social structure. The discovery of silver in Yaqui territory in 1684 caused some tensions between natives and Europeans, but did not cause the Yaquis to revolt. The next big uprising would be in 1740 when 5,000 Yaquis and 1,000 Spaniards were killed. The central government in Mexico City then decided to tighten control over these people. The Jesuits, long-time advocates for the Yaqui, had been losing power in the region by the mid-1700s and by the 1760s they were completely expelled from Mexico. With the departure of the Jesuits and the closing down of some of the missions, the Yaquis and the Spanish maintained an uneasy peace until the Mexican Revolution began in 1810 and the Yaquis faced new challenges from a new group of people who now attempted to rule them from faraway Mexico City. During the Mexican fight for independence, while the government of Sonora and the Spanish elites of the area sided with the Spanish Crown, the Yaquis remained neutral and refused to participate in the conflict. To the new authorities in Mexico City, this indicated that the Yaquis considered themselves not to be subject to outside rule. The newly formed Mexican government, seeking to integrate all of former New Spain into the new political unit called Mexico, sent tax collectors to Yaqui lands proclaiming that the Yaquis were citizens of a new nation which needed money in its treasury. Given the Yaqui history of resistance to outside intervention, the tax collecting project did not go well. A revolt in 1825 beat back the new central Mexican government, but it returned intent on controlling every inch of Sonora. Thus began a series of minor revolts, skirmishes and guerilla attacks for the next 50 years until Cajemé proclaimed the new Yaqui republic in 1876.

Cajemé was not born to any high station that prepared him to be a leader. His decisive role in the Yaqui independence movement came from a solid set of life experiences that made him ready when circumstances called on him. Born in 1835, he left his native land in 1849 to accompany his father Fernando to California which had been ceded to the United States in the Mexican War just a year before. His father was part of the large influx of people to the San Francisco/Sacramento area looking for gold. While in California helping his father as a gold prospector, Cajemé learned English and gained valuable experience in the larger world. Cajemé returned with Fernando two years later and because of his father's success in the California gold fields, Cajemé was enrolled in an exclusive private school located in the town of Guaymas and excelled in his coursework, learning to read and write Spanish with ease. He impressed the schoolmaster, Cayetano Navarro, who was also the prefect of Guaymas. After leaving school Cajemé joined the local militia called the Urbanos which was captained by Navarro. When Cajemé was 18 he had his first taste of battle with the Urbanos as they had assisted Sonoran state authorities and the Mexican Army in quelling a series of rebellions in Sonora instigated by foreign mining interests. In the latter half of 1854, the 19-year-old Cajemé decided to leave Sonora and traveled to Tepic in the state of Nayarit where he became a blacksmith. Drawn to military service once again, he joined the Mexican Army, San Blas Battalion, but grew tired of it after 3 months. He deserted the army and fled to the mountains of Nayarit to work as a miner. Knowing that the army was searching for him for desertion, Cajemé went to Mazatlán and joined a battalion comprised mostly of indigenous fighters, specifically soldiers from the Pima, Mayo, Yaqui and Opata tribes. As a trooper in the army, Cajemé caught the attention of General Ramón Corona due to his ability to speak 3 languages and his previous military experience. In the nearly dozen years as General Corona's aide-de-camp, Cajemé participated in the War of Reform and fought against the French during the reign of the Habsburg Emperor of Mexico, Maximilian. As an aside, most Yaquis back in Sonora at the time liked having the French in power in Mexico City because Maximilian represented weak central government control in a faraway capital which would leave them alone for the most part. Cajemé rounded out his military career by serving under the command of Ignacio Pesqueira who made Cajemé a captain in the cavalry. When Ignacio Pesqueira became governor of Sonora, he had big plans for Cajemé. He named him to the office of *Alcalde Mayor* of the Yaqui people, an appointment Pesqueira had hoped would end the Yaqui problem forever. Cajemé had proved his loyalty to Mexico and Pesqueira thought him perfect for the job. This was 1872.

Instead of pacifying the Yaquis once and for all, Cajemé announced that he did not recognize the Mexican government, united the 8 Yaqui towns and surrounding lands, and declared and independent Yaqui republic. The government of the new nation would be based on the traditional Yaqui social structure with each town having 5 governing groups called *yau'uras*. There was a *yau'ura* for civil authority, one for military authority, one for fiesta authority, another for religious authority and one called the *kohtumbre yau'ura* which preserved the sacred customs surrounding Holy Week, including the Deer Dance. The governing bodies would be elected from groups of elders In each town and each *yau'ura* would vote democratically on issues facing it. As a social reformer, Cajemé reinstituted the notion of communal ownership of Yaqui lands within the Yaqui territory. He initiated taxation and foreign trade controls. Cajemé told the Mexican authorities that his new nation would not recognize Mexico if they did not give the Yaquis the autonomy they had craved for centuries. It all seemed good and well, but while the Yaquis were fortifying themselves and building a new nation with enthusiasm and hope for the future, the central government in Mexico City had other plans for the so-called Yaqui Republic.

The new war between the Yaqui and Mexico featured a succession of battles and brutalities on both sides. By 1885, there was dissent coming from the ranks of the Yaqui military. One of Cajemé's officers, Loreto Molina, tried to take over the government of the new republic, and with the help of Mexican authorities, had a plan to assassinate Cajemé. Cajemé heard of the plot and fled, but by then he was a marked man. The Mexican government sent a well-equipped force of 1,200 men to end the Yaqui independence movement once and for all. Of note to military historians, this force carried two primitive machine guns which would be the first to be used in major combat. When the force arrived at the Yaqui River, the first Mexican company met with defeat and retreated. By the middle of 1886, however, it seemed as if the Mexican forces would win, as they had captured Cajemé's fort at El Añil and destroyed much of the Yaqui military's other fortifications. On a tip from a woman who was loyal to Loreto Molina and who opposed the endless wars with Mexico, Cajemé was captured in the small Indian village of San José de Guaymas, just north of the town of Guaymas, on the 13th of April, 1887. His captor was General Angel Martínez who would later rise to the position of Vice President under the reign of dictator Porfirio Díaz. Martínez put Cajemé on a gunboat that sailed up the Yaqui River and paraded him around the Yaqui towns to make sure everyone knew he was captured. On April 23, 1887, at eleven in the morning, Cajemé was shot by firing squad, thus ending his life and the dreams of the new indigenous republic that briefly existed in Sonora.

As a postscript, the Yaquis did not fare well immediately after Cajemé's execution. Tired of the endless wars and skirmishes, the Mexican government decided to end the Yaqui "problem" once and for all. Although many Yaquis went into hiding and escaped to the mountains or fled to neighboring states, many were captured by the Mexican government and sold into slavery. The slaves were taken to the Yucatán to work on plantations and many Yaquis did not survive the alien tropical climate or the harsh living and working conditions. The more troublesome members of the tribe were either executed or deported to faraway places such as the islands of the Caribbean or the nation of Bolivia in South America. In spite of all of this, the remaining Yaquis in Sonora continued to resist the Mexican government in one way or another. After the "last stand" of the Yaquis at what has been called the Battle of Cerro del Gallo in 1927, Mexico established armed garrisons in each village with a majority Yaqui population. This was a solution that seemed to keep the people at bay. It is amazing that in the face of all of the aggression used against them in their struggle for sovereignty that the Yaqui still exist today in Sonora, living life much as they have for millennia and maintaining their cultural institutions as they always have. The Yaqui language has even seen a revival in recent years as classes and schools have popped up to focus on the language. In spite of everything that the Yaquis have gone through it is quite evident that nothing can completely break the spirit of the Yaqui. The tribe, and the memory of the Yaqui Republic, live on.

WILLIAM LAMPORT, MEXICO'S IRISH WOULD-BE KING

The year was 1633. A ship in the chilly North Atlantic near the ancient French city of Saint-Malo found itself under siege by pirates. Among the passengers captured by the buccaneers was a boy of 13 who was fleeing England. The teenage boy had no money or valuables but explained to the pirates that had escaped from an English prison and was heading for the European continent. The boy had been convicted of sedition by Crown authorities for publishing pamphlets against the English king and had been arrested and jailed. He escaped the prison and found himself on that captured ship. The pirates took him in and for several years the boy fought alongside them and distinguished himself in battle.

The boy's name was William Lamport. He was born in County Wexford, Ireland, around 1610. His parents, Richard and Alonsa Lamport, were from English merchant families which had settled in southern Ireland centuries before. The Lamports, as with similar merchant families of the area, saw their autonomy diminish throughout the 16th Century as English Tudor control over Ireland increased. Their Catholic faith was also threatened by new laws enacted by King Henry VII of England starting in the 1530s. William Lamport's grandfather, Patrick Lamport, aligned himself with the traditional Irish nobility against the increasing power of the English in Ireland and actively resisted rule from London. In 1617, when William was 7 years old, his grandfather was captured and executed on the personal orders of King James I of England. Soon after the execution, William Lamport and his brother John left Wexford for a Jesuit school in Dublin. The tutelage of the Jesuit fathers lasted for a few years, William then went to school in England at Gresham College, located in central London. He excelled in mathematics and Greek and it was there, as a young teen, where Lamport expanded his political conscience. It was at this time, as previously mentioned, when his activities landed him in jail and eventually into the hands of the pirates.

Young William said good-bye the pirates while harboring in Bordeaux, France sometime in the 1630s and made his way to a community of expatriate Irishmen living in La Coruña in northwestern Spain. He soon enrolled in the Colegio de Niños Nobles, a school for Irish exiles living in Spain located near the shrine of Santiago de Compostela, the notable destination of the Catholic World's Spanish Pilgrimage. It was here in Spain where William Lamport Hispanicized his name to Don Guillén Lombardo. It was also here where Lamport got the attention of Spanish and Irish nobles alike, and even the king of Spain, when he secured the allegiance to the Spanish king of the 250 members of the two pirate ships with whom he previously sailed. Thereafter, Lamport's former pirate friends proved to be important mercenaries for the Spanish Crown and helped win victories in a few Spanish naval battles. Lamport was still a teenager when he received a scholarship to study at the College of the Irish in Salamanca. While at the college Lamport's star seemed to be on the ascent and he was noticed by the Count-Duke of Olivares, the Spanish king's principal minister. Lamport was then offered another scholarship to study at the elite Colegio de San Lorenzo de Escorial, a training ground for ambitious public servants of the Spanish government. When Lamport left his schooling he distinguished himself in the service of Spain's King Phillip the Fourth on the battlefield, helping Spain win many campaigns in Europe. As the protégé of the Count-Duke of Olivares, the young Irishman also served in espionage and diplomatic missions on behalf of Spain throughout the European continent. Lamport even adopted Olivares' principal last name, Guzmán, and later added that to his Hispanicized name thus becoming Don Guillén Lombardo de Guzmán. A favorite at the Spanish court in Madrid, Lamport became well connected with people in power and involved himself in politics. He became the chief architect of a plot to have the Spanish take over Ireland, which would have made the Emerald Isle a tribute-paying state within the Spanish Empire. Ultimately, Lamport's plan was dismissed, but his ambitious nature was not squelched by this temporary setback.

While in Madrid Lamport fell in love with a minor noblewoman, Doña Ana de Cano y Leyva. It's unclear whether Lamport married her of if they were in a state of unwed cohabitation. Doña Ana became pregnant with Lamport's child at which point we see him flee Spain for the New World, perhaps to avoid a scandal or to leave an unhappy marriage. He was on a boat bound for Mexico on April 21, 1640, along with a new Viceroy, the Marqués de Villena. Some historical accounts state that Lamport was sent to Mexico City as a spy for his benefactor, the king's chief minister the Count-Duke of Olivares. There was some unrest and dissatisfaction in Spain's colonies in the Americas at the time and the minister needed someone whom he could trust to send accurate reports back to him in Spain. The causes of concern were coming from the population of New Spain's *criollos*, or those of pure Spanish descent born in the New World. The *criollos* were protesting unfair treatment with regard to taxation and access to participation in government. In colonial Mexico, there existed a rigid social and racial hierarchy with *peninuslares*, or those newly arrived Spanish subjects born in Spain, at the top.

In late 1640 Lamport arrived in Mexico City and rented a room from Don Fernando Carrillo, the *Escribano Mayor*, or Chief Clerk, for the Spanish government in Mexico City. The well-educated Lamport, who knew 14 languages, became the tutor to Carrillo's son, Sebastián. It wasn't long before Lamport began to move in influential circles among the *criollo* elite of New Spain, and sent a steady stream of well detailed reports to his benefactor the Count-Duke back at the Spanish Court in Madrid. Lamport appears to have gotten a little too close to his espionage subjects, though, and seemed to play a crucial role in the *criollo* conspiracy to overthrow the new Viceroy, the Marqués de Villena. The conspiracy was led by the Bishop of Puebla, Juan de Palafox y Mendoza. Lamport, who was sympathetic to the concerns of the *criollos*, served as a messenger between Bishop Palafox and Madrid, and eventually got the go-ahead from the Count-Duke of Olivares to oust Viceroy Villena. With the backing of Spanish troops, Bishop Palafox deposed the viceroy in June of 1642. Because of his pivotal role in this change of power, Lamport sought a position in the new regime of Bishop-Viceroy Palafox. As he was Irish and not a

Spanish *peninsular* or even a *criollo*, Lamport was denied any role in the new Palafox government, and again his ambition was frustrated.

A visit at the Carrillo residence from an indigenous miner from Taxco named Don Ignacio would change the course of Lamport's life once again. Don Ignacio came seeking legal advice about the abuses the indigenous miners suffered at the hands of their Spanish overlords. Lamport met with Don Ignacio frequently and during one of the visits, the indigenous man introduced Lamport to peyote, the cactus with hallucinogenic properties. During one of the mescaline-induced peyote sessions, Don Ignacio claimed to see the future, where Lamport ruled over all of New Spain as an emperor. This fed Lamport's ego and this ambitious young Irishman began a new project in the fall of 1642: laying out the first ever plan for Mexico's independence from Spain.

Lamport worked diligently on his plan. His dream was to create a society in Mexico free of the rigid social and racial caste-like divisions imposed by the Spanish. Lamport envisioned Mexico as one of the most prosperous countries in the world if freedoms were granted and the economic restrictions from the mother country eliminated. As a colony of Spain, the Mexicans were required to send a fifth of everything mined back to Spain. Without the siphoning off of this "royal fifth," or *quinto*, and with taxes imposed on New Spain kept in-country, Lamport imagined a land of unending prosperity. Additionally, there were severe trade restrictions in colonial Mexico that were hindering its progress. Under Lamport's vision of an independent nation of Mexico, trade with the Orient and other nations of the world would flow freely, thus appealing to the sensibilities of the members of the wealthy *criollo* merchant class who had complained about trade restrictions for generations. Social reforms would come with the economic ones. Lamport proposed complete legal equality under the law for all races and socio-economic classes, and in his plan he proposed the end of slavery and the elimination of forced labor drafts and tributes paid to the Crown by indigenous communities. Indian communities would be allowed to keep their languages, customs and laws. Popular assemblies would sprout up all over Mexico with an emphasis on decentralized power. The state would be ruled by a limited monarch, initially Lamport himself, who would be the first emperor of Mexico, who would lead the country with the consent of an active parliament elected by the people. If the monarch was a tyrant, he could be deposed by popular vote. In Lamport's idyllic image of his new country, freed African slaves, wealthy *peninsulares* and marginalized members of impoverished indigenous communities would all participate in government and would have equal rights under a strictly codified law.

Lamport was way ahead of his time with this line of thinking. What were his influences? Where did he get his sense of egalitarianism? Historians often credit Lamport's sharp intellect and his ambitious nature for wanting to create a merit-based society free of ethnic and social barriers that he himself could not overcome in colonial New Spain. Others suggest that he was influenced by the writings of the 16th Century Dominican Friar Bartolomé de las Casas, an advocate for the rights of the indigenous in the Spanish colonies of the New World. What historians seem to overlook is Lamport's time aboard the pirate ships in his formative teenage years. Modern-day historians and sociologists who have studied social organization and power structures on pirate ships in the 16th through 18th Centuries have discovered mini egalitarian, multicultural, floating democracies among pirate communities during this time. Decisions were generally made collectively among the pirates whose crews were comprised of men of various races and ethnicities, social strata, ages and religious beliefs. Leaders arose in the pirate world not from noble birth or through courtly political connections but through ability. If leaders of pirate ships became tyrannical, they were deposed by popular consent, much like what Lamport proposed with regard to his limited monarchy. Perhaps Lamport formulated his ideas of creating an egalitarian society with merit and more democratic ideas replacing ancient social and racial norms as a result of his time as a teenage boy with the pirates.

In the fall of 1642, while working on his grand plans for an overhaul of Mexican society, Lamport tried to gain support for his plans from disgruntled *criollo* merchants, dissatisfied militia men and freed African slaves. He shared his vision and confided in a local *criollo* named Captain Méndez who eventually had Lamport arrested, but not on the charges of plotting against the Spanish government of New

Spain. In October of 1642, Lamport was charged with heresy and arrested by the Spanish Inquisition for his use of peyote to invoke visions. The Spanish were generally appalled by indigenous drug use and saw it as something demonic and against the Catholic Church's authority. Thus began Lamport's lengthy incarceration, a full seventeen years behind bars. During his time in jail Lamport had access to pen and paper and was a prolific writer, authoring over 900 Latin psalms along with extensive political treatises and his own memoirs. During his time in jail it was rumored that Lamport was the illegitimate son of King Phillip the Third of Spain and thus the brother of the current Spanish king. Historians generally agree that this rumor was started – perhaps by Lamport himself – to give him a noble legitimacy in the eyes of the Mexican populace who had not yet been won over by his views of egalitarianism. Lamport escaped prison once, on Christmas of 1651. Many believe that the escape was allowed to happen and was helped along by Lamport's cellmate who was acting as a spy. During his brief time free, Lamport tried contacting the Viceroy and also plastered central Mexico City with pamphlets denouncing the Spanish Inquisition which had imprisoned him. After his recapture, the escape was given as a justification to treat Lamport even more harshly and he was sent to solitary confinement. He was then sentenced to a public execution in 1659, to be burned at the stake as was customary for heretics under the rules of the Inquisition. Lamport remained defiant to the end, and before the flames of the executioner's pyre could reach him, he strangled himself to death with the ropes they used to tie him to the stake, thus depriving the Inquisition of its public burning. So ended Mexico's first, and perhaps most dramatic, bid for independence.

DOÑA BERNARDA'S KITCHEN TABLE

The year was 1802. In a far-flung province of the Spanish Empire called Alta California in the Presidio of Santa Barbara a little girl was born. Her name was María Bernarda Ruíz Lugo. Her father was a Spanish military officer who was stationed at the Santa Barbara presidio and her mother hailed from the relatively new California

landed aristocracy. Her mother's parents, members of the powerful
Lugo family, had been granted tens of thousands of acres by the
Spanish king in what is now some of the most expensive areas to buy
property in the United States: the present-day California counties of
Santa Barbara, Ventura and Los Angeles. It is often difficult to imagine
a California in Bernarda's early days. It was not yet the United States,
it was not yet Mexico. Spain was busy quarrelling with Napoleon in
Europe and fighting off and on with the British. Even though the
Spanish Empire had once ruled the seas and had conquered some of
the greatest civilizations on earth, by the early 1800s it had become
worn down and its foundation had begun to crack. Its domestic
problems were exacerbated by grumblings throughout their many
colonies, from Asia to the Americas, by people who wanted more
rights or more political autonomy. By the time of Bernarda's birth
many believed that the Spanish Empire would not be able to hold on
for much longer. In this declining empire's remote backwater called
California, its Spanish inhabitants called *californios*, although loosely
governed by military outposts and under various degrees of clerical
supervision, were mostly left to themselves. Most of the members of
California's various indigenous communities lived settled lives in the
Spanish mission system, and many still held on to their pre-European
ways of life away from the Spanish settlements. The California coast
attracted Russian fur trappers, Yankee trading vessels, English pirates
and an assortment of miscreants from all parts of the world. Local
landowning families had a great deal of informal political power and
influence in the late 18th and early 19th Centuries. The young Bernarda
would grow up in the prosperous and independently minded world of
the Spanish California landed gentry. As a young girl she had no idea
of the history she would witness or what amount of that history she
would help shape.

By the time Bernarda was 8 years old, the persistent colonial
grumblings turned into the Mexican War of Independence from Spain.
By 1821, the Viceroyalty of New Spain, with Alta California as its most
northwestern province, became the independent nation of Mexico.
By that time Bernarda was 19 and had been married for almost 4 years
to a wealthy *californio* only known to history by his last name of
Rodríguez. After bearing him 9 children Doña Bernarda became a

widow and took on the added responsibilities of running the family businesses. Principal among these businesses was an express mail service that linked California to Mexico City through Santa Barbara and Los Angeles. Just 5 years after Mexican independence, a man by the name of Jedidiah Smith became the first American to make it to California by an overland route. Many more would soon follow. The central government in Mexico City felt almost the same way about California as the Spanish once did. It was far away, remote, and was hard to manage from such a long distance. The Mexicans were aware that foreign powers coveted the province, especially Russia, Great Britain and France and to a lesser degree the United States which had only been an independent nation for a few decades. They were also aware that if vast tracts of land were left unoccupied they might be perceived as being ripe for the taking. To deal with the California population issue, Mexico City was eager to grant all newcomers to California ample rights to land along with citizenship if they pledged allegiance to the new nation of Mexico. As a result of this the population of California increased and by 1840 over 20% of the non-Indian inhabitants were foreigners. With the foreigners came an influx of new political ideas and philosophies that countered the status quo the independently-minded *californios* had grown accustomed to. At the same time, the Californians had begun to view Mexico City's involvement in their affairs as quite meddlesome. An example of this intrusion occurred in 1834 when the nation of Mexico declared all Catholic missions in California to be federal property. In spite of the interference from a faraway central authority, *californios* under Mexican rule had enjoyed a small degree of political autonomy by the 1840s. The governor of California was elected by the Alta California popular assembly instead of being appointed by the central government thousands of miles away. By the middle of the 1840s, when Doña Bernarda had established herself as an educated middle-aged matriarch, *californios* had raised their own army and had kicked out the Mexican *federales*. The doña's 4 eldest sons belonged to the California militia groups. The high degree of autonomy enjoyed by this rebel province would be short lived, as the Americans were coming.

In 1846, in the wake of the American annexation of the Republic of Texas the year before, hostilities increased between the United

States and Mexico. The Mexicans never recognized the independence of Texas and with the annexation came a border dispute. Both Mexico and the US claimed the land between the Nueces River and the Rio Grande and when an offer made to Mexico to purchase the disputed land was rejected, the newly elected American president, James Polk, sent Major General Zachary Taylor to occupy the disputed territory. The Mexicans burned an American fort on the Rio Grande only after they attacked Taylor's force, killing a dozen men and capturing over 50. Two days after President Polk's message to Congress calling for war with Mexico, the United States Congress approved the declaration of war. The date was May 23, 1846.

In California the war took an altogether different turn. As previously mentioned, there was already unrest in this faraway Mexican province. According to the history books, word of the war with Mexico took three months to get to California, the region's inhabitants only finding out about the conflict in August of 1846. Perhaps with information ahead of everyone else, on June 14th 1846 a group of 30 Americans attacked the Mexican barracks at Sonoma, took it over, hoisted a flag with a bear on it and proclaimed California to be an independent country, the "California Republic." No government was formally organized and this event has gone down in California folklore and serves to motivate modern-day California secessionists. As the war became known on the Pacific Coast, and direct orders from Washington were issued for California, the Americans mobilized in a more organized fashion. The Mexican inhabitants had mixed thoughts about the war after it got underway. The governor of Alta California, Pío Pico, had openly expressed his support for California to become a colony of the British Empire and was prepared to swear his allegiance to Queen Victoria. Others welcomed the Americans and saw their possible occupation as a temporary thing, and one step closer to true independence. Still others vowed to fight for their land against all invaders and would do anything to repel the foreigners whether they be Russian, British, French, American or the out-of-touch bureaucrats and politicians from Mexico City. One thing was certain: As war loomed, Doña Bernarda saw the world around her changing once again and she was concerned about her sons who were eager to fight.

The three major American players in the Mexican War in California were Stephen Kearny, Commodore Robert Stockton and John C. Frémont. Kearny and Stockton were cut from the same cloth. Both were seen as by-the-book ruthless military commanders. Kearny had hoisted the American flag at Santa Fe, the capital of the Mexican province of New Mexico, and with 100 men he marched across the deserts to join the fighting in California. Stockton commanded 3 naval vessels and his 650-man fighting force, comprised mostly of US Marines, Navy men and militiamen, was the largest American ground force in California. Stockton ordered Frémont to put together a force of 100 men to join with his forces. Frémont had stopped over in California after surveying newly acquired American lands in the West with the US Army Corps of Topographical Engineers and his being in California at the time was pure coincidence. Frémont's scraggly force of surveyors were joined by some 60 other men and later 150 others who had been sympathetic to the Bear Flag Revolt. The somewhat flamboyant and agreeable Frémont had very little trouble attracting future fighters who would follow him, and as mentioned earlier, he was not as strictly military minded as Stockton or Kearny. After a few months of mostly token resistance, the combined forces of Stockton and Frémont easily controlled the northern part of what is now the state of California. The Mexican capital at the Pueblo of Los Angeles was the true prize and all forces were directed to head south.

By the end of 1846 Doña Bernarda had seen the handwriting on the wall and had a strong feeling that California would become part of the permanent territory of the United States. She was well connected with all of the established families in what is now the counties of Santa Barbara, Ventura and Los Angeles. Her family's express mail service kept her on top of news of the war and other valuable information. She had several concerns about her future. What would happen to her sons who were involved in the fighting? What would happen to the *californios* under Yankee rule? What would become of her own property, wealth and status? She had grave concerns as the Americans came closer to her home town of Santa Barbara.

At San Luís Obispo the forces under Frémont captured José de Jesus Pico who was cousin to the Mexican governor of Alta California, Pío Pico. José was sympathetic to the Americans and told Frémont he

would help him in his campaign heading south. By the time Frémont
got to Santa Barbara it was the week after Christmas, 1846. His troops
were weary and he needed fresh horses. Frémont commandeered all
of the horses in Doña Bernarda's corrals that were used in her express
mail business. The Americans took over Santa Barbara without firing a
shot, as the sleepy town of 900 was relatively defenseless. As the
doña was well connected and well respected among the *californio*
families of influence, she approached José Pico and asked him if she
could have 10 minutes of Lieutenant Colonel Frémont's time. The
American forces were staying at the San Carlos Hotel which was within
walking distance of her home. Frémont, a fluent Spanish speaker,
agreed to the private meeting. The 10 minutes that the doña had
asked for turned into 2 hours. During the time she had the "ear of the
emperor" Doña Bernarda appealed to Frémont's ego and ambition
and voiced her concerns and spoke on behalf of the *californio* families
in her circle. Did Frémont have political ambitions in what would be
the new US territory of California? She could help him secure his
political future. Doña Bernarda felt like she could work with Frémont,
who she saw as an officer and a gentleman and a stark contrast to the
more bellicose Stockton and Kearny, to come to some sort of peaceful
end to the hostilities. In their conversation she told the American that
californios would gladly lay down their arms and submit to the
Americans peacefully provided that the United States would honor
certain conditions. There were rumors coming from the Stockton and
Kearny camps that all Mexicans involved in fighting against the
Americans would be shot and their property taken away. The doña
wanted the Americans to grant clemency to all those involved in the
fighting for a guarantee that all fighting would cease. Additionally, she
wanted equal status given to the conquered people of California; that
they would become full American citizens with equal rights and equal
protection under the American legal system. The last thing she
emphasized was the respect for property; that all current property
granted by the Spanish Crown or the Mexican government, including
grants to indigenous groups, would be honored by the new American
government. What Doña Bernarda wanted was a peaceful and
seamless transition to her new overlords that would minimize loss of
life and would have the least possible impact in the status quo.

Frémont was not only sympathetic to what Doña Bernarda was saying, it became the foundation for the peace treaty signed to end the Mexican War in California called the Treaty of Capitulation or the Treaty of Cahuenga, and later became the basis for the grander Treaty of Guadalupe Hidalgo that formally ended the Mexican War a few years later. From his own memoirs we see what Frémont thought of this Mexican matriarch:

"And she wished me to take into my mind this plan of settlement, to which she would influence her people; meantime, she urged me to hold my hand, so far as possible. Naturally, her character and sound reasoning had its influence with me, and I had no reserves when I assured her I would bear her wishes in mind when the occasion came, and that she might with all confidence speak on this basis with her friends."

The doña did speak with her friends and one person of note whom she told of her meeting with Frémont was Andrés Pico, the younger brother of former governor Pio Pico, who put him in charge of California while he left to make an appeal to the federal authorities to send more Mexican troops to support the war in the province. As the person in charge, Doña Bernarda urged Andrés Pico to meet with Frémont to sign a capitulation treaty. He agreed to do so.

While writing about the days of the treaty, Frémont also said about Doña Bernarda: "I found that her object was to use her influence to put an end to the war, and to do so upon such just and friendly terms of compromise as would make the peace acceptable and enduring."

Doña Bernarda accompanied Frémont to a small rancho near modern-day Universal Studios to witness the signing of the capitulation treaty that she had a major hand in authoring and brokering. The day was January 13, 1847 and it was pouring rain. The house at the rancho was abandoned and from out of the kitchen the signers of the treaty took a small wooden table to sign the documents on. Doña Bernarda and other influential *californios* stood under the porch and witnessed the peaceful transfer of power to the Americans. At the end of the day, in accordance with the treaty, Frémont even

returned Doña Bernarda's horses to her. She was allowed to keep her
properties and businesses and her family flourished under the new
regime enjoying the rights and privileges she had secured in her
fateful two hour meeting with Frémont. John C. Frémont amassed
great wealth during the California Gold Rush and with the alliances he
had made with the *californios* starting in that Santa Barbara hotel,
Frémont realized his political career, becoming one of the first two US
senators from the new state of California in 1850 and later the
Republican Party's nominee for President of the United States in 1856.
Doña Bernarda Ruíz de Rodríguez who was born a subject of the
Spanish Crown, became a Mexican citizen and then proudly became
an American, died peacefully in her Santa Barbara home in 1880 at the
age of 78.

The table on which the Treaty of Cahuenga was signed is now in
the Natural History Museum of Los Angeles County, safely protected
under glass and illuminated with a bright light. While it really didn't
belong to Doña Bernarda, and she didn't have a seat at it either
literally or figuratively, what was done on that kitchen table on that
rainy day in California back in January of 1847 was the doña's doing.
That was her treaty. That was her moment. And that was her table.

LEE HARVEY OSWALD IN MEXICO

It is a tragic story familiar to most Americans and to many around
the world. The date was Friday, November 22, 1963. It was a sunny
day in Dallas when the motorcade of the 35th President of the United
States, John F. Kennedy, found itself in Dealy Plaza near the Texas
School Book Depository. At 12:30 in the afternoon, shots rang out and
the young American president was killed. Within hours the Dallas
Police apprehended Lee Harvey Oswald, a 24-year-old former US
Marine, and later that night charged him with the killing of the
president. On Sunday, November 24, while Oswald was being
transferred to the county jail, he was shot by a man named Jack Ruby
who claimed he wanted to spare Mrs. Kennedy from the horrors of a
murder trial. Oswald died an hour and a half later at Parkland
Memorial Hospital, the same medical facility that tried to treat

Kennedy. As Oswald would never stand trial, the public would never know a complete picture of the Kennedy assassination, including why Oswald did it - if he did do it – and if he had help. Right before he was shot Lee Harvey Oswald declared publicly that he did not do it and that he was set up as a patsy.

The nation and the world mourned the president's death and sadness quickly turned to questions. The Warren Commission was formed by President Lyndon Johnson on November 29, 1963, less than a week after the killing of Kennedy, to investigate the assassination. The commission presented its 888-page report to President Johnson on September 24, 1964 and it was released to the public three days later. The report concluded without absolute proof that Oswald acted alone in killing President Kennedy and that Jack Ruby acted alone in killing Oswald. The Warren Commission was not the only government-sponsored investigation into the JFK assassination. Because of public skepticism of the commission's findings and due to increasing concern about the lack of transparency of certain government agencies, in September of 1976 the United States House Select Committee on Assassinations (HSCA) was formed to look further into both the assassinations of John F. Kennedy and Dr. Martin Luther King, Jr. After 18 months of investigation, the HSCA disagreed with the conclusions of the Warren Commission that Oswald acted alone stating that Kennedy was "probably assassinated as a result of a conspiracy". The second investigation was not able to identify any individuals or groups involved in the conspiracy, however. The House Select Committee left the American public with even more questions and in the 40 years since this last formal government investigation into the JFK assassination a whole cottage industry has sprung up to look more closely at this major historical event. There are thousands of books and articles written about this with hundreds upon hundreds of theories as to what really happened, who was involved in this tragedy and to what degree. In fact, the very term "conspiracy theory" was popularized right after the assassination, some say, to discredit the multitude of ideas spawned by this event. Speaking at a conference in September of 2014 titled "The Warren Report and the JFK Assassination: Five Decades of Significant Disclosures," Dan Hardaway, a young law school student who was hired as a researcher for the House Select Committee on Assassinations in the late '70s said this about conspiracies:

"If you're involved in a conspiracy, one of the primary things you don't want to happen is to have the people you are conspiring against discover the conspiracy. The essence of a conspiracy is that it stays secret. In the eventuality that information about the conspiracy should come out, the alternative that you want to do is to make it so confusing, to sow so many red herrings, plant so many false trails, to create so much disinformation that no one could be absolutely certain whether or not if there really was a conspiracy."

Lee Harvey Oswald, while never able to defend himself publicly in a courtroom setting, has gotten the lion's share of the scrutiny of all the complex characters involved in the Kennedy killing, and there are many of the "false trails" and "red herrings" mentioned by Hardaway to make investigating Oswald very difficult and confusing. The days and months of Oswald's life leading up to November 22, 1963 have been examined in great detail but remain cloudy at best. Those familiar with the Kennedy assassination story and the cast of characters involved might not know that in September and October of 1963, just weeks before that fateful date in Dallas, Lee Harvey Oswald was in Mexico City. What were his activities while in Mexico? Was he alone? What role does Oswald's visit to Mexico City play in the Kennedy assassination?

Before looking into the particulars of Oswald's time in Mexico, we must first examine the context. The early 1960s saw the United States on high alert in Latin America. Cuba had just fallen to communism and the axis between Havana and Moscow had solidified. Numerous attempts were made to dissuade or oust Fidel Castro, but he held on to power, and as it seemed like he would be head of state for good, the American government began to fear the spread of communism in the Western Hemisphere. Mexico City in the early 1960s may have well been the center of Latin American Cold War intrigue. Using the latest surveillance equipment, the American CIA and FBI monitored the diplomatic compounds of a variety of communist countries, with special emphasis on those of the Soviet Union and Cuba. Across the street from the Cuban Embassy was the CIA surveillance post in a 3rd-floor apartment. From here an agent photographed visitors entering and exiting the front door. The door to the Cuban Consulate, on the side of the Cuban Embassy, was monitored by a pulse camera that snapped photos of people coming and going based on movement. This camera was installed on September 27, 1963, an important date to remember. The Soviet Embassy was monitored by manual cameras by CIA agents focusing on 3 different locations: 1 on a yard in the embassy and 2 on the front entrances. Many of the phones at the Cuban and Soviet embassies were tapped. A total of 30 wiretaps recorded incoming and outgoing calls from the embassies. Agents at remote CIA listening posts would transcribe relevant phone conversations - whether they be in Spanish, English or Russian – translate to English if need be and consolidate the transcripts in what were called daily "resumas." The resuma from the previous day would be on the desk of CIA Station Chief Winston Scott by 9:00 every morning. In addition to the video and audio surveillance of the Soviet and Cuban diplomatic compounds there were what was termed "penetration agents" inside the embassies. These penetration agents were covertly working for the CIA while holding low-level clerical jobs for the Cubans or Soviets. Often times the identities of these secret agents were only known by the station chief himself, who received regular reports and updates from them. There was very little that could get through this complex monitoring system down in Mexico City, and station chief Win Scott was known throughout the agency for running a tight ship.

Lee Harvey Oswald's movements and activities in Mexico were lightly touched upon in the original Warren Commission Report in 1964 but further expanded in the report generated by the House Select Committee on Assassinations some 15 years later. Oswald allegedly arrived by bus in Mexico City's *central camionera*, or central bus station, at 10:00 am on Friday, September 27, 1963, and departed for Texas on Wednesday morning, October 3, spending 5 full days in Mexico. While in Mexico City he made contact with the Soviet and Cuban consulates by phone and in person. His objective was to secure two travel visas: one "in-transit" visa to Cuba and then another visa to his ultimate destination, the Soviet Union. Oswald had lived in the

Soviet Union before. After an honorable discharged from the US Marines in 1959, he defected to the USSR and settled in the city of Minsk where he married a Russian woman, Marina Nikolayevna Prusakova. He returned to the US with his Russian bride in February of 1962. He had special interest in Cuba because not only was he an avowed Marxist, he was also the New Orleans president of the Fair Play for Cuba Committee.

When Oswald arrived in Mexico City on Friday, September 27, he immediately got down to business. He secured a hotel room and then, according to the government investigations, made two calls to the Soviet Consulate, one at 10:30 am and one at 10:37 am, asking routine questions having to do with hours of operations and when the consul would be available to process visas. The caller spoke perfect Spanish. This is troublesome, as Oswald did not know how to speak Spanish. At 11:00 on this same Friday morning, Oswald showed up at the Cuban Consulate, which is located in the Cuban Embassy compound, requesting an in-transit visa to travel through Cuba on his way to the USSR. His contact at the Cuban Consulate was a 26-year-old, very attractive Mexican national named Silvia Duran. Oswald showed Duran various documents to complete the visa application, but none of the documents had a passport-type photo that was required for the paperwork. One of the documents Oswald proudly showed to Duran was his Fair Play for Cuba ID card and declared himself to be a communist. Silvia Duran thought this strange, as it was routine for the American Communist Party to send its members down to the Cuban Consulate in Mexico City to get immediate visas. They had a special deal with the Cuban Communist Party for properly vetted communists to have a hassle-free paperwork experience for their travel to Cuba. The man before Duran was going about this the hard way, she thought, or something else was going on. As he didn't have the proper photographs, Oswald left the Cuban Consulate and came back with the appropriate pictures at about 12:15 in the afternoon. He filled out all of the paperwork in Duran's presence and then she explained to him that he needed to get a Soviet travel visa first before the Cuban Consulate would issue the in-transit visa to get him to Cuba. On this, Oswald walked to the Soviet Consulate and arrived at around 12:30. On arrival, he met with Embassy worker Valery Kostikov, who had long been watched by the CIA as a possible KGB agent. Kostikov handed Oswald off to a man named Oleg Nechiporenko. Nechiporenko explained to Oswald that all travel matters to the Soviet Union are handled by the Soviet Embassy in the country of the traveler's origin. Since Oswald was not a Mexican citizen, the Soviet offices in Mexico could not help him. He would have to go to the Soviet Embassy in Washington DC. Oswald explained that he didn't want the FBI to arrest him for establishing contact with the Soviets, so he figured that getting a visa through Mexico was a better option, and, as previously mentioned, he wanted to make a stopover in Cuba. Nechiporenko explained to Oswald that they could make a special exception in his case, but the paperwork would take 4 months to process. This made Oswald very angry, so much so that Nechiporenko ended the meeting and escorted the American off the premises with no visa paperwork filled out. At around 4:00 pm that afternoon Oswald returned to the Cuban Consulate and spoke with Silvia Duran. He lied to her and told her that there were no problems with his Soviet visa application and that they should proceed with his Cuban paperwork. Duran called the Soviet Consulate to verify Oswald's story and in about 20 minutes they called her back, confirming that they had not processed any paperwork for him and that a visa to the Soviet Union would take about 4 months to get. Silvia Duran put down the phone and explained the situation to a very unhappy Lee Harvey Oswald. The tirade drew the attention of the other Cuban staff members including the consul himself, a man named Eusebio Azcue. Azcue explained to Oswald that Cuba had to be very careful as to who it let into the country and that he was obviously not a man of the revolution if he could not understand that. Oswald received an escort out of the building and never returned to the Cuban Consulate. He did however, return to the Soviet Consulate the next morning, Saturday, September 28 to try one more time to get a visa to the USSR. This time Oswald was calm, and faced with the reality that he was not going to get a quick visa, he left the Soviet compound and didn't even take the visa paperwork that was offered to him. It is the next event on the Oswald-Mexico City timeline that makes little sense. According to the House Select Committee report, a call recorded and transcribed by the CIA came into the Soviet Consulate from the Cuban Consulate that same Saturday morning at 11:51 am, about an hour and a half after Oswald left the Soviet compound. On the line to the Soviets were who had been identified as both Silvia Duran and Lee Harvey Oswald. The purpose of the call, it seems, was to clarify details on the visa paperwork. The call is strange for a few reasons. First, the Cuban Consulate was closed on Saturdays. For Silvia Duran to be working that day, she would have had to have been called in for a special situation. Second, by reading the transcript of this call, it seems like the people who are doing the talking are fishing for information and are not really sure of the sequence of events that had already happened. Third, the person identified as Oswald spoke broken, almost incomprehensible Russian. Oswald was a fluent speaker of that language. The fourth strange aspect of the call is that there was no need for it to have been made in the first place. If Oswald left the Soviet Consulate that morning and had resigned himself to the fact that getting a quick visa was hopeless, why would there be any need for a follow-up call? The House Select Committee theorized that this Oswald may have been an impostor. It was not uncommon for the CIA station itself or other intelligence agencies to impersonate people successfully for whatever ends. This voice impostor would make perfect sense. On Tuesday, October 1, the day before Oswald left Mexico, two more calls came in to the Soviet Consulate, one made at 10:31 and the other at 10:45. The people transcribing the calls noted that it was the same person who was on the Saturday morning call to the Soviets. The man on the line identified himself as Oswald by name, spoke poor Russian and was checking on the status of his visa. Again, this makes no sense because there was no visa to check and the speaker's Russian was bad. There can be very little doubt that the person who made the two calls on Tuesday and the one on Saturday was some sort of voice double for Oswald. The story does not end here and nor does it get any less complicated.

After Lee Harvey Oswald left the Soviet diplomatic compound on Saturday morning we have a few days – the rest of Saturday, Sunday, Monday and Tuesday – that are not properly accounted for. In the original Warren Commission Report there is next to nothing about what he was doing on these missing days. It was after the commission published its findings that rumors began to circulate about Oswald's whereabouts in Mexico from September 28 to October 3, 1963. The two big rumors that ended up being investigated by the House Select Committee in the late 1970s had to do with Oswald's involvement with a leftist student group and Oswald being spotted at a party of a private home.

The House Committee eventually tracked down a man named Oscar Contreras who was part of a pro-Castro student group at the National Autonomous University of Mexico, or UNAM. Silvia Duran from the Cuban Consulate allegedly told Oswald that getting a solid recommendation from a pro-Cuban source might expedite his visa paperwork and so this was the reason for the university visit. Contreras and other Mexican students interacted with Oswald at a lecture at UNAM's School of Philosophy. Besides Contreras, no other students from the group were ever identified or found. No photographs or other physical proof that Oswald was at the university have ever surfaced. In the course of an investigation undertaken by Jim Garrison, the District Attorney from New Orleans, Contreras was interviewed and provided vague details of his interaction with Oswald, but Contreras never spoke to the House Committee.

Another rumor that Oswald had been spotted at a party either Monday or Tuesday night comes from a very interesting source, the wife of Mexican poet and diplomat, Octavio Paz. This woman, a poet in her own right, was Elena Garro. Garro was at this party which was being held at the home of Rubén Duran Navarro, the brother-in-law of Silvia Duran, the Mexican employee at the Cuban Consulate. Rubén was Elena's cousin. Garro claimed that she saw Oswald at the party with two other young "beatnik-looking" American men. No one at that party spoke to the three Americans and after the assassination the Durans stated that Oswald was never at any of their parties. Elena Garro claimed to see Oswald and the other two Americans the next day on Avenida de los Insurgentes, one of the main boulevards of the Mexican capital. No photographs of the party exist and there are no other witnesses to Oswald at the party. The House Select Committee on Assassinations tried to get a statement from Elena Garro in the late 1970s but could not. Garro was also responsible, in part, for perpetuating another rumor that Silvia Duran, the Mexican employee at the Cuban Consulate who supposedly helped Oswald with his visa issues, was having an intimate relationship with Oswald while he was in Mexico. This allegation deserves further investigation. In the mid-1960s, when rumors initiated or perpetuated by Elena Garro began to swirl around Mexico City, Garro was already being discredited as a reliable source for information. She didn't like the Cubans and she didn't like her cousin's sister-in-law, Silvia Duran. After the assassination of Kennedy, Elena Garro had her own personal reasons for connecting the alleged assassin to Duran and the Cubans. CIA Station Chief Winston Scott was aware of Elena Garro's allegations and dismissed her as being "nuts."

A very interesting figure connected to Lee Harvey Oswald's time in Mexico City and who keeps popping up in the research was Silvia Duran, the attractive 26-year-old Mexican employee at the Cuban Consulate who helped Oswald and was accused by the rumor mill of having an affair with him. Perhaps Silvia was an easy target to victimize because it was well known around the diplomatic circles in Mexico City that a few years before she had had an affair with the then Cuban ambassador to Mexico. At some point after the Kennedy assassination, Silvia Duran was picked up for questioning by the Mexican police, and possibly tortured. While the full contents of the Duran interrogation were not made available to the Americans, it was made public that Duran confessed to having had intimate relations with Oswald. This piece of information was also reported in the Mexican newspapers. The House Select Committee on Assassinations could not verify the veracity of Duran's testimony and in its final report speculated that Silvia Duran could have been a penetration agent placed in the Cuban Embassy either by the American CIA or by the Mexicans, hence the reason why the Mexicans apprehended her and coerced a statement out of her. Silvia Duran's role in all of this could be pivotal, especially in light of the great doubt that later researchers have placed on the possibility that the real Lee Harvey Oswald was never even in Mexico.

Researchers who allege that the real Lee Harvey Oswald never was in Mexico City cite several anomalous pieces of information to strengthen their case. As previously mentioned, the House Select Committee believed that 3 calls allegedly made by Oswald were fake, including the last call from the Cuban Consulate to the Soviet

Consulate, which supposedly involved Silvia Duran. The man calling himself Oswald spoke incomprehensible Russian while the real Oswald was fluent in that language. But what do we know of the other visits and calls? What tangible proof exists that Oswald was really there? It was well known that the Cuban and Soviet embassies in Mexico City were under heavy scrutiny. The CIA as well as intelligence agencies from other governments closely monitored the comings and goings of the people there. In all the photographs that were taken during the highly scrutinized time of Oswald's visit, not a single photograph of Lee Harvey Oswald has surfaced even after two government investigations. During a trip taken to Havana, Cuba to investigate this case, investigators of the House Select Committee on Assassinations met with Castro representatives who shared their own surveillance materials from the Cuban Embassy and Consulate from late September and early October of 1963. The Cubans had books of photographs taken outside their own diplomatic compound and those photos showed everyone coming and going. Oswald was not to be seen among the pictures. In addition to this lack of photographic evidence we also have conflicting statements made by eyewitnesses who were in the presence of the man claiming to be Oswald at the Cuban Consulate. These witnesses reported that he was blond, muscular and about 30 years old. The real Oswald was 24, skinny and no more than five foot six. Wiretapping and recording device evidence of Oswald's time in Mexico is also non-existent. Either tapes were erased, misfiled or destroyed. All we have left are transcripts.

Speaking of transcripts, a curious transcript of a phone conversation between President Lyndon Johnson and FBI Director J. Edgar Hoover was uncovered by intrepid JFK assassination researchers. It starts with President Johnson asking, "Have you established any more about the (Oswald) visit to the Soviet Embassy in Mexico in September?" The FBI director replies, "No, that's one angle that's very confusing for this reason. We have up here the tape and the photograph of the man who was at the Soviet Embassy using Oswald's name. The picture and the tape do not correspond to the man's voice, nor to his appearance. In other words, it appears that there is a second person who was at the Soviet Embassy."

So, was Oswald even in Mexico? Some researchers believe that the real Oswald had information about plots to kill Cuban president Fidel Castro and that he was really working for the CIA. Castro stated publicly that he felt like he was being set up to take the fall for the Kennedy assassination. Did some sort of "blame the Cubans" plot get thwarted and Oswald was sacrificed? Could missing photos and conflicting reports of various Oswalds in Mexico City be part of what Dan Hardaway from the Select Committee said about conspiracies? Has all of this been part of the red herrings, false trails and disinformation that Hardaway was talking about? There are many JFK-related documents that still have not been released to the public, but even after their release we may never know the full story of Lee Harvey Oswald's 5 days in Mexico.

PART FIVE: CRYPTIDS AND LEGENDARY CREATURES

MEXICAN GIANTS

In March of 2015 the internet was abuzz with a strange photo that popped up on social media and paranormal/fringe sites. It showed what appeared to be at least two gigantic human skulls that had been exposed to the surface by heavy rains. The photo was allegedly taken in a small village in the Sierra de Tapalapa in the southern Mexican state of Chiapas. By the size of the people standing next to and on top of the skulls, one could assume that the skulls belonged to humans that stood almost 20 feet tall. After hundreds of thousands of clicks, likes and shares, the hive mind of the internet came through to solve the mystery of the picture. In October of 2008 the web site worth1000 dot com had a contest for graphic artists to come up with the most convincing depictions of absurd or anomalous archaeological finds. An image that made it to the top ten was this image of rural Mexicans marveling at the newly uncovered skulls of giants. The image was attributed to an online graphic artist who calls himself "YearOfTheDragon," a self-described single father raising his daughter alone who lives off of illustration gigs solicited online. While some online fringe researchers were fooled by YearOfTheDragon's intriguing work, others were quick to point out that there are ample amounts of firsthand accounts and even some physical evidence that Mexico once might have been inhabited by a race of giants in the not-so-distant past.

When the Spanish first explored and conquered Mexico they heard of mythical races of giants wherever they went, from the Baja Peninsula in the northwest part of the country to the Maya areas of southern and eastern Mexico. Some researchers have even uncovered what they consider tangible proof that some conquistadors came into contact with actual giants, based on diary entries and early writings of the first people who made contact with living and breathing pre-Hispanic civilizations. The Spanish heard the myths and legends from the natives that seemed to correlate with their own biblical stories about giants as found in the Book of Genesis: that sometime in some part of the distant past giants roamed the earth alongside modern-looking humans. The giants were responsible for much of what was left behind by previous civilizations and the giant explanation was common in many parts of the New World. To the people of central Mexico at the time of the Spanish contact, giants featured so prominently in their belief system that they even named their capital city, Tenochtitlán, after a man called Tenoch, who belonged to an entire ancient race of giants called the *quinametzin*. In recent fringe research literature and websites the Nahuatl word *quinametzin* has been mistranslated to mean "The Old Ones." A closer look at the etymology of the word we find that *quinametzin* almost directly translates to "giant people." In the beginning of the Aztec "Fifth Sun," or the epoch of time in which we currently live, there were four giants who held up the sky. Their names were Cuahtémoc, Izcóatl, Ixcaqlli and Tenexuche. The Mixteca people, referred to as "Mixtecs" by modern anthropologists and historians, were supposedly fathered by a member of the *quinametzin*, a giant by the name of Mixtécatl. As briefly mentioned before, giants were often used by the ancient Mexicans to explain colossal ruins that had unknown builders. According to the Aztecs, the Toltecs had help from giants in building their capital city of Tula. The ancient central Mexican city of Teotihuacán, with its large pyramids and broad avenues had giants as its initial builders. Finally, the great pyramid at Cholula, the largest pyramid in the world, was said to have been built by Xelhua, a 20-foot-tall member of the *quinametzin* tribe. Xelhua was also credited with founding 7 cities in central Mexico in the times before the coming of the Aztecs. Unlike the Aztecs, the Maya did not believe that a race of giant humans existed before them, but giants were part of the ancient Mayan religious belief system in the form of chaacob, a group of demigods who would serve the god Chaac, and who take human form in the shape of dwarves or giants. Some researchers cite a Maya belief in giants as evidenced by larger human figures being depicted in murals, carvings and other works of art. Mainstream archaeologists claim that these depictions of larger humans speak more to class and societal position than belief in a race of actual giants, as there is very little in Maya oral tradition that would indicate such a belief. As recently as the 1690s, almost two centuries after the Spanish Conquest, Jesuit missionaries to the remote desert areas of Baja California were still being told by the local Cochimi people that the large rock wall art, carved so high up in the cliff surfaces in the rugged mountains of Baja was done by a race of giants who were tall enough to paint so high on the wall.

Many researchers of giants point to actual modern post-Conquest historical references to races of larger humanoids and claim that the Spanish encountered the remnants of tribes of giants throughout Mexico, citing writings from the 16th Century. One often-used reference to giants comes from a book written by an Italian count called *Decades*, which was a history of New Spain commissioned by King Charles V and published in the 1520s. Here we have an updated version in English about conquistador Diego de Ordaz and his discovery of what appears to be the remains of giants:

"I wish to end this chapter with a gigantic story, which, like the formidable Atlas, comes to support my claims. Diego de Ordaz, whom I have before mentioned, knew many hidden places in those lands, especially in the land of cacao, where he learned to plant and grow the tree of money, as I have explained on that occasion. He found in the vault of a temple the thighbone of a giant, worn and nearly destroyed by age. The licentiate Ayllón, one of the most learned jurists in Hispaniola, brought this bone to the city of Victoria a short time after Your Holiness left for Rome. For some days I had that bone in my home; it measured five palms in length, and its width in proportion. Those who were afterwards sent by Cortés into the mountains if the south returned, saying that they had discovered a country inhabited by giants; in proof of this claim it is said that they brought back many ribs of the dead."

Another story of the remains of giants being found in Mexico comes from a Spanish source from the late 16th Century, a book titled *The Natural and Moral History of the Indies* by José de Acosta. Acosta writes:

"When I was in Mexico, in the year of our Lord one thousand five hundred eighty six, they found one of those giants buried in one of our farms, which we call Jesus del Monte, of whom they brought a tooth to be seen, which (without augmenting) was as big as the fist of a man, and, according to this, all the rest was proportionate, which I saw and admired at his deformed greatness."

The True History of the Conquest of New Spain by Bernal Díaz, written around 1570, is one of the most read books on the topic of the Spanish Conquest of Mexico and early colonial life in New Spain. It also has a passage referring to giants in Chapter 78 in which conquistador Hernán Cortés is asking local kings about the history of their kingdoms. Here is the 1844 English translation of the passage by John Ingram Lockhart:

"Our friends told us how and whence they came into this country, and how they had settled themselves there; how it came that, notwithstanding their vicinity to the Mexicans, they resembled each other so little, and lived in perpetual warfare with each other. The tradition was also handed down from their forefathers, that in ancient times there lived here a race of men and women who were of immense stature with heavy bones, and were a very bad and evil-disposed people, whom they had for the greater part exterminated by continual war, and the few that were left gradually died away.
In order to give us a notion of the huge frame of this people, they dragged forth a bone, or rather a thigh bone, of one of those giants, which was very strong, and measured the length of a man of good stature. This bone was still entire from the knee to the hip joint. I measured it by my own person, and found it to be of my own length, although I am a man of considerable height. They showed us many similar pieces of bones, but they were all worm-eaten and decayed; we, however, did not doubt for an instant, that this country was once inhabited by giants. Cortés observed, that we ought to forward these bones to his majesty in Spain by the very first opportunity."

Those researchers who propose that there were giant humans roaming the earth in pre-historic times cite these early Spanish accounts of remains as proof positive of a lost race of gargantuan humanoids. Others claim that these are stories of stories and that the gigantic bones may have most likely been the remains of large ancient megafauna such as giant sloths and mastodons. In spite of the stories of giant bones being found by the Spanish, we have no intact giant human skeletons or even parts of giant human skeletons from the time period to study. As with many "fringe" topics from Bigfoot to the Loch Ness monster, scientists have a simple question: Where are the remains for them to study? Researchers counter that there has been a long history of government and academic suppression of the evidence of giants, beginning with the number one villain in the cover-up story, a villain with long arms that stretch across borders and into Mexico: The Smithsonian Institution, established in Washington DC in 1846.

There is, however, one curious account that is pretty well documented of a Spanish encounter with a living, breathing giant during the siege of Tenochtitlán, in the final stages of the subjugation of the Aztec Empire. When forces commanded by Pedro de Alvarado arrived in at Tlatelolco, just north of the main city of Tenochtitlán in the Aztec home island in the middle of Lake Texcoco, no people came to fight the Spanish except for a warrior named Tzilcatzin. According to eyewitness accounts, Tzilcatzin stood over 10 feet tall and repelled the Spanish by throwing at them rocks the size of watermelons. Tzilcatzin's bravery motivated other men of Tlatelolco to fight. As a consequence, the standoff with the Spanish lasted several days. In the Twelfth Book of Franciscan friar Bernardino de Sahagún's colonial treatise titled *General History of Things in New Spain*, the friar writes:

"The brigantines came to the neighborhood called Xocotitlán, and as they came ashore, they jumped ashore in the neighborhood fighting. And when that Indian captain, named Tzilacatzin, saw them fighting, he came to them with other people who followed him, and they fought them out of that neighborhood and made them return to the brigs."

When it comes to the topic of Mexican giants, while interesting and somewhat romantic, very little evidence exists that an actual race of giants walked the deserts, jungles and *altiplano* of Mexico. The medical condition commonly referred to as gigantism existed in ancient Mexico as it does today throughout the world, as evidenced in the stories of the warrior Tilcatzin. This condition is rare and only occurs in less than 1% of the population. A mythical and/or magical race of giants inhabiting ancient Mexico is something altogether different. While there may be truth to ancient legends, Mexican giants might be proving to be a bit more elusive than some researchers want them to be.

THE ALUX AND THE CHANEQUE: MEXICO'S ELUSIVE ELVES

It was a foggy and rainy day in London. The year was 1844. American showman extraordinaire PT Barnum had traveled to the court of Queen Victoria with his human circus act. Barnum bowed before a dour-faced queen as he presented to her two special members of his performing troupe, a pair of microencephalic dwarves from the jungles of Mexico. The dwarves bowed and greeted Her Britannic Majesty in Spanish and in their native Maya dialect. In his introduction, Barnum claimed that the dwarves were "the last degenerate remains of a caste of high priests found, at great expense, in a lost Maya city." As the acrobatics show in the palace commenced, the serious queen - who would later be crowned Empress of India and would rule over one quarter of the earth's population - WAS amused. She showed her delight openly for these tiny Mexican visitors and other nobles and notables at the English court did so, too. It was only later, in reflection in her personal diaries, that the queen expressed a sense of sadness for these two, who she thought were relegated to a most miserable existence. While Barnum was known for his exaggeration and tall tales, there might have been a part of him that actually believed that the two Maya dwarves he was traveling with were part of a small race of magical, feral, humanlike beings who lived in the mountains and forests of Mexico and Central America. He had heard the story of the Alux from the tiny Mayan acrobats themselves.

There are many cultures around the world that have myths of magical little people who live their lives outside of the view of normal humans. Gnomes, leprechauns, elves, fairies and pixies are some of the European manifestations of this phenomenon. In Mexico we also see a tradition of powerful, nearly invisible, small-statured, human-like creatures, in two areas. We see what is called the Alux – or plural, Aluxob – in the Maya heartland, encompassing the Yucatán Peninsula and modern-day Mexican states of Chiapas and Tabasco. In the eastern and southern portions of the former Aztec Empire – notably in the present-day states of Veracruz, Oaxaca and Guerrero – the "wee folk" were called Chaneques. The word "chaneque" comes from the Nahuatl word meaning, "those who inhabit dangerous places." So we see the magical little people legends confined to the eastern and southern parts of the modern-day nation of Mexico. To this day, people believe in these creatures and the Alux/Chaneque phenomenon has been studied by serious Mexican and international researchers.

The concept of the Alux or Chaneque in Mexico may date back thousands of years. The Olmec culture, considered the "mother civilization" of ancient Mexico, flourished in the area of the gulf coast from around 1600 BC to 300 BC. Although the Olmecs had no written record, they left behind much in the form of sculpture, pottery and monumental architecture. Among the artifacts of this civilization we see depictions of dwarflike humans engaging in service to the elites or as court entertainers much like PT Barnum's tiny Mexican duo. Some investigators believe these cultural remnants illustrate actual human dwarves who held special status in Olmec society. Others see the depictions of smaller humanoids in the archaeological record as proof that the belief in a mythical race of little people dates back thousands of years. By the time the Maya become prominent in Mexico in the few centuries before Christ we also see similar depictions as we saw with the Olmecs and we are left wondering if the archaeological "evidence" of smaller humanoids is indicative of a belief of a race of supernatural beings or if it was just the fact that human dwarves were accorded a special status in the ancient Maya world. When the

Spanish encountered the living cultures of the New World, they found
that the people of the Aztec and Maya lands had a powerful belief in
Aluxes and Chaneques, a belief that is still strong in these areas today.

So, if people believe in these creatures and have actually seen
them in some cases, what do they look like? They are generally
described as fully human but in smaller form, sometimes standing no
more than two feet tall and sometimes clothed. They tend to have
larger eyes, which are sometimes described as a glowing red, and their
noses are larger than a normal human's. Their ears are pointed, much
like those of European elves. Often they are said to wear straw hats
and cloth shoes, and they carry bags made of cloth or agave cactus
fiber, their "bag of tricks," so to speak. In some legends, the alux or
chaneque carry around slingshots to use in hunting or to shoot stones
at disagreeable humans. Other stories of this creature give it a less
friendly and more diabolical appearance. In some recent sightings in
Mexico, the creature has been depicted as a hairless, almost alien-
looking humanoid with a large forehead, big black eyes and claws on
its feet and hands. In some legends, the creature is said to have
backwards-facing feet and is covered in fur, much like the Mexican
jungle-dwelling version of Bigfoot called the Sisimite. According to
some accounts, these creatures have been known to shape-shift from
their diminutive humanlike form into the form of animals found in
their domains.

Besides the possibility of shape-shifting, Aluxes and Chaneques
possess many powers that either help or serve to confound humans.
According to Maya legend, aluxes pre-date humans and even pre-date
the arrival of the sun to the earth, so they are accustomed to working
in darkness. They sometimes work together with local spirits and gods
to affect changes in their environments, like summoning rain, for
example. These beings are seen as caretakers of the wild areas in
which they live and look after the animals and the plants in their
respective areas. Certain aluxes and chaneques inhabit forests,
mountains, rivers and beaches. In the Maya area, certain aluxes may
be assigned to individual *cenotes* or water-filled sinkholes in the
limestone earth. Wherever there is a distinct natural formation, a
chaneque or alux is usually nearby living its life in harmony with its
surroundings. If their happy coexistence with nature is upset by

human intrusion, there is often hell to pay. As the alux or chaneque may exact retribution for disrespect, great care is shown to respect the magical being before a problem arises. For example, if a farmer plants a new field of corn in a forested area, he may ask permission of the local alux or chaneque or give up offerings before he starts digging. A farmer will leave behind food or cigarettes as a kind gesture for permission to use the land. There are two famous modern-day stories in the Yucatán in which care was taken by authorities to appease the local aluxes. One has to do with the construction of the Cancun-Nizuc Bridge near the international airport. Several times during the different phases of construction of the bridge, workers would return in the morning to the site to find the bridge mysteriously destroyed. Some locals suggested that the recurring destruction of the bridge was caused by a mischievous alux who didn't want the bridge built. The government then contacted a local Maya shaman to perform a ceremony at the construction site to acknowledge the alux and to ask its permission to carry on with the construction. After the shamanic ceremony, no further incidents occurred. Today, you can see a small stone house constructed under the Cancun-Nizuc Bridge as a sign of respect for the alux where offerings are periodically left by locals who believe. In 2010 we see a similar situation with regard to an Elton John concert at the Maya archaeological site of Chichén Itzá. In a spring concert, days before the performance, the massive main stage collapsed and as there was no weather disturbances at that time, the destruction of the stage left the show promoters scratching their heads. Locals were quick to point out that the organizers of the show failed to secure the permission and blessing of the local aluxes before constructing the stage. Concerts held at this location in previous years by Placido Domingo and Sara Brightman had no problems because proper precautions were taken by calling in local shamans to appease the temperamental spirits of the location. The Elton John concert organizers then brought in a local Maya religious leader to conduct the proper ceremonies and the concert went off without a hitch.

As seen in the two examples and in many others, the changing temperaments of aluxes or chaneques are legendary. The creature may be playful and joyful like a child, and then be quick to anger.

Because they are somewhat childlike, these creatures are said to have an affinity for children. Sightings of aluxes or chaneques are more common by children than by adults. Of course, sightings by children are often dismissed as imaginary friends or parts of made up stories, but parents who believe in these creatures often tell their children to be careful while playing in the wilder areas as there are stories of children being kidnapped by upset aluxes or chaneques.

While many believe that the aluxes and chaneques have been around long before humans, there are parts of the Maya area where people believe that aluxes can actually be created by humans through shamanic ceremonies. Property owners will fashion an alux out of clay with a heart made of honey. In the creation process, the effigy must also include 9 drops of blood from the landowner. The size of this small humanlike statue is similar to that of a garden gnome familiar to most Americans. When finished, they take the clay figure to a shaman or priest who calls upon the wind, sun, rain and earth for the proper alignment to create the perfect guardian spirit that will enter the clay figure. After the ceremony the small alux statue is placed in an inconspicuous corner of the person's property. At night, it is said, the alux comes to life. It is the responsibility of the person who created the clay figure to maintain the statue, to leave offerings and to ask the alux for permission or forgiveness. The shaman who creates the alux also has the power to counteract the being's malevolent power. If an alux is up to bad tricks – like breaking windows, or stealing keys, for example – the shaman may intervene on behalf of the landowner by making special offerings in a ceremony specifically dedicated to troublesome aluxes. In extreme cases, especially when the alux has been blamed for diseases or pestilence, the shaman will conduct a ceremony in which the clay figurine is shattered by a big rock, thus releasing any curses of the alux or obligations to it.

The alux/chaneque phenomenon garnered the attention of cryptozoologists – those who investigate and describe unknown and legendary creatures – after a farmer claimed to have captured a chaneque in the early 2000s. Although no photos exist of this incident, investigators determined that the alleged chaneque was really a howler monkey that was suffering from a type of mange and had lost all its hair. It was unknown whether or not this was just a mistake or a hoax. For those serious investigators, it might be hard to get any sort of physical proof of the existence of aluxes and chaneques. Elusive and temperamental by nature, it will be difficult to capture a creature that does not want to be found. For those who believe in these beings, no proof is necessary and no further investigation is advocated, just the proper respect is given and precautions taken to make sure the creatures are not upset. A hands-off approach may be the best solution here, with the aluxes and chaneques best left to human legends and their own little worlds.

THE MAN-BAT OF NORTHERN MEXICO

It was a chilly morning a few hours after midnight on Friday, January 16, 2004. The young twentysomething police officer Leonardo Samaniego Gallegos was patrolling the neighborhood of Valles de la Silla in the municipality of Guadalupe, an eastern suburb of Monterrey. Officer Samaniego was driving his patrol car down Aldama Street when he saw something big and black fall from a tall tree. The big black figure did not touch the ground, but seemed to hover over it. Samaniego turned on the patrol car's high beams and before him in the short distance stood a humanoid with big black eyes, brownish skin and what appeared to be black clothing or fur. According to the officer's report, when the car's lights shone on it, the creature covered its eyes and became angry, and then lunged at the car. It grabbed the patrol car and shook it violently. In a panic, Samaniego spun the car in circles to try to shake off whatever had gotten ahold of his car. He grabbed the police radio and desperately called for reinforcements. The creature then started to smash his windshield at which point the young policeman shifted the car into reverse, gunned the engine, lost control of the vehicle, crashed it and was knocked unconscious. When he came to, revived by paramedics, the creature had been long gone. Samaniego was rushed to University Hospital and in addition to being treated for his physical wounds he was subjected to psychological and toxicological tests to determine whether he was under the influence when he had his supposed encounter. All the tests came up negative.

The police department was left with a mangled car and the strange testimony of a very trusted officer.

Samaniego's story spread quickly and it caught the attention of local news stations throughout the Mexican state of Nuevo Leon. In an on-camera interview the next day the police officer recounted the horrible night, and gave a detailed description of the creature. Newsmen wondered exactly what Samaniego had seen. Was it a gigantic bird of prey? A huge bat? Was it some unknown or unclassified animal? Was it a ghost? Something otherworldly? One interviewer even put forth the idea that it could have been some crazy person dressed up in a costume, although that would not account for the creature seeming to hover over the ground or the severe damage done to the police car. At the conclusion of one of the news stories, the announcer asked the public to come forward if they had any information about that specific incident or if anyone had any knowledge of a big, black, flying creature seen at other times in the region. The response to this plea was quick. A resident of Monterrey and a member of the OVNI Club de Nuevo Leon, or, in English the UFO Club of Nuevo Leon, came forward with a video showing a strange black humanoid-looking being flying over the hills just outside the city. The station played the video on the air and afterwards many reports came in about what would later be called *"La Bruja de Guadalupe"* or, "The Witch of Guadalupe." Three policeman from the municipality of Santa Catarina, another suburb of Monterrey, claimed to have seen the creature several times flying over the Sierra las Mitras, the site of a natural wilderness preserve just north of town which is known for its jagged peaks. Another policeman named Gerardo Garza Carvajal, of the same town of Santa Catarina, claimed to see a creature standing a meter and a half tall with dark feathers or fur and black claws in the town's cemetery. He thought it was a gigantic bird or bat, but it had the face of a human. In this sighting Officer Garza said that soon after the creature appeared it was joined by another one of the same size and type. Garza ran to a guardhouse and locked himself there until the creatures left. The theory that these are gigantic birds is supported by the eyewitness testimony of Francisco Peña who lives near the Santa Catarina Cemetery. He claims that when the creatures make noise, they sound like, "laughing turkeys." Of all the stories coming out as a result of the newscasts, perhaps the most interesting came from a man named Manuel Sifuentes who is also a policeman for the municipality of Guadalupe and a colleague of Samaniego. He describes a sighting that occurred almost 2 weeks before Samaniego's. According to Officer Sifuentes, he was leaving the police station on foot when suddenly a black creature with a large stick swooped down out of the sky. He instinctively closed his eyes and according to his report, "I felt much cold as if I had gotten into a freezer full of ice." The creature did not do physical harm to him but he had felt that the creature's energy had pierced his body. It all happened so suddenly, but Sifuentes claimed that he was attacked by a classic witch and that the stick the creature had was more like a broom that it used to fly around. He had the distinct impression that the *"bruja"* was a humanoid woman. No other sightings in early 2004 had described the creature in quite this way. In the wake of the flurry of news stories of Officer Samaniego's initial sighting, Guadalupe's mayor, Juan Francisco Rivera, in an attempt to calmly address the public on the issue, declared that officer Samaniego was a good public servant and had good character, but sometimes the stress of being a police officer or excess work might get to some people. The mayor believed the young policeman thought he saw something, but "sometimes life puts us in weird situations that we cannot explain." However, the politician had no comment on the many dozens of other sightings throughout the area made by other police officers and average citizens alike. The sightings of this huge, black, flying humanoid in the Monterrey area petered out within two years or so of the initial report.

In another part of northern Mexico, in the rural parts of the neighboring state of Chihuahua, a similar creature has been sighted. As the largest state in Mexico, Chihuahua, along with its namesake desert, boasts huge forests, deep canyons, rugged mountains and sweeping prairies. Many parts of the state are still wild and somewhat inaccessible and would make perfect habitat for an unknown creature or creatures. We see reports of the tall, dark, flying humanoid creature occur again in the year 2009 in a few small towns throughout Chihuahua. Just west of the capital of the state, Chihuahua City, near the Sierras, in the town of La Junta, a young man was returning home from his studies along a very infrequently traveled road. The date was

March 6, 2009. He came across something hunched over in the middle of the road. When the man's jeep got closer to the hunched-over figure it stood up and what he saw was similar to the sightings in Nuevo Leon just a few years before: It was a being standing upright, black, covered in fur, with a face similar to a human's and with wings. According to this eyewitness, the creature had two sets of wings and also red eyes. When it started to leap toward the jeep, the young man sped up his vehicle and for 15 minutes, the creature flew next to him, looking into the passenger window. The story made the newspaper, *El Heraldo de Chihuahua*, and much like what happened in the neighboring state a few years before, once the story hit the mainstream media, other people started coming forward with stories of other sightings. Two women, Angela Mendez and Viviana Ledezma, both from a town south of La Junta called Miñaca, claimed to have seen and heard the creature in an apple grove near the town's cemetery. This is only the second time that it was reported that the creature made noise. In most of the sightings it is silent. Although this gigantic man-bat might scare people, physical attacks on humans are almost nonexistent. Animals are another story. Many ranchers and other rural people have blamed the creature for destruction of livestock. The phenomenon of cattle mutilation, which has occurred with some frequency in the American Southwest, has also occurred in northern Mexico and once the stories of the man-bat became public, many people put the blame of mutilated livestock on this mysterious flying creature. A farmhand working a ranch near Huerta el Rosario claimed that he saw the creature struggling when caught up in some netting used to shield young plants from hail. Within days of this report, at nearby ranches sheep had been found with their throats slit and their tails cut.

Later in 2009 governmental authorities became involved to try to assuage the panic of the people in rural Chihuahua and to try to come up with some answers once and for all. The police department of the town of Guerrero joined forces with the Civil Defense Department of Chihuahua to try to track down the creature. The joint task force concluded that if this man-bat were real that it probably lived in the mountain wilderness outside of Miñaca but they could never track down the elusive nocturnal creature or find any physical evidence of its existence.   Not a single track or a single tuff of fur was ever found. After this formal investigation the sightings seemed to fall off and there hasn't been a sighting in northern Mexico of these creatures for years.

The northern Mexico man-bat got the attention of Loren Coleman, an American cryptozoologist, someone who seeks to identify and describe cryptids, or legendary creatures and unknown animals. He noted that the appearance of this being in rural Chihuahua coincided with outbreaks of the H1N1 swine flu in this region, but a direct cause-and-effect relationship did not necessarily exist. Coleman and other cryptid and paranormal researchers have compared the northern Mexican man-bat appearances to the American "Mothman" sightings, which occurred starting in the mid- 1960s in rural West Virginia. The Mothman was described as an upright-standing, flying humanoid with a large wingspan and red eyes, sometimes seen as being covered in either black or brown fur. Like the man-bat of northern Mexico, a few eyewitness accounts of the Mothman caused widespread panic and possible copycat sightings. Both were also subjects of serious investigations by authorities that came up empty. Could these creatures be related or are we seeing a similar psychological phenomenon apparent in both cases? Until one of these creatures is actually captured for further examination, the man-bat of northern Mexico will just remain an interesting unsolved mystery and the stuff of legend and the imagination.

JOSÉ AND THE SKYFISH

In May of 2016, Alberto Ignacio Alejo Ibarra whipped out his phone and with his camera feature he recorded a strange anomaly in the skies of his hometown of Guadalajara, Mexico. The video shows a translucent object with a tail appearing to "swim" over the skies of Jalisco. It lazily moves through the air and looks somewhat like a manta ray or a fish with a long tail. The video lasts for a few minutes and has been analyzed by many. For some, the anomaly looks like a blue plastic grocery store bag carried aloft by wind currents. Others have claimed that it is the remains of a weather balloon coming down to earth or that the object is simply a blue, heart-shaped balloon with a thick ribbon attached to it. With advanced computer technology in the hands of everyone these days, was this video simply a clever fake? Away from the earthly and computer-generated explanations of this video we have a whole group of people, investigators in the paranormal and cryptozoologists, who think that Alberto's video shows a previously unclassified group of creatures called "skyfish," to include what has been termed "rods," or in Spanish, *los rods*, supposed quick-flying, nearly invisible creatures that live in the far reaches of the stratosphere.

Perhaps the first person ever to see skyfish was a man named José Bonilla, an astronomer working at the observatory at Cerro de la Bufa which overlooks the city of Zacatecas. The date was August 12, 1883, and Bonilla was taking pictures of sunspots when he observed nearly 300 unidentified flying objects crossing the sun. The photos were taken on wet plates with an exposure of one one-hundredth of a second. This 1883 sighting is considered to be the first UFO sighting in modern Mexican history. José Bonilla noted the irregular movements of the objects he saw and when he made his photographs public the objects were dismissed as high-flying geese. A 2011 investigation of Bonilla's plates by UNAM, the National Autonomous University of Mexico, stated that the objects were possibly the fragments of a billion-ton comet that was passing by earth at the time. Other investigators with a more paranormal bent claim that the 1883 José Bonilla photographs not only represent the first tangible records of UFOs in Mexico, but they depict the elusive skyfish.

A century after Bonilla's photographs, sophisticated camera equipment became more affordable for average people. By the middle of the 1990s, with more anomalies in the skies recorded on film, we see the beginnings of the classification of skyfish as a possible cryptid or previously unknown animal. According to paranormal investigator Fon Ramos creator of the website *Atraviesa lo desconocido* – "Across the Unknown" in English – and author of the book, *Nuestro origen extraterrestre y otros misterios del cosmos – Our Extraterrestrial Origins and Other Mysteries of the Cosmos* – skyfish were first recorded in our era in the mid-1990s when an American cameraman named Mark Lichtle was filming parachutists jumping into a deep cave just outside of San Luís Potosí, the capital city of the Mexican state of the same name. The mysterious flying objects, classified as the rod-like skyfish, were only noticed later when the film was being reviewed by Lichtle in slow motion. Various skyfish darted around the base jumpers, some even going around the jumpers to avoid collision. The creatures appear to be somewhat translucent, about one to two meters long, and thus ruled out the possibility of birds or insects. The American photographer had a mystery on his hands and didn't know what to do with the footage.

Slightly earlier than the San Luís Potosí photographic anomalies, we have similar objects being filmed outside the town of Real de Palmas in the Mexican state of Nuevo León. On March 19, 1994 a man named Santiago Ytturia set up his video camera in anticipation of recording the UFOs that neighbors had spoken of seeing the past few evenings. Nearly discouraged after hours of waiting, Santiago was about to give up when he saw strange flashing lights in the sky. He filmed the darting lights and thought that was all he captured with his video camera. Later Santiago reviewed the film in slow motion and after the UFO had disappeared from view he noticed something highly unusual: spear-like images with strange small appendages, only seen when he reviewed the film frame by frame. They flew by so fast that they were nearly invisible to the naked eye. Had he discovered some strange atmospheric disturbance previously not described or was this some special type of UFO?

In the same month in 1994, a few hundred miles away from Santiago's home in Nuevo León, a man named José Escamilla was also setting up his camera in hopes of filming UFOs. He had had a UFO sighting in the 1960s when he was with other members of his local rock and roll band. He had seen strange lights outside his home in March of 1994 and wanted to record them. Escamilla recorded 16 minutes of footage and like the previous people he only saw the anomalous rod-like flying things when he slowed down the footage. At first he thought they were insects flying too close to the camera, but dismissed this because the objects were far and not close. José's curiosity was unrelenting and that began for him a lifetime of trying to figure out what these images were. He is considered to be the most expert researcher in this topic and has appeared on various TV and radio shows and participates actively in the UFO and paranormal lecture circuit. Through his internet presence and fame within the UFO and paranormal communities, José has amassed quite a bit of information on the skyfish, including much video evidence submitted from all parts of the world showing these strangely moving objects in the sky.

These anomalies have several things in common, according to José, and he has his theories as to what they could be. They move very fast – hundreds of miles per hour – and are almost never visible to the naked eye. They seem to be very common in Mexico, the southwest US, and parts of South America. There have also been reports of them in parts of Europe and China. They are cylindrical in shape and measure from about 4 inches to up to 9 feet in length. The have many appendages on their sides which run the full length of their bodies and may be attached to light wings.   They appear to fly through the air by using an undulating solid membrane which vibrates very rapidly on each side of their bodies very similar to how squids propel themselves through water. Skyfish are usually translucent. Skyfish have been observed flying in and out of large bodies of water. Escamilla theorizes that these are living organisms, animals that have adapted to predators over the years by developing translucence and by flying fast. Although not resembling any known animal currently living on earth, they are not extraterrestrials but a creature that has lived on earth for many years. Why has a body of a skyfish never been found? Like an octopus, it is theorized, the skyfish may be comprised mostly of soft tissue and may decompose quickly. Skyfish sightings are increasing and that may be just because camera technology has become more sophisticated and more widespread than ever. Also, there are just more people living in concentrated areas than ever before in human history. Take, for example, the mass sightings of rod-like skyfish sighted over Mexico City in May of 2015 seen by untold thousands. With a population of almost 25 million people – that's 50 million eyes – there is a greater chance for mass sightings of any sort of UFOs in the skies. José Escamilla claims that governments of the world are aware of this flying creature and he has alleged that his phone has been tapped and that his skyfish activities are being monitored. He remains determined to continue with his research and remains a clearinghouse of information for all things skyfish to this day.

As with everything decidedly "fringe," the skyfish phenomenon is not without its critics. When trying to debunk the skyfish the critics usually begin with camera errors and camera lens effects. Many of these supposed skyfish photos and videos can be explained away by tricks and aberrations of light. In other words, these images are simply just byproducts of photography. In general, when an image moves too fast in front of a still camera, the image blurs. When you take a picture of a person running, for example, there might be a slight blur in the arms and legs of the subject. It doesn't mean the person is morphing into something else, it is just a camera effect. The use of outdated or poorly maintained cameras in Mexico as an explanation for these anomalies is dismissed by counter-critics as racism. The seemingly easy explanations for photographs do not explain images seen in video and digital camera footage, but most critics have chalked up these motion picture examples to insects or the wind blowing small objects like airborne seeds through the air. Much like with Bigfoot, a body has yet to be produced of a skyfish for scientific examination. There has also been no biological precedent for this supposed cryptid. If they exist, what did they evolve from? In spite of the critiques, José Escamilla still pursues his studies, thus continuing the research of another José, his 19th Century counterpart from Zacatecas. Perhaps with better technology and more people investigating this phenomenon worldwide, José might finally have answers to this curious mystery.

THE NAGUAL

On a Sunday in October of 2013 the small church dedicated to *Nuestra Señora de la Asunción* – Our Lady of the Ascension – held a special mass for the worried townsfolk of the sleepy seaside town of Chicxulub Puerto located on the northern coast of the Yucatán. It was a very hot day, but the church was packed with parishioners searching for answers and comfort. Among the attendees was Alejandra, a gas station worker who had beheld a terrible sight just days before: a tall, clawed, hairy, growling creature crossed her path while she walked to work. Alejandra's encounter was tied to the many horrible deaths of chickens throughout the town and the surrounding area. Hundreds of chickens were found dismembered and half eaten with feathers and parts strewn about large areas. Soon after Alejandra's sighting, and a few other brief sightings about the town, the people in the town had collectively come to the conclusion that the strange creature lurking in their area and destroying their poultry stock was a demonic nagual.

The modern Mexican folklore idea of a nagual, a cryptid on par with Bigfoot or the Chupacabra, has generated recent interest from cryptozoologists, or those who study unknown animals, and is much different from the nagual of old. The concept of the nagual has seem to shape-shift with the times and has been used to describe any number of hideous, evil creatures spotted throughout Mexico's backcountry and mostly relegated to the darker hours of the day. There are few common threads in the modern nagual story: It is big and hairy, makes growling or howling noises and has the snout of a dog or sometimes the face of a cat. The nagual is blamed for disappearances of animals or people and destruction of property. Today's version of the nagual is not what we see in the historical record.

Some claim that the Codex Borgia, a pre-Hispanic pictographic bark book features naguales on page 22. The codex, which is essentially a calendar book created by Aztec scribes and used for purposes of divination, contains no written language, so there is no explanation of the figures claimed to be naguales on the page of the illustration. Most likely, the claim of modern-day analysists that these images are of "shape shifters" is not an accurate one. The word nagual is definitely pre-Columbian in origin. In the various languages in Mesoamerica, that word and similar words from the same stem or root, mean different things. For example, in Nahuatl, the language of the Aztecs, there is the word *naualli*, which means sorcerer, magician or enchanter and the word *nauallotl*, magic, enchantment or witchcraft. In the Quiché Maya language we have *naual*, a witch or sorcerer and the word *naualin*, which means "to tell fortunes," or "to predict the future." In the Tzental language spoken in the Mexican state of Chiapas there are similar words having to do with wisdom and memory. A *Ghnaoghel* is a wise man. That word is related to two other words, *naoghi*, "art, science" and *naoghibal*, "memory." Yet another set of examples of similar words are found in the Zapotec language of Oaxaca. We have *nayanii*, which loosely translates to "the superior reason of man." There are also two other similar words *nayaa*, and *naguii*, which mean "superior or powerful man." Although these words have existed in their respective languages for millennia, one researcher in the 1950s named Gustavo Correa has argued that the idea of the nagual and the mystical practices surrounding the nagual called "nagualism" were wholly imported from Europe and did not exist before the arrival of the Spanish. In his work titled *El espíritu del mal en Guatemala*, the author compared the idea of the nagual to the werewolves of medieval Europe and claims that because the nagual is so close to its European counterpart that it must have come to the Americas centuries ago with Spanish colonization as part of European folklore. Others counter Correa's claim by citing evidence in stone of shape-shifting creatures, notably the were-jaguar figurines of the Olmecs dating back over 2,000 years and the more recent pre-Hispanic stone monuments of the Zapotec which show people turning into animals.

The first mentioning of a nagual or nagualism by Europeans occurred in a 1530 writing by Antonio de Herrera called *Historia de las Indias Occidentales*. He was reporting, specifically, on the Maya. Translated from the Spanish, the author writes:

"The Devil was accustomed to deceive these natives by appearing to them in the form of a lion, tiger, coyote, lizard, snake, bird, or other animal. To these appearances they apply the name *Naguales*, which is as much as to say, guardians or companions; and when such an animal dies, so does the Indian to whom it was assigned. The way such an alliance was formed was thus: The Indian repaired to some very retired spot and there appealed to the streams, rocks and trees around him, and weeping, implored for himself the favors they had conferred on his ancestors. He then sacrificed a dog or a fowl, and drew blood from his tongue, or his ears, or other parts of his body, and turned to sleep. Either in his dreams or half awake, he would see some one of those animals or birds above mentioned, who would say to him, 'On such a day go hunting and the first animal or bird you see will be my form, and I shall remain your companion and *Nagual* for all time.' Thus their friendship became so close that when one died so did the other; and without such a *Nagual* the natives believe no one can become rich or powerful."

In another colonial account, this time from a priest named Father Bernardino de Sahagun, who was assigned to Aztec country, we see that the nagual is not an animal at all, but a person. In his work, *Historia de Nueva España*, the priest writes:

"The *naualli*, or magician, is he who frightens men and sucks the blood of children during the night. He is well skilled in the practice of this trade, he knows all the arts of sorcery (*nauallotl*) and employs them with cunning and ability; but for the benefit of men only, not for their injury. Those who have recourse to such arts for evil intents injure the bodies of their victims, cause them to lose their reason and smother them. These are wicked men and necromancers."

The church was very concerned in colonial times about the continuation of previous "pagan" religious practices and fortunate for the modern-day researcher there is a lot of material about Mesoamerican religious and folk-belief practices documented by the clergy. In an instructional book for confessors written in the year 1600 for priests with a predominately Indian congregation, Father Juan Bautista writes:

"There are magicians who call themselves *teciuhtlazque*, and also by the term *nanahualtin*, who conjure the clouds when there is danger of hail, so that the crops may not be injured. They can also make a stick look like a serpent, a mat like a centipede, a piece of stone like a scorpion, and similar deceptions. Others of these *nanahualtin* will transform themselves to all appearances, into a tiger, a dog or a weasel. Others again will take the form of an owl, a cock, or a weasel; and when one is preparing to seize them, they will appear now as a rooster, now as an owl, and again as a weasel. These call themselves *nanahualtin*."

The type of animal used has to do with the day on which the conjurer was born, as each day in the Mesoamerican calendar is associated with a specific animal. It is unclear from Father Bautista's writings if the person practicing nagualism is claiming to actually turn into these animals or if he is casting spells on witnesses to make others believe he is shapeshifting into something else.

The practice of nagualism was not completely erased during the Spanish colonial period for curious reasons. When the Spanish Inquisition ramped up in the Spanish colonies of the Americas, the primary focus of the inquisitors were the Europeans or mixed bloods who were part of the European society of the New World. No great attention was paid to the Indians, especially those living their traditional ways away from urban centers, because, they were seen as ignorant and "not knowing any better." Over the long course of the colonial period, the concept of the nagual thus became better documented by those who wished to learn more about the Mesoamerican natives.

Another primary source observation about the nagual from a Spanish historian Orozco y Berra writing in the latter colonial period states:

"The *nahual* is generally an old Indian with red eyes, who knows how to turn himself into a dog, woolly, black and ugly. The female witch can convert herself into a ball of fire; she has the power of flight, and at night will enter the windows and suck the blood of little children. These sorcerers will make little images of rags or of clay, then stick into them the thorn of the maguey and place them in some secret place; you can be sure that the person against whom the conjuration is practiced will feel pain in the part where the thorn is inserted. There still exist among them the medicine-men, who treat the sick by means of strange contortions, call upon the spirits, pronounce magical incantations, blow upon the part where the pain is, and draw forth from the patient thorns, worms, or pieces of stone. They know how to prepare drinks which will bring on sickness, and if the patients are cured by others the convalescents are particular to throw something of their own away, as a lock of hair, or a part of their clothing. Those who possess the evil eye can, by merely looking at children, deprive them of beauty and health, and even cause their death."

For most of the recorded history of this phenomenon, the nagual has been considered a powerful person who, through the use of what is collectively known as "witchcraft", changes into an animal or causes other people to think that he or she has changed. The term nagual has also been used by some Mesoamerican groups to denote a lifetime spirit guide represented by a real-world animal. The notion that the nagual is a cryptid, or unknown animal, is a more recent belief, as old memories of the real meanings of nagualism have died out or become murky down through the generations. Folk tales of legendary beasts and shape-shifters have changed over time and have developed into the mysterious creature we have today. Those claiming sightings of large, hairy, snarling, feline or doglike creatures in Mexico may have something altogether different on their hands not even related to anything conjured from old Indian magic.

LA LECHUZA

What's that huge creature in the skies of Chihuahua? Gigantic bird sightings have been happening all over northern Mexico and the Rio Grande Valley of Texas for centuries. The massive bird has been called La Lechuza for its resemblance to an owl. Is this creature real, or is it part of folklore and myth or maybe something else?
There are many descriptions and stories about the Lechuza. Depending on which telling one hears, the massive bird is the size of a small human to 7 feet tall and can have a wingspan of 15 feet. It is sometimes described as black in color and sometimes as white as snow. In most cases it has been said to resemble an owl. In other cases it is more like a huge raven. Some accounts say that the Lechuza's face is that of an old woman, or of something more otherworldly with large, dark, almond-shaped eyes. In all cases the Lechuza flies and is seen at night. It has been reported only in the Mexican states of Chihuahua, Coahuila, Durango, Nuevo Leon and Tamaulipas and on the American side of the Rio Grande in Texas.

There are many different legends surrounding the sighting of this creature. What could the large variety of explanations mean? The fact that there are so many different legends may indicate that sightings occurred over a large geographical area over the years among people who were isolated from one another. One town may have made sense of their sighting one way, while another town a thousand miles away may have made sense in another, without ever communicating with each other about it.

One of the main themes running through stories regarding the Lechuza is that the creature was once a woman who was wronged and who is seeking revenge. Some say the Lechuza is a woman by day and turns into a huge owl by night. Some say that the Lechuza snatches kids because her own child was killed by angry villagers for a crime he did not commit. In a variation of this, the child was killed by a drunk and so now the Lechuza exacts revenge by hanging around bars, waiting until closing time to attack bar patrons who stumble out into the street after hours not knowing the danger from the sky about to rain down on them. In some of the legends, La Lechuza is not a shape-shifting person at all, but a witch's familiar, much like a black cat, and does the bidding of the witch, attacking people and destroying property on her command. Other stories say the bird is a minion of Satan himself. Not only is the Lechuza said to take humans as prey, it also preys upon the negative emotions of humans, acting as a psychic vampire, drawing power from emotions surrounding human conflict and distress. The Lechuza has been known to appear outside of houses during domestic quarrels, waiting for one of the people involved to storm out of the house to then be snatched and carried to the Lechuza's lair. The Lechuza has a special fondness for children, especially for those who wander away from home after dark. If you feel secure in your home, the creature will make crying sounds like a baby to lure you out of your house. It's also been known to make a whistling sound, like a human whistling. If you answer it back with a whistle of your own, the Lechuza will swoop down and carry you away. If you wake up in the morning and see large scratches on your doors or windowsills it means that the Luchuza was there and is coming for you, so you must prepare yourself accordingly.

Can the Lechuza be killed? How can you protect yourself?
Because the creature is magical, according to legend the Lechuza
possesses supernatural powers and care must be taken to kill it or to
ward it off. If you shoot at it and it doesn't die, you die instead. If any
part of the Lechuza touches you – even a feather from its wingtip –
you will die. If you dream about the creature that means someone in
your family will die. In many stories, the Lechuza has been killed, but
when the sun comes up the body of the bird transforms back into the
body of a haggard witch. There are several things one can do to ward
off an attack by the creature. Hanging a rope with 7 knots in it outside
your front door or on your porch shows the creature that you
acknowledge and respect it and it will leave you alone. If you see the
creature flying at you, an attack can be repelled with a combination of
salt and chile powder thrown into the Lechuza's face. If salt and chile
powder are not handy, you can always recite The Magnificat – in
Spanish, *La Magnifica* – a Catholic prayer taken from the Gospel of
Saint Luke where the Virgin Mary is praising the power of God. It is
also called the Canticle of Mary and celebrates the Visitation, the
second Joyful Mystery of the Holy Rosary. The prayer must be recited
in the normal manner AND backwards. There would probably be very
little time to say this payer forwards and backwards if a massive bird
came out of the sky and was swooping down on you, but in any event,
it made the list of possible Lechuza repellants.

Some stories of Lechuza encounters have happened well into the
21st Century and continue to this day. In one recent story, near the
town of El Tigre, Chihuahua, a man was driving on a dirt road outside
of town when the creature began swooping down on his truck. At one
point, it hit the truck's windshield and bounced on to the road in front
of the vehicle. The driver gunned the engine, ran over the Lechuza,
backed up over it and ran over it again to be satisfied that the creature
was dead. Unfortunately, from the rear-view mirror the man saw the
Lechuza rise again and instantly had a heart attack and died at the
wheel. This, according to the passenger in the truck.

In another story, the Lechuza was hanging around a small town
near Nuevo Laredo sometime in the 1950s. The townsfolk gathered
together to come up with a plan to kill it. One person lured it out of
the trees using his young child as bait. When the Lechuza swooped

down to take the child, several men shot at the bird, but only hit it in the claw before it flew off. The next morning, members of the town went to the house of a supposed witch and she answered the door with a crutch and a bandaged leg. The story ends there and we don't know what happened.

In the United States, in the town of Santa Rosa, Texas, near the border with Mexico there was a mass sighting of La Lechuza in 1977. The bird was spotted on a tree and then flew to the front door of a woman, scratching the door as if it wanted to get in. By then the neighborhood dogs arrived, barking, and the Lechuza flew away. The dogs ran after the bird as far as they could, but gave up when the Lechuza flew too high. The next morning, all of the neighborhood dogs were dead. Several people saw the massive bird and all were mystified by the death of the dogs.

Could the legends of the Lechuza exist because they are describing an actual animal? If so, is there physical evidence to the animal's existence? Among the many reports on the internet about this creature – most of which is written in Spanish – there exists only one photo of a supposed Lechuza killed in northern Mexico. The bird appears to be a huge white barn owl with a 15-foot wingspan. Some dismiss this as a hoax or a fake, something cropped and photoshopped. This, however, is the only piece of photographic proof of the creature's existence. No gigantic feathers, bones or massive nests have been discovered or uncovered thus far.

On the American side of the border there are many native groups who have similar legends of gigantic birds collectively classified as "Thunderbirds." These huge nocturnal birds are in the oral histories of the peoples of the Southwest and the Pacific Northwest and can be found among the Algonquin, the Ojibwe and Winnebago of the northern US and Canada. The Thunderbird has garnered serious interest from cryptozoologists – those who study fabled or yet-unknown animals – as sightings of these massive birds have also continued through to the 21st Century.

The Lechuza might turn out not be the stuff of legend or a mysterious animal yet undiscovered. It could have a more otherworldly origin. Many people connected with the alien abduction phenomenon have reported the sighting of owls before and during their supposed abduction experiences. Many alleged abductees, or "experiencers," claim that the owl is used as a "screen memory" to take the place of the aliens themselves so as to cause the human less trauma in dealing with the abduction experience. Owls are often associated with arrival of The Greys, the short, menacing, spindly, hairless creatures with big black eyes who carry off humans for experimentation and tests in UFO lore. The topic of screen memories and the alien use of owls is discussed at length in a nearly 400-page book by Mike Clelland titled *The Messengers: Owls, Synchronicity and the UFO Abductee*. Whitley Strieber, the author of the famous book about the alien abduction phenomenon, *Communion*, also links owls to the arrival of The Greys. Could this legend be used to manipulate people during an alien abduction? The possibility that the Lechuza is being used by off-world intelligences in their nefarious doings is not off the table.

So, is this massive bird a figure of the collective imagination? Is it a genuine cryptid? Is it part of something not of this earth? There has been very little serious investigation into the Lechuza and for now the creature remains mostly the stuff of legend and a way to keep children inside and safe. It's an interesting phenomenon, but it is waiting for some serious examination.

THE SISIMITE: MEXICO'S JUNGLE-DWELLING BIGFOOT

Does Mexico have its own version of Bigfoot? The answer is "yes." It's called the Sisimite and he is only found in 3 Mexican states: Campeche, Chiapas and Quintana Roo. It has been spotted in the jungle-covered tropical areas of these states and is said to range all the way down the heavily forested Central American cordillera to Colombia where he has been nicknamed the Darien Monster. The Sisimite has also been called "The Olmec Ape" based on a figurine found at an Olmec archaeological site in the state of Campeche. The figurine dates back 2,000 years.

So, what does this creature look like and what are its origins? The Sisimite has been described as a hairy ape-like creature, much larger than a human, with the face of a human. It has only 4 fingers and no thumbs, and in some cases it has been described as having backwards-facing feet. Sisimites walk upright, like humans. They let out high-pitched screams but have no language. They are generally regarded as being hostile to humans and have been accused of kidnapping people. Their apelike fur has been described as ranging from a chestnut color to pitch black. They have no protruding ears and their noses are flat. Cryptozoologists, those who study unknown or mythical animals, suspect that the Sisimite came across the Bering land bridge with humans – and its northern cousin, Bigfoot – some 40,000 years ago. Why it is confined to the dense jungles of southern Mexico, thousands of miles away from the closest Bigfoot sighting, is unknown. Perhaps the northern offshoots of this creature were killed off by early humans, or if this is something unrelated to Bigfoot, the habitat of the north and central parts of Mexico were not conducive to the survival of the Sisimite. Some believe that the creature is a surviving remnant of Gigantopithecus, a large prehistoric ape native to Asia that stood almost 9 feet tall and supposedly died out over 100,000 years ago.

Briefly, it is worth mentioning that the Sisimite has a smaller cousin who lives in the same region. The creature's little cousin is simply called the Duende by Spanish-Speakers and the Dwendi by the English-speaking people of the country of Belize, which is in the heart of the Sisimite's territory. People who still speak one of the many Maya dialects refer to the Duende as Nukux Tat. The word *duende* in Spanish literally means "elf" or "dwarf". It is described as a much shorter hairy humanoid and is often seen or depicted wearing a sombrero or woven palm leaves on his head. This 3 to 4 foot tall creature is described as a trickster and is seen as more of a mythical creature possessing magical powers. Often he has been described carrying a stick or machete and can be clad in rags or animal skins. The Duende has been described as a creature perpetually engaged in mischief, he has alternatively been known to rescue lost people in the forest and kidnap them. He is also seen as being a protector of all the animals in the jungle. The Duende is used to scare children not to play in the forest alone as it is said he may kidnap kids and take them to his cave to hold them hostage. Farmers may blame the tricks of the Duende for bad crops. Many people who have studied the Sisimite have categorized the Duende as more of a mythological creature whereas his larger cousin could most likely be a real and yet undiscovered animal. The Duende is mentioned here because it also may be an embellished cryptid and has some of the same characteristics as have been ascribed to the Sisimite, notably, a body covered in a course fur and backwards-facing feet. The country of Belize even issued a postage stamp as part of a folklore series that depicts the Duende.

To return to the larger cryptid, the Sisimite, this creature has long been part of the animal make-up of the forest according to the Maya who still live in the creature's territory. The traditional Maya beliefs, going back to ancient times, divide the world of spiritual beings into three categories. There are the main powerful deities that lord over the universe, the gods of the sky, the earth, the water, etc. Then there are the local spirits that may inhabit certain areas of the forest, or a geographical feature such as a mountain or a landmark tree. The last group of spiritual beings include certain animals of the forest that are connected to the gods or local spirits. The jaguar has special powers because it is connected to the higher spirits, for example. The Sisimite is considered to be another animal that is "plugged in" to the spirit world while being a real, living, breathing animal of the forest.

Although native to the world of the Maya, the name Sisimite comes from a Nahuatl – Aztec – word *tzitzimitl* which loosely means "demon" or "supernatural creature." While known to the Maya for centuries, the first outside report of the Sisismite came from a group of Spanish gold prospectors in the 18th Century. On an expedition in what is now Honduras, a member of this group supposedly shot and killed one of the creatures that was raiding the mining camp.

The Sisimite made its debut in the English-speaking world through the writings and reports of a man named Edward Jonathan Hoyt, who was nicknamed "Buckskin Joe." Hoyt was born in Lower Canada – modern Quebec – in 1840. He headed south in 1861 to take part in the American Civil War, fighting on the Union side. Between the end of the war and a trip to tropical Mexico and Central America in 1898, Buckskin Joe traveled with circuses across America and was an aerialist and acrobat in addition to playing 16 musical instruments. On that 1898 gold prospecting adventure he would encounter our horrible hominid, shooting a Sisismite that crawled onto his bunk while he was sleeping. The account made the papers back home.

The Sisimite appeared again in a 1961 compendium compiled by author Ivan T. Sanderson titled, *Abominable Snowmen: Legend Come to Life*. In the book the author compiled stories of the Central American Bigfoot, mostly concentrating on British Honduras, the former name of what we now call Belize. The Abominable Snowmen book prompted Bigfoot researcher Mark Sanborne to track the creature in 1992, and he, too, compiled stories from tropical Mexico, Belize and Guatemala. Both works are full of eyewitness accounts of the creature.

So, then, is the Sisimite real or imaginary? Is it like the Giant Panda and the Mountain Gorilla, a real animal that managed to evade human investigation until modern times? Or is it just a myth created to scare children? We have many stories and eyewitness accounts and in spite of people claiming to have shot the creature, we have no physical evidence of the Sisimite. Like Bigfoot, no one has yet produced a body or captured one alive. Perhaps more investigations and expeditions into Mexico's dark jungles are necessary to finally figure out conclusively whether or not the creature is real.

THE CHUPACABRA

The word Chupacabra comes from two Spanish words, *chupa* "suck" and *cabra* "goat." Sometimes the pluralized form is used: Chupacabras. Unlike many myths and legends that stretch back to times before people can recall dates, investigators know when the Chupacabra first appeared: March of 1995. Yes, that means it is a newly hatched cryptid, the new kid on the block of demons and monsters. Where did it come from? What does it look like?

There are two types of creatures that have been sighted by people that have been classified as a Chupacabra. The first is one that looks like a reptile with spikes on its back, standing about 4 feet tall, often times with red eyes and wings like a flying squirrel. Creatures in the second group look like a skinny, larger, hunched over dog with patchy fur or no fur.

As previously mentioned, the Chupacabra first appeared in March of 1995 which makes him a relatively new monster. It first appeared not in Mexico but in Puerto Rico. In the spring of 1995 the residents of 2 small Puerto Rican towns had discovered dead farm animals on their properties, and the animals had two incisions on their necks, and reportedly, all the blood drained from them. The creature was not actually spotted until 5 months later and its description was very vivid: It was almost reptilian, with bat-like wings, claws and spikes on its back. This first Chupacabra encounter was described in great detail at the time by the Puerto Rican tabloids and later in a book published in 1997 by Scott Corrales called *Chupacabras and Other Mysteries* which received attention from the curious outside of Puerto Rico. A flurry of sightings happened right after the creature was talked about on the pan-Latin American talk show hosted by the bleached blonde, Cuban-born Cristina Saralegui called "Cristina". The first sighting in Mexico happened right after that broadcast. This made people wonder, did the show give people permission to talk about this phenomenon or were people just hallucinating because of ideas put in their heads by this television program?

One well-publicized story of a sighting of this creature involved an older lady who woke up to find a chupacabra in her house. According to the reports based on interviews with the woman, the creature understands Spanish. She yelled at the chupacabra and called it a *pendejo,* and almost in a reaction of shame, the creature covered its face with a wing, shivered a bit and then disappeared behind her washing machine. Perhaps what happened speaks less about the chupacabra's ability to understand human language and more about the powers of intimidation of the Mexican *nana*.

A wave of reports occurred in the late 1990s across northern Mexico and the state of Jalisco in central/western Mexico. Many of these sightings were of the wingless, hairless doglike creature. In May of 1996 there was a rash of sightings in the rural parts of the state and many dead animals with the characteristic bite marks on the necks, especially in goats and sheep. The director of the Guadalajara Zoo went out to some of the ranches and took plaster casts of footprints and said that the creature was probably a large dog. Two investigators from Mexico City, Patricia and Mario Mendez Acosta also traveled out to rural Jalisco to look into the phenomenon. They even set up traps to catch the chupacabra and each time caught wild dogs. A local police official made a comment at the time saying that locally the chupacabra phenomenon could be explained away by wild dogs and that the wave of sightings was part of *"una gran psicosis,"* a great psychosis. Many Mexicans believe that the whole thing is a joke and that only the gringos would take the story seriously enough to investigate such nonsense. Ironically, throughout Mexico, sightings of the chupacabra have been decreasing with time. Sightings are now few and far between.

The early sightings in Puerto Rico, of the slightly winged reptile kind were blamed on UFOs and even the U.S. military. America has long used Puerto Rico as kind of a dumping ground, according to locals, and some people suspected that the chupacabra was some sort of chimera, or blend of two or more animals, and the product of a biological experiment gone wrong. One Puerto Rican tabloid even alleged that eyewitnesses saw the creature being transferred by the US military from a crashed saucer site. Somewhere along the way the Chupacabra got loose after a wreck on a back road. No other news outlets could confirm this story.

Some Mexican and Texan chupacabras have actually been tested and examined. A famous photo made its rounds on the internet of a chupacabra supposedly killed in south Texas near the Mexican border. Animal experts have claimed that these are dogs, coyotes or even raccoons with types of mange or scabies, diseases that stress the animals and cause their hair to fall out, make them look disheveled and give them a foul odor.   The diseases may also weaken the animals to such an extent so as to cause them to go after domestic livestock instead of hunting or foraging normally. There have been formal DNA tests on some of these animals to determine that they are indeed dogs or other known animals.

But what would explain those other sightings? The ones where the creature is standing upright or that it has spikes on its back or even wings? Is it part of a *"Gran Psicosis"* or an entirely new creature either recently discovered, manufactured in a lab or imported from another world? As with so many other legendary creatures, a body to examine would really help investigators, but until the time that one of these animals can be trapped or killed, the chupacabra will remain a mystery.

PART SIX: ANCIENT MYSTERIES

TEOTIHUACÁN, THE LOST CITY OF THE GODS

Just a short bus ride from Mexico City, following the brown signs with one word – *Piramides* – is the most visited archaeological site in all of Mexico. Our name for the place is Teotihuacán, which is the Hispanicization of the Aztec name for the place, Teotihuácan, which has been interpreted to mean "the place where the gods were born." While being the most visited archaeological site in Mexico, not much is known about it. No one knows what the inhabitants of the city actually called the city as no formal writing system existed there. The common language used at Teotihuacán is unknown, along with the ethnicity of its rulers. No one knows exactly who built the city of for what purpose. Archaeologists and historians are unclear whether or not Teotihuacán was an empire, a city-state or just a religious and commercial center with little or no territorial ambitions. It was one of the largest population centers in all of Mesoamerica at the time and some historians say that at its height of population in the first centuries AD it was easily the 5th or 6th most populous city in the world with over 125,000 people living there. In spite of its grandeur and scope and impact on Mexico many centuries after its collapse, Teotihuacán today largely remains a huge mystery.

What do we know of this place? When the Spanish arrived here in the early 16th Century, squatters lived among the ruins. The Aztecs, who ruled the surrounding area at the time of the Spanish Conquest, did not build Teotihuacán. In fact, the Aztec Empire only came to prominence about a thousand years after the height of the city. The Aztecs thought the place holy and it was said that the gods and the sun itself came from there. Emperor Montezuma, it was said, would take regular pilgrimages from his capital of Tenochtitlán to Teotihuacán. While revered by the Aztecs, no Aztec knew anything about the city's origins, who lived there or why the place even existed.

Teotihuacán is located in the modern Mexican state of México just 25 miles north of present-day Mexico City. The city was built on a north-south axis aligned to precisely 15.5° east of north. The city's grid extended uniformly across a vast land area. At the city's height, around 450 AD, the area included in Teotihuacán proper covered some 32 square miles. Dominating the core of the city is the Avenue of the Dead, or *Calzada de los muertos* in Spanish, which is over 130 feet wide at its thickest point and runs over 3 miles long. The name Avenue of the Dead is a direct translation of the Nahuatl word for the road, *Miccoatli*. The Aztecs named it that because they believed the platforms lining the road contained tombs. Besides the platforms, on the side of this great road we see some of the most impressive pieces of monumental architecture in the ancient world. Two massive pyramids, the Pyramid of the Sun and the Pyramid of the Moon, dominate the ceremonial heart of the city along with large palaces and temples. Besides the pyramids the more notable buildings include the Temple of the Feathered Serpent, the Court of the Columns and the Quetzal-Butterfly Palace. On the western side of the Avenue of the Dead, across from the Temple of the Feathered Serpent is what is called the Great Compound, which served as the city's massive marketplace. Most of these structures are surprisingly well preserved. The signs leading to Teotihuacán say *piramides* for a good reason; the Pyramid of the Sun and the Pyramid of the Moon dominate the ancient city. The Pyramid of the Sun is the largest pyramid at the site and the third largest pyramid in the world behind the Great Pyramid at Giza in Egypt and the Great Pyramid of Cholula found just south of Teotihuacán. Teotihuacán's largest pyramid measures 720 feet by 760 feet at its base and is 260 feet tall. It has a volume of 41.8 million cubic feet of stone, rubble and a conglomeration of other materials. This massive structure, just like the Great Pyramid at Giza in Egypt, once was covered in a bright white, smooth limestone facing. This structure was most likely slightly larger in the past than it is now, as quarrying and reconstruction efforts have reduced the size of the pyramid slightly. Outward from the ceremonial center were living quarters and workshops for the various commercial trades found throughout the city. Teotihuacán may represent the first place in the Americas where multi-level apartment-house dwellings were built. The city was divided into barrios where peoples of different areas of Mesoamerica lived, notably the Otomi, Zapotec, Maya, Nahua and Mixtec peoples. Many of the buildings were fashioned in what would later be termed the talud-tablero architectural style, in which an inwards-sloping external side of a structure called a *talud* is surmounted by a rectangular panel called a *tablero* and repeated. This style was adopted by other sites throughout ancient Mexico. Many intricate and colorful murals survive throughout the city and depict everything from mythological allegories to scenes from everyday life. Many of these paintings were done in the fresco style ala the Italian Renaissance and are regarded as some of the best in the ancient Americas. There were also many canals for irrigation to support farming and many of the living areas had their own small gardens for food. There is a surprising lack of any evidence for fortifications at Teotihuacán.

Occupation at the site of Teotihuacán began around 200 BC. During this time many small urban centers began to emerge in central Mexico. At the time of Teotihuacán's ascendency another competing urban center in the southern part of the Valley of Mexico called Cuiculico was threatened by the eruption of the volcano Xitle. Scholars believe that the threat of the volcano caused people to emigrate from the southern shores of Lake Texcoco to the Teotihuacán Valley, thus encouraging the growth of the city. By 100 AD, the Pyramid of the Sun and most of the other massive buildings were completed. Building continued at a steady pace until 450 AD. Although the political structure of Teotihuacán is unknown, it is clear that a highly structured civil society was necessary to complete such organized and massive building projects. As found in graves and in the architecture of dwellings, there was definitely a hierarchy and a marked social order to the place. It's long been debated whether or not Teotihuacán was the center of an empire, but we know of its influence both politically and culturally. Without a doubt, the city was the center of industry as hundreds of workshops employed craftsmen working in stone, clay, wood and feathers. Stamped decorations found on Teotihuacán pottery is indicative of mass production. Fashioned obsidian and pottery from Teotihuacán has been found as far away as the Maya sites of Kaminalyjuyú in Guatemala and Copán in Honduras, almost a thousand miles away. To the north, the Teotihuacán trade network reached as far as the area of modern-day Santa Fe, New Mexico, with turquoise mined from the mountains around Cerillos found 1,400 miles away at Teotihuacán. There was definite contact between Teotihuacán and the ancient civilization of the Hohokam in Arizona, as the Mesoamerican ball game began to appear in the ancient cities around modern-day Phoenix around 500 AD. Some scholars believe that one of the major functions of Teotihuacán was religious. Archaeologists have discovered caves and tunnel structures underneath the pyramids in the city. These caverns may be related to the Mesoamerican creation myth and the center of the city may have been a place of pilgrimage, much as what had been witnessed in the latter days with the Aztecs visiting the ruins at Teotihuacán for religious reasons. Those scholars who propose Teotihuacán as a political empire that conquered or exacted tribute from surrounding areas much like the Aztecs, cite historical writings from the Maya, who had a written language at the time. The Maya called Teotihuacán *Puh*, or "The Place Where the Reeds Grow," and references to the great city have been found at various Maya sites. An inscription found at the lowland Guatemalan Maya city of Tikal references a ruler called *Jatz'om Kuh* which has been translated as "Owl that will Strike" or "Spearthrower Owl", a Teotihuacán ruler who reigned 60 years and died in the year 439 AD. Some say this king installed his relatives to rule over the Maya cities of Tikal and Uaxactun in modern-day Guatemala. A group of Mesoamerican scholars proposing an "internalist view" with regard to the relationship between Teotihuacán and the Maya world theorize that the ancient Maya only emulated the elites of Teotihuacán and were linked to that city through trade and copied elements of their culture and religion, but were politically separate from it. The "externalist view" believes that Teotihuacán militarily invaded the faraway cities of the Maya civilization and directly ruled over some of them. So, it is unclear whether or not Teotihuacán was the center of a political empire or merely the center of a commercial, cultural and/or ideological one.

Perhaps one of the biggest mysteries of this "Lost City of the Gods" is why it collapsed. There are many theories. These theories range from external warfare to environmental degradation to the "return of the star people" beliefs. The latest theory now in fashion is climate change, which is not surprising because many theories of collapses of ancient civilizations throughout the world tend to mirror our own contemporary ideas of doomsday. Many scientists believe that lengthy droughts occurring in the years 535 and 536 caused famine and pressure on the population and with that came social discord and the abandoning of the city. Smaller skeletons and remains showing malnutrition began to appear in the archaeological record at this time. In around the year 650 AD we know the city suffered a great fire, but the fire did not engulf the entire city. It was restricted to the ceremonial centers and the neighborhoods of the elites. This was accompanied by destruction of sacred objects and an overall looting of the wealthier areas of the city. 100 years after the fire Teotihuacán was a shadow of its former self.

Researchers have not, up to this point, proposed this alternate theory of the demise of this great city. Perhaps the collapse of Teotihuacán may also be rooted in a somewhat contemporary vision of our own doomsday held by some. As Teotihuacán grew in size and wealth, it attracted more and more foreigners. A few centuries after the city's founding, the impact of the foreigners was measurable. The barrios mentioned before that housed people from the Gulf Coast, the Maya regions of Central America and other far-flung parts of Mexico increased in size with time. This is evident in the archaeological record; over time there is an increase in foreign pottery styles and religious iconography that was coming from outside the traditions of the city. Did these foreign groups assimilate into the wider culture of Teotihuacán or did they butt heads with the ruling class? According to the studies by Harvard professor Robert Putnam, increased cultural diversity in a limited geographical area causes increased strife. The mantra heard in modern America in the past two decades, "diversity is our strength," is called to question here. Back in Teotihuacán, it is quite curious that the Great Fire of 650 AD and its accompanied looting only raged through the elite areas of the city. This suggests great internal social turmoil. With foreigners outnumbering the natives who ruled the city, one could only imagine the tensions stemming from a variety of causes. The droughts that happened a century before the calamities of 650 AD had little effect on the collapse because, for one, the droughts were brief, and also, other cities in the area were on the rise while this one was on the decline. A drought would have affected the other major cities in the area, too, like Cholula, and it did not. Perhaps the theory of cultural diversity causing the collapse belongs on the pile of unfounded speculations and misdirected musings regarding the end of Teotihuacán. Perhaps with more reflection on our own current situation with regard to immigration in the West this may cause archeologists and political historians to formulate similar theories with regard to Teotihuacán. Until we come up with a concrete and indisputable reason or set of reasons for the collapse of this great city, it will remain one of the greatest mysteries of ancient Mexico.

MAYA ASTRONOMY

One of the most popular tourist sites in all of Mexico is the ancient Maya city of Chichén Itzá. Just a short air-conditioned bus ride through scrub jungle from the resort towns of Cancún or Playa del Carmen, the ruins are visited by almost 1.5 million people annually. As one of the largest of the Maya cities, the ceremonial center of Chichén Itzá is dominated by several very large buildings and ceremonial complexes. One of the buildings that stands out is one unique to the Maya world because of its cylindrical shape. It is called in Spanish El Caracol – "The Snail" in English – because of the circular staircase inside the building. In the middle of the 20th Century the building acquired the nickname "The Observatory" because its collapsed roof and circular body are reminiscent of modern observatories and planetariums. Since the nickname became popular, writers and amateur archaeologists have turned the building into an actual ancient observatory not just based on its shape, but based on the fact, like most other ceremonial buildings, that it is aligned to celestial bodies. To this day the purpose of "The Observatory" at Chichén Itzá remains open to scholarly speculation. There is no doubt, though, that the ancient Maya were quintessential stargazers and compiled massive almanacs over hundreds of years to chart the movements of the sun, moon, stars and planets. What did the Maya know about their physical world and how did astronomy integrate into their religious beliefs?

As the Maya were the only group in ancient Mexico with a fully developed written language, much of what we know about Maya astronomy and what they thought of their physical reality has come from firsthand sources. In addition to inscriptions made in stone found in the ruins of Maya cities, the ancient Maya also wrote in bark paper books called codices. In the few codices that survived the massive Maya book burning of Archbishop of the Yucatán Diego de Landa in 1562, we find astronomical tables and texts about the movements of celestial bodies. We also find pieces of the Maya creation myths and what the members of this civilization thought of the makeup of their physical world. In addition to the archaeological evidence of what the Maya thought in their own words, we have written accounts from the initial Spanish contact with descendants of the ancient Maya. Although classic Maya civilization collapsed five to six hundred years before the arrival of the Spanish, much of what was gleaned by the Spanish chroniclers at the time of first contact has been interpreted by scholars as being part of the unbroken chain of Mesoamerican belief systems passed down from antiquity and much of it reinforces what archaeologists have learned from studying ancient texts and inscriptions. It's also important to note that the Maya had an advanced number system and were skilled at mathematics. They even developed the concept of zero, seemingly independent from the rest of the world in their jungle isolation. Their applications of math and written language to understanding their world helps us in the modern age understand what the Maya thought about their physical world and its relation to the cosmos.

The Maya practiced naked-eye astronomy, as no instruments were used to view the heavens except for crude hollowed-out pointing sticks held close to the eye. Certain buildings in ancient Maya cities were arranged to serve as astronomical observatories. The set up usually consisted of a pyramid oriented due east which was used in conjunction with three temples situated to give the observer on the pyramid's staircase points of reference to view sunrises and sunsets and thus determine the occurrences of the equinoxes and solstices. Archaeoastronomers and modern-day scholars who study astronomical alignment of buildings or settlements often call this "sacred geometry."

With their advanced knowledge of math and ability to make keen observations, the ancient Maya never thought of the earth as a ball moving in an endless Universe. The Maya thought that the earth was the center of all creation and that it existed on a flat plane instead of a sphere spinning through space. The earth extended into infinity on this endless plane with layers below making up the underworld and layers above making up the heavens. While some authors claim the Maya believed there were four corners to the earth, there is nothing uncovered so far to indicate that they believed that the earth plane ended, only that it had 4 directions and that somewhere away from the center of the earth plane off into those directions were symbolic jaguars called *bacabs* holding up the sky. Each jaguar corresponded to a color: east-red; north-white; west-black; south-yellow. We can see an illustration of the four jaguars in the Codex Madrid, one of the surviving bark painted books described earlier. In these four directional areas were also four ceiba trees topped with birds of the appropriate colors. From inscriptions found at the ancient cities of Palenque and Piedras Negras, it is also believed that a fifth green tree was found in the center of the earth plane. It is unknown if the trees were there to help hold up the heavens or as pathways to the heavens. It is also unknown whether or not the Maya felt they could know the exact location of the gigantic ceiba tree in the center of the earth plane, or even if they had interest in looking for it. We do know that the ceiba was looked upon by the ancient Maya as a tree of abundance from which food for mankind first came. In the Maya cosmology, Earth has often been symbolized as a gigantic crocodile or lizard, sometimes with two heads, which has led some to write that the Maya believed that the earth traveled on the back of a crocodile or lizard, but this would not fit in with the structural or spatial view the Maya had of their universe. To them, the earth was stationary and fixed and only the objects in the heavens moved.

The Maya believed that the heavens were divided into seven sections and symbolized by thirteen steps in which certain gods resided. Six steps ascended in the east, and six descended in the west, with one step or platform at the top. Much of what the Maya saw in the skies was allegorical or based on myths and fables, but most of why these ancient people tracked the movements of the celestial bodies were for practical uses. Like many other ancient peoples, they relied on the heavens for clues as to when to plant and when to start the harvesting process. The Maya also looked skyward for other reasons we might consider more astrological instead of astronomical, like when to go to war, for example.   The planets were called "stars that travel" and not seen as spherical worlds made of rock orbiting the sun. The sun, of course, was the most important heavenly body, and the Maya tracked it and recorded it, and predicted its eclipses with high accuracy. The rulers of the Maya world co-opted the sun and often Maya kings were shown alongside the powerful sun symbol. The sun was not considered to be a star, but a separate type of entity. In the Maya creation story, the sun and the moon were the first people on the earth. The sun was a great hunter and the creator of music and poetry. The moon was a weaver, a protector of plants and later the patroness of childbirth. She had a fight with the sun and lost one of her eyes and that is why her light is so much dimmer than the sun's. The ancient Maya often bestowed honorific titles on the sun and moon, such as "lord" or "lady", or "our mother," or "our grandfather." In art and in inscriptions, the sun's path in the sky was often illustrated by a double-headed serpent. The planets, while tracked and catalogued meticulously by the astronomer-priests, also had their allegorical sides to them. Saturn and Jupiter were two types of falcons. The planet Mars was considered to be twin monkeys. Venus, which was probably the most important planet to be studied by the ancient Maya, was associated with the feathered serpent god Quetzalcoatl. The famous "Venus Tables", an 8-year almanac of the planet, can be found in the Dresden Codex, with a detailed description of the 584-day average Venus cycle which is very close to our modern-day astronomical observations. Venus, it seemed, also played important roles in fertility and warfare. So-called Venus cults existed throughout Mesoamerica, and not just in the Maya area. As it is the brightest star-like celestial body in the night sky, Venus is often conflated with the sun in some Maya imagery. Very little is known about how these ancient people regarded the planet Mercury. It has been loosely associated with an owl image, but not much else is known about how this planet fit into the Maya universe.

As mentioned earlier, the Maya believed that the heavens had seven layers, so they did not think that the universe was infinite in an upward and outward direction as we do. In this contained space, existed the sun, the moon and planets along with the stars. To the Maya, the stars were metaphorically described as jaguar spots, flowers, fireflies and "the eyes of the night." Like other peoples throughout the world, the ancient Maya saw constellations in the night sky. The Pleiades was thought to be a rattlesnake's rattle called *Tz'ab*. Orion's Belt was part of a turtle constellation. In Sagittarius they saw a gigantic fish-snake. In a strange coincidence, the people in the northern Maya area saw the constellation Scorpius as we see it, in the shape of a scorpion. The Milky Way holds a special place in the beliefs of the ancient Maya. To them it was the extension of the World Tree whose roots begin in the layers of the underworld and stretches from the earth plane to the heavens. When oriented in a north-south direction, the Milky Way makes a cross with the elliptical path of the sun. This cross is called the *K'an* and is very popular in Maya iconography. The center of this cross is where all creation began. The dark center of the Milky Way, called *Xibalbá Be* by the Maya and often referred to as "The Great Rift," was also important in that it was seen as the pathway of souls to another world, a belief held by many other cultures.

While most of what the Maya knew about their world and the universe can be understood by us today, the decipherment of Maya writing is ongoing and new discoveries are constantly being made to further our current understanding of how the Maya saw the universe and their place in it. The jungle astronomer-priests continue to speak to us and teach us hundreds of years after the collapse of Maya civilization. Apparently, there is still more yet to be revealed.

MONTEZUMA'S ZOO

Digging 3 meters down from the floor of the National Museum of Cultures in Mexico City, the archaeological team headed by Doctor Elsa Cristina Hernández Pons hit a curious basalt slab. Ever since Hernández was a little girl she had been lucky at finding things. On trips to the sprawling ruins of the ancient city of Teotihuacán in the early 1960s, accompanied by her father, she would find pieces of obsidian and fragments of pottery for her collection while digging just below the surface. She would nurture her curiosity of the past and later studied to become an archaeologist, earning her PhD from the National Autonomous University of Mexico, or UNAM. After her dissertation, Hernández was hired by Mexico's National Institute of Anthropology and History in July of 1978 to work at the site of the Templo Mayor, the main ancient pyramid complex, in the heart of Mexico City. Over the course of her career she has had some amazing finds, including the discovery of a 500-year-old Aztec sculpture called "The Cuauhxicalli Eagle" in 1985, an intact stone carving of a gigantic bird that was so detailed one could see the fine lines of the feathers on its back. Her latest discovery in 2015 may be her most important find yet. Like so many other buildings in the older part of Mexico City, the National Museum of Culture was built on top of a building that was once another building. Hernández' excavation is like a time tunnel going all the way back to the epoch when Mexico City was the imperial capital of the vast Aztec Empire and was then called Tenochtitlán. The basalt floor she found is not to any ordinary building. Archaeologists believe that Doctor Hernández has found the section of the imperial palace of the Aztec emperors called *Las Casas Nuevas*, which would be loosely translated into "the newer additions" in English. These newer additions to the palace complex were made by Emperor Montezuma the Second, the 45-year-old ruler of the Aztecs who lorded over the Aztec Empire at the time of the Spanish Conquest led by Hernán Cortés in 1519. According to Spanish written accounts from the time, in the newer part of the palace complex we find Montezuma's meditation rooms as well as the emperor's legendary zoo, a private menagerie that would have been the envy of any European ruler at the time and may have been much larger than the fabulous zoo of the Great Khan as described by Italian adventurer Marco Polo on his visit to China in the 13th Century. Work continues beneath the culture museum and the possible find of Montezuma's zoo may be the crowning achievement of the career of Doctor Hernández which has solidly spanned 4 decades.

At the time of the Spanish arrival in Mexico, the Aztecs were the rulers of the majority of the lands and peoples of the central part of the country. The Aztecs ruled over people directly or through small client kingdoms which paid the empire tribute. A vast trade network radiated outward from the capital of Tenochtitlán, which was built on an island in the middle of Lake Texcoco and later became the modern-day capital called Mexico City. The trade network penetrated the dense jungles of Central America and extended as far north as the Indian villages in present-day Arizona and New Mexico. Tenochtitlán was the center of what has been termed as a dendritic system; all roads eventually led back to the capital with a positive flow of wealth coming to Tenochtitlán as the center of empire. When the Spanish arrived here in 1519 they were not met with hostility. The emperor knew Cortés was coming, and curious about the Spaniard's intentions, he welcomed the visitor and his men as honored guests. Because of this cordial reception we have many first-hand European accounts of a living and breathing Aztec Empire. All of Cortés' contingent were amazed at the city. Many of the Spanish soldiers had visited the major metropolises of the Old World: Jerusalem, Rome, Constantinople. Nothing prepared them for the magnificence they would experience once they crossed the narrow causeway spanning the lake and were welcomed to Tenochtitlán by Montezuma. The majestic buildings, the abundance and efficiency of the markets, the cleanliness and attention to detail throughout the capital city were unlike anything they had ever before seen on earth. The massive imperial palace complex drew much attention. There were swimming pools, lavish apartments for the emperor's family and foreign dignitaries, lush gardens where thousands of flowers bloomed and the often-wrote-about legendary private zoo of Montezuma.

The zoo consisted of two aviaries, one for larger birds of prey and one for smaller birds. There were 20 ponds – 10 of freshwater and 10 of saltwater – which were stocked with various fish and served as habitat for waterfowl. There was a section for mammals, including large carnivores, and one for reptiles. As they were unfamiliar with the names of the many animals, the Spanish could only briefly describe what they saw in their journals and other written accounts. A member of the Cortés expedition named Bernal Díaz del Castillo writes this about the aviaries in his book, *Historia verdadera de la conquista de la Nueva España, The True History of the Conquest of New Spain*:

"I am forced to abstain from enumerating every kind of bird that was there and it peculiarity, for there was everything from the Royal Eagle and other smaller eagles, and many other birds of great size, down to tiny birds of many-colored plumage, also the birds from which they take the rich plumage which they use in their green feather work. The birds which have these feathers are about the size of the magpies of Spain, they are called in this country 'quetzals' and there are other birds which have feathers of five colors – green, red, white, yellow and blue; I don't remember what they are called; then there were parrots of many different colors, and there are so many of them that I forget their names, not to mention the beautifully marked ducks and other larger ones like them. From all these birds they plucked the feathers when the time was right to do so, and the feathers grew again. All the birds that I have spoken about breed in these houses, and in the setting season certain Indian men and women who look after the birds place the eggs under them and clean the nests and feed them, so that each kind of bird has its proper food. In this house that I have spoken of there is a great tank of fresh water and in it there are sorts of birds with long stilted legs, with body, wings and tail all red; I don't know their names, but in the island of Cuba they are called 'ypiris,' and there are others something like them, and there are also in that tank many other kinds of birds which always live in water."

The zoo had thousands of specimens and the Spaniards noted that it employed over 300 zookeepers to tend to the animals. As turkeys were an abundant source of food in the Aztec Empire, chroniclers wrote that 500 turkeys a day were used as food for the carnivorous animals, which not only included the birds of prey but also included wolves, large dogs and the great cats such as jaguars and pumas. These animals also, it was noted, fed on the remains of human captors or sacrificial victims, which were many.

While writing of the mammalian part of the zoo which included sloths, monkeys, bears, rodents and canines of all kinds, Bernal Díaz recounts the most curious area of the zoo to the Spanish visitors, the reptile house, filled with alligators, lizards and snakes of all kinds. He says:

"They also have in that cursed house many vipers and poisonous snakes which carry on their tails things that sound like bells. These are the worst vipers of all, and they keep them in jars and great pottery vessels with many feathers, and there they lay their eggs and rear their young, and they give them to eat the bodies of the Indians who have been sacrificed, and the flesh of the tiny dogs which they are in the habit of breeding."

Díaz concludes his account of the zoo by writing the following:

"Let me speak now of the infernal noise when the lions and tigers roared and the jackals and foxes howled and the serpents hissed. It was horrible to listen to and it seemed like hell."

Montezuma's zoo had a section not seen in any modern zoo: an area for human curiosities. Dwarves and people with various deformities and disabilities who hailed from all parts of the empire were housed in the zoo. As these people were separated from their families, the State compensated family members generously, taking care of them for life. It was almost seen as a blessing to have a relative living in the imperial palace's human zoo.

To the Spanish, the most unbelievable animal at the zoo was called "The Mexican Bull." A member of the Cortés expedition named Solís described the animal thus:

"It has crooked shoulders, with a bunch on its back like a camel; its flanks dry, its tail large, and its neck covered with hair like a lion. It is cloven footed, its head armed like that of a bull, which it resembles in fierceness, with no less strength and agility."

Solís was describing a familiar sight to those Natives of the North American Great Plains. The Mexican Bull was really and American bison, more commonly known as a buffalo. At the time of the Aztec Empire's height, North American bison were found over a thousand miles from the capital city. There were small herds that roamed the northern scrub prairie areas of the modern-day Mexican states of Durango and Nuevo Leon. One could only imagine how an animal like that was transported all the way to Montezuma's zoo, given that the Aztecs had no use of the wheel.

And what became of Montezuma's zoo? The story has a tragic ending. When the "honeymoon period" between Cortés and Emperor Montezuma ended, the Spanish decided to take over the Aztec capital and laid siege to the city. The siege lasted 75 days during which the capital – which had a population of over a quarter million people – was cut off from the mainland and was subjugated through mass starvation. During the two and a half months of the siege, the inhabitants of the once-mighty capital became desperate for food. By the time the population was completely demoralized and surrendered to the Spanish, all animals in the emperor's private menagerie had been eaten and the grand zoo of Montezuma became the stuff of legend.

THE GIGANTIC ATLANTEAN STATUES OF THE TOLTECS

The Aztecs called this place Tlahuizcalpantecuhtli, the Temple of the Morning Star. It is a massive pyramid in the center of the ancient city of Tula, the civic-ceremonial capital of the Toltecs. On the top of the pyramid are curious stone carvings. They are giants. Standing over 15 feet tall and weighing several tons each, these basalt carvings in human form are the masters of all they survey. Called the Atlantean Statues – or in Spanish, *los atlantes* – these huge sculptures are perhaps the most enigmatic surviving artifacts of the Toltec civilization which ruled central Mexico about 1,000 years ago. No one knows how these figures were made or how they were transported to the top of the pyramid.

In order to understand the Atlantean figures we must first understand the context in which we find them. The statues dominate the abandoned ancient city of Tula located in the central highlands of Mexico in the present-day Mexican state of Hidalgo about 45 miles from Mexico City. According to archaeologists and anthropologists, the name "Tula" comes from the Aztec phrase *Tollan Xicocotitlan*, which means "place where the reeds grow." The Aztecs later shortened this to Tollan which has been more generally used to denote any urban center. The city of Tula has long been believed to be the capital of the Toltec Empire, although some archaeologists describe the Toltecs politically as having a kingdom rather than an empire. Some believe that the term "Toltec" is best used to describe a civilization instead of a political entity. In any event, the Toltecs came to prominence in the power vacuum left by the fall of Teotihuacan at around the 8th Century AD. The first village at the site of the present-day ruins of Tula was established around 400 AD. Archaeologists call the first phase of occupation at this site "Tula Chico" or "Little Tula." At its height, Tula Chico had well over 20,000 people and covered about 6 square kilometers in area. Between 850 and 900 AD the site known as Tula Chico was mysteriously abandoned. Soon after people abandoned this site, a new city was built on top of the old one and archaeologists call this city "Tula Grande," or "Big Tula." This new Tula grew to be the largest city in Mexico at its height around 1,000 years ago with an urban population of over 50,000 with 20,000 or so people living in the immediate countryside surrounding the city. The extended urban area stretched to about 1,000 square kilometers. As the center of trade, some believe that half of the population of Tula was engaged in some sort of craft production including work in stone and ceramics. In fact, the very word "Toltec" in the Nahuatl language of the Aztecs means "skilled worker" which later broadly meant "urban person." The items produced in Tula were traded for goods coming from distant places such as Costa Rica. The influence of the Toltec civilization in Mexico can be seen as far away as the Yucatán, specifically at the sites of Chichén Itzá and Mayapán. In the former set of ruins we also see Atlantean figures at the Temple of the Warriors, but they are smaller in scale compared to the ones found at Tula. Archaeologists have debated for years about whether or not the sites identified as Toltec in the faraway Yucatán were just copying Tula, were colonies of the city or were conquered by it. All can agree and plainly see the strong influence coming from the Toltecs, including the smaller Atlanteans. Whether a trading empire, influential kingdom city-state or cultural movement, the Toltec civilization ended with the fall of Tula to outside northern invaders sometime in the 12th Century. Most of the living quarters around the ceremonial center were abandoned by 1150 AD and there is evidence of a huge fire sweeping through the city at about this time along with the destruction and looting of much of the massive buildings of Tula. A disputed king's list created by ethno-historians show that the last ruler of Tula, and perhaps the Toltec civilization, was a king called Ce Acatl Topilitzin and the last year of his rule was 1179 AD. In the 1400s, one of the early rulers of the Aztec Empire, a king called Izcoatl, burned all the books related to the Toltecs. Much knowledge about Tula and the Atlantean statues was lost as a result of this ruler's zeal to get rid of all things from the previous civilization that might have challenged his power or legitimacy. When the Spanish arrived to Mexico in the early 16th Century, Tula was occupied by a fraction of the population it had once had, and most of the people were ethnically Aztec, as the surrounding lands were part of the Aztec Empire. The city never saw its former glory again. Early Spanish chroniclers noted that craftspeople still lived in Tula creating things out of stone, feathers and pottery. As with the great monuments of Peru or Egypt, or the gigantic stone heads of Easter Island, surviving people living in and around the ruins of Tula at the time of Spanish contact had no idea how the Atlantean statues were made or what their significance was.

Given their Mesoamerican context, modern archaeologists have established a firm interpretation of what the Atlantean statues at Tula mean. Structurally, they were said to support a wooden or thatched roof at the top of the pyramid, like columns. Artistically, they are said to represent warriors, possibly soldiers following the god-king Quetzalcoatl. Quetzalcoatl, also called the Feathered Serpent, is associated with Venus; as the story goes when he died here on earth he went up to the sky and became the Morning Star. The name of the pyramid – Tlahuizcalpantecuhtli – means "The Temple of the Morning Star." The statues, according to archaeologists, are wearing hats of snakeskin and feathers, solidifying the claim to be associated with the feathered serpent god. The colossal figures have breastplates in the shape of butterflies, also symbolic of Quetzalcoatl, shields on their backs and they are carrying weapons. The conclusion is that the statues represent warriors. Further support is given to the warlike nature of the figures by the association made with their counterparts. The similar figures found in the Yucatán can be found in a place called the Temple of the Warriors. Whatever their definitive purpose, the Atlantean figures took much time to make and for that reason alone they are very significant. In the modern age, we are just a little unclear as to their exact meaning.

In the 1970s alternative theories about the Toltecs and the Atlantean figures began to emerge. Before we begin this part of the podcast, we must explain that the word "Atlantean" was given to these statues because of their supposed stance and their similarity to load-bearing figures of the mythical character of Atlas of the Old World. Many people misinterpret the very word "Atlantean" to mean that the statues had a direct connection to the fabled lost continent of Atlantis. The meaning and origin of the word aside, researchers in the alternative histories and "ancient astronauts" fields have tied these statues to everything from a forgotten super civilization that spanned the earth before the Biblical flood to ancient extraterrestrials. One online researcher has connected the word "Tula" with the ancient reference to "Thule," a mythical island on par with the lost continents of Atlantis or Lemuria. The early Greek astronomer Geminus of Rhodes first mentions the mythical land of Thule a few centuries before Christ and calls it "The place where the sun goes to rest." This would place Thule somewhere in the Atlantic Ocean or beyond. This mythical western land was later referenced by the Roman poet Virgil in his 29 BC 4-book work, *The Georgics*, in which he introduces "Ultima Thule" which is poetically described as a faraway land or unattainable goal. Did these ancients writing over 2,000 years ago know of a lost continent whose refugees founded a Mexican civilization? Mainstream academia, of course, says "no." Others cite similarities in the way the Atlantean figures look compared to other statues around the world, specifically to those found in the pre-Inca site of Tiahuanaco in South America and those discovered from Ancient

Egypt. Archaeologists chalk up all similarities to sculptures from other parts of the world to pure chance.

In the 1970s, with the popularity of the ancient astronaut movement came greater scrutiny of the massive statues atop the Tula pyramid. In popular pulp paperbacks such as *Chariots of the Gods?* and *The Outer Space Connection*, the figures become representatives of an ancient space-faring race. It's important to note here that the ancient city of Tula was astronomically aligned, like many larger cities in ancient Mexico, and its inhabitants were cognizant of the movements of the planets and stars. The city was abandoned suddenly and the mystery of what happened to the people and where they went is easily solved by saying the Toltecs may have not only abandoned Tula, but they left the earth. Back to the statues themselves, the snakeskin/feather hats become spacesuit helmets. The butterfly breastplate and its corresponding shield on the backs of the gigantic figures become elements of a jetpack. Much has been discussed about what the Atlantean statues have in their hands. While archaeologists see arrows and the common Mesoamerican spear-thrower called an atlatl, ancient aliens theorists see advanced laser-based weaponry. Upon closer examination, some of the statues do indeed look like they are carrying something reminiscent of a phaser cannon from *Star Trek*. As mentioned earlier, as no written records exist from the time that the statues were supposedly carved and placed on top of the pyramid, no one knows exactly what they mean, who carved them and for what purpose, or how they were transported to the top of the pyramid. Again, we are confronted with an unsolved mystery of the ages which begs more investigation and research.

THE ANCIENT DINOSAUR FIGURES OF ACÁMBARO

In the late 1960s American detective author Erle Stanley Gardner stood before a collection of over 30,000 figurines. He had heard about this collection many years before and felt a deep sense of astonishment when seeing it in person at this modest house in the small rural town of Acámbaro in the state of Guanajuato, Mexico.

Gardner, the writer who came up with great titles like *The Case of the Black Cat* and *Granny Get Your Gun,* and who created such memorable characters as Perry Mason, Della Street and Lester Leith had a real life mystery in front of him. The figurines were fantastic and seemingly out of place. Many of them featured people of various races and some 10 per cent of them looked like our modern depictions of dinosaurs. These dinosaurs were sometimes accompanied by humans; some of the figures had dinosaurs wrestling with people or men even riding dinosaurs. Of course, dinosaur representations in ancient art were unheard of because humans did not coexist with these prehistoric creatures. The creator of Perry Mason, who was considered to be the best-selling American author at the time of his death, was asked to examine the collection by a friend, the Harvard-educated anthropologist Charles Hapgood, who was one of the many voices chiming in on this controversy at the time. Hapgood knew that Gardner's love of sleuthing did not just apply to fiction writing and Gardner's many years as a trial attorney would be helpful in solving the mystery of these anomalous figurines.

Over the years the massive collection has been proclaimed to be an elaborate hoax by people in the more traditional fields of science and has been shunned by most mainstream archaeologists. While many have thought that the whole discussion was put to rest years ago, the Acámbaro figures have begun to generate interest again among fringe scientists, Christian "young earth" proponents, believers in alternative universe theories and those who follow the "New Chronology" writings of Russian Anatoly Fomenko which claim that written history itself has been adjusted over time to fit the agendas of the elites. Some investigators in more traditional scientific fields have also been recently drawn to these figures once again, as the controversy has become debated online. The figures, which for many years have been literally and figuratively "crated up" and not been available for examination are now on display for all to see at the Waldemar Julsrud Museum in Acámbaro, Guanajuato.

The story of the Acámbaro figurines begins in 1945. A German merchant named Waldemar Julsrud was riding his horse along the edges of a mountain called El Toro just outside of town. In a dried out riverbed he noticed an unusual part of a clay figurine sticking out of the dirt. He began digging and found a number of curious figures near the riverbed. Julsrud was already quite familiar with pre-Columbian ceramics as he had one of the largest collections of artifacts from the pre-Classic Chupicuaro culture then amassed. While he wasn't selling hardware, he was digging up or acquiring pieces for his collection and over the years Julsrud became quite the amateur archaeologist. He had never seen the types of figures that he had uncovered at the base of El Toro, so he asked one of his employees named Odilon Tinajero, if he could find more of these figurines for him. Julsrud would pay Tinajero one peso for each figurine brought to him intact or with pieces that were easily put together. Thus began his collection, and over a 5 to 6 year period, Julsrud gathered over 35,000 of these strange figures.

In 1947 when Julsrud published a booklet on his discoveries called *Enigmas del pasado – Enigmas of the Past –* the figurines began to receive international attention. In March of 1951, Lowell Harmer, a veteran writer for the *Los Angeles Times* published an article titled: "Mexico Finds Give Hint of Lost World: Dinosaur Statues Point to Men Who Lived in Age of Reptiles." Harmer had visited Acámbaro earlier that year. Amazed by the sheer volume of the collection in Julsrud's house, the author wrote that the figurines "filled the floors, the tables and the wall cabinets to overflowing." The *Times* writer also wondered in his article, "How could it be a hoax? Not even in Mexico, where money is so scarce, could anyone afford the labor of these thousands of statues at the low prices Julsrud is paying." While seemingly convinced of the collection's authenticity, as an objective writer Harmer finished off his article by saying, "I am a writer, not an archaeologist. It will be up to the experts to decide." In the next few years the story was picked up by the tabloid press and made it to the magazines specializing in stories of the fanciful and the bizarre. One article of note appeared in the February/March 1952 issue of *Fate* magazine titled "Did Man Tame the Dinosaur?" A clear reference to some of the figurines showing men roping and riding the creatures.

The following year, 1953, the Mexican government got involved in the Acámbaro mystery. It sent 4 archaeologists from the Instituto Nacional de Antropología e Historia – also called INAH – in Mexico City to investigate. They set up a dig site about a mile from Julsrud's original discovery location near the base of the mountain called El Toro. They dug a test pit going about 2 meters down and discovered dozens of figurines similar to Julsrud's, including dinosaurs. INAH then issued a statement that the figurines did correspond to the pre-Classic civilization of the Chupicuaro and could date to as early as 800 BC, but not the dinosaur ones. The scientists concluded that even though the dinosaurs were found among other similar figurines in the same archaeological strata, they couldn't possibly be anything but modern productions as human interaction with dinosaurs was impossible. The Instituto did no further excavations and after the 1950s refused to issue permits for other archaeologists to make new excavations.

On the American side of the border an anthropological organization dedicated to preserving Native American culture, the Amerind Foundation, sent archaeologist Charles Di Peso down to examine the figurines. Di Peso published his findings in volume 18 of the scientific journal *American Antiquity* in the year 1953 and in the prestigious *Archaeology* magazine the same year. Those who do not believe the figurines to be part of a hoax have pointed out that Di Peso went down to Mexico with a clear bias to expose the figures as fakes and that he did not approach the problem of the figurines with an open mind. Although having the backing of the scientific establishment, Di Peso did make claims that should be scrutinized more closely. For example, in his *American Antiquity* article, Di Peso states:

"None of the specimens were marred by patination nor did they possess the surface coating of soluble salts... The figures were broken, in most cases, where the appendages attached themselves to the body of the figurines... No parts were missing. Furthermore, none of the broken surfaces were worn smooth. In the entire collection of 32,000 specimens no shovel, mattock, or pick marks were noted."

He also stated, "Further investigation revealed that a family living in the vicinity of Acámbaro make these figurines during the winter months when their fields are idle." In his writing Di Peso alleged that after the figures were made that they were "planted" in certain locations, and in his *American Antiquity* article he tells the tale of a botched excavation in which he witnessed figurines coming up out of a hole mixed with fresh backfill and even fresh manure. In the end of his article Di Peso states, "Thus the investigation ended: it seems almost superfluous to state that the Acámbaro figurines are not prehistoric nor were they made by a prehistoric race who lived in association with Mesozoic reptiles."

It was not long before Di Peso's articles and claims were shot full of holes. For one, Di Peso only spent 2 days in Acámbaro and only spent 4 hours examining Julsrud's collection in his home. Di Peso did not set up and conduct an excavation on his own. He also did not take into consideration that Julsrud's collection included near-perfect figurines purchased from villagers as per Julsrud's own request. When he began his collection, Julsrud specified that he would pay one peso for each intact figure. There were plenty of pieces and broken figures that did not make it to the over 30,000 in Julsrud's home.

The Di Peso articles caught the eye of Charles Hapgood, the Harvard-trained archaeologist and friend of Perry Mason creator Erle Stanley Gardner. Hapgood had years of experience and the academic credentials to analyze the Julsrud collection and in 1954 he spent a considerable amount of time in Acámbaro. Hapgood refuted most of Di Peso's claims point by point. Di Peso claimed that there were no missing pieces. Hapgood found boxes and boxes of parts that could not be put together. Di Peso claimed that there was no discoloring or encrusted dirt on the figures. Hapgood observed that dirt and patination were evident on the figures in spite of Julsrud's requirement for cleaned, intact figurines to earn the one peso reward. Di Peso alleged that there were no pick marks from shoveling on any of the figurines. Hapgood documented the opposite. One of the big elements of the hoax proposed by Di Peso was his observation that one of the excavations he witnessed was bringing up fresh dirt from a recent backfill. Hapgood had an answer for this, too. In documenting the excavation procedure, Hapgood wrote, "An important point that came out was that when the digger stopped work in the middle of excavating a cache, he filled in the hole, to protect it from the many small boys of the neighborhood. This may have a bearing on the accusations of fraud…" The final point dispelled by Hapgood was that the villagers were making the figurines during their "off time" in the winter. The sheer number of figures, both intact and partial, would take many families an incredible amount of time to produce. In the next decade, Erle Stanley Gardner would add to this sentiment in his 1969 book about Acámbaro called *The Host with the Big Hat*. He writes, "I don't believe that it would have been at all possible for any group of people to have made these figures, to have paid for the burro-load of wood necessary to 'fire' them, take them out and bury them, wait for the ground to resume its natural hardness which would take from one to ten years, and then 'discover' these figures and dig them up—all for a gross price of twelve cents per figure." Gardner also concluded "It is absolutely, positively out of the question to think that these artifacts which we saw could have been planted."

As a scientist, Charles Hapgood knew of the need for concrete dating of the pieces using the most up-to-date methods. In 1968 he submitted three samples to Isotopes Incorporated of New Jersey for radiocarbon dating. The first sample came back as three thousand five hundred and ninety years old, plus or minus 100 years. The second sample came up as six thousand four hundred and eighty years old, plus or minus one hundred and seventy years. The third sample came up with a date of three thousand and sixty years old, plus or minus one hundred and twenty years.

To be thorough, Hapgood also submitted four samples to the University of Pennsylvania Museum for thermoluminescent dating, a more accurate way to date pottery. All four samples came up with a date of 2,500 BC, plus or minus one hundred and ninety years. Dr. Froelich Rainey, realizing the importance of accuracy in the dating of these pieces did 18 runs on each of the 4 samples and came up with the same results.

The last attempt to date the figures occurred in 1976. Gary Carriveau and Mark Han also used the thermoluminescent dating technique on 20 of the figures. All of the samples failed the "plateau test" which indicated that dates obtained from these figurines using high-temperature thermoluminescent dating were not reliable and lacked significance. Based on the signal regeneration found in some of the samples, the Carriveau-Han team estimated that the figurines were fired sometime in the late 1930s or early 1940s.

So, are these dinosaur figurines authentic archaeological finds of great importance, or are they part of an elaborate hoax? One must ask if this were a hoax, who would benefit from it? Waldemar Julsrud made no money from the sales of the figurines or from tourism connected to his collection. No archaeologists have made names or reputations for themselves because of the dinosaurs of Acámbaro. The Mexican government wants to ignore these figures and prohibits any excavations in the area. Why do they not want more investigation into these figures? For now, the little-known "Dinosaurs of Acámbaro" remain an enigma.

HUEYATLACO: THE 250,000 YEAR OLD ARCHAEOLOGICAL SITE

In the highlands of Mexico in the state of Puebla just 75 miles southeast of Mexico City there exists an archaeological site that is possibly the most controversial in all of Mexico. It is called Hueyatlaco, the location of some amazing discoveries in 1962. Amid the bones of mastodons, extinct camels, mammoths and smaller animals was evidence of human activity and man-made artifacts of flaked flint, quartz and bone. Spearheads were embedded into bones and some of the bones showed evidence of deliberate butchering leading investigators to believe that Hueyatlaco was a "kill site" where animals were hunted and butchered. A team led by Mexican paleohistorian Juan Armenta Camacho, who had grown up in the area, and a young Harvard anthropologist named Cynthia Irwin-Williams investigated the site over several field seasons. They discovered human artifacts in several layers of sediment with the more simple tools in the lower levels and more complex tools in the upper levels.

While excavating the site the investigators realized that they might have a problem dating their findings. Carbon 14 dating up until that time was the most common radiometric dating method in the Americas for assigning ages to archaeological sites. At Hueyatlaco there were no remains of anything containing carbon – wood, charcoal, shell, etc. – to extract dating samples from. The animal bones that were found at the site were all fossilized. Whatever carbon that was contained in them was now gone.

By the mid-1960s it had been theorized that the Hueyatlaco site could be 22,000 years old. If this date were true it would cause all sorts of history and science books to be re-written. The peopling of the Americas, according to the longstanding theory, began some 13,000 to 16,000 years ago when hunters and gatherers from Asia crossed the Bering Land Bridge to North America and migrated southward. Early big game hunters called the Clovis People existed some 13,500 years ago in the Americas and left behind distinctive knapped stone tools. If the Hueyatlaco site were older by some 10,000 years, this site would have revolutionized what scientists and researchers thought about the arrival of humans to the Americas from Asia. Armenta had a big problem on his hands. How to date the site?

In 1966 a young PhD student from Harvard who was looking for an interesting doctoral dissertation joined the team. Her name was Virginia Steen-McIntyre and she was trained in the field of tephrochronology. Tephrochronology is a dating technique that uses discrete layers of volcanic ash from specific eruptions of a given volcano to create a chronological framework in which ancient artifacts or environmental samples can be placed. A layer of ash, for example, can be dated, and thus things occurring within, above and below the layer can be dated with some degree of accuracy. In the area around Hueyatlaco there were several volcanic and pumice layers and the region had hundreds of other volcanic deposits. Some of the volcanic layers had already been dated by using the Carbon 14 dating method which was applied to wood burned during the corresponding volcanic eruptions. Using a microscope and techniques learned at Harvard, Steen-McIntyre's plan was to match the undated layers at the Hueyatlaco site to the already-dated layers of the nearby volcanoes. It seemed simple enough, but after hundreds of samples and testing spanning years, Steen-McIntyre could find no correlation between the volcanic layers and could not date the site this way. The dates would have to be arrived at through some other method. Steen-McIntyre gave up having Hueyatlaco as the subject of her doctoral dissertation, but the site so fascinated her that she never gave up on Hueyatlaco.

During the '60s the site had garnered a lot of attention from the Mexican government and the Instituto Nacional de Antropología e Historia in Mexico City. In 1967 Jose Lorenzo of the *instituto* claimed that the artifacts at Hueyatlaco were faked and planted at the site. The authorities in Mexico City sent their own scientist to the area and set up test pits near Armenta's digs to begin their own excavation. Eventually, Armenta's artifacts were confiscated and moved to Mexico City and he was banned by the authorities from doing any sort of fieldwork of any kind, ever. Armenta's field partner and co-excavator at the site, Cynthia Irwin-Williams came to Armenta's defense, but to no avail. In spite of this big bump in the road, the quest to date the site continued.

Irwin-Williams was dead set on believing the date of 22,000 years based on the carbon dating of snail shells associated with a similar kill site very close to Hueyatlaco called Caulapan. A new dating technique called the "uranium series method" had also been applied to two samples from this nearby site and yielded similar dates going back 22,000 years. Irwin-Williams was satisfied that these dates could also apply to the larger, main site of Hueyatlaco, even those these dates did not come as a result of testing items found at Huetatlaco proper. After those dates were firmly established from Caulapan, a butchered camel pelvis that actually came from Hueyatlaco was tested using the uranium series and the results were astounding.

They came back with a date suggesting the site was almost 250,000 years old. Virginia Steen-McIntyre was excited about the findings, while the now-sole head of the excavation, Cynthia Irwin-Williams was not. She stuck to her original date of 22,000 years old for Hueyatlaco and would not compromise. Steen-McIntyre knew that more tests were needed, so she spearheaded an effort to get more dating done at the site. She also shifted her focus to compare the layers at Hueyatlaco to even older layers of volcanic ash at the nearby volcano.

The next dating method they would use came from the paleoanthropologists in Africa who were using it to date some of the earliest human ancestors yet discovered. This dating method was called "zircon fission-track dating" where small crystals of zircons in the layers at Hueyatlaco were tested. The date that came back from the tests was more in line with the quarter-million-year-old date found from the camel bone sample than the 22,000-year-old more "politically correct" date advocated by Cynthia Irwin-Williams.

There were two other dating methods that were applied at Hueyatlaco. One looked at the volcanic ash deposits again and was called tephra hydration dating. The other method involved studying the mineral weathering to determine the age of the artifacts uncovered at the site. All 4 dating methods, which all concluded that the site was almost a quarter of a million years old, were explained and explored by Virginia Steen-McIntyre in a 1981 publication in the journal *Quaternary Research* titled "Geological Evidence for Age of Deposits at Hueyatlaco Archeological Site, Valesquillo, Mexico." The article was subject to a ferocious backlash even from Cynthia Irwin-Williams, the original excavator, who wrote a rebuttal to the article. People in mainstream science shunned Steen-McIntyre for her challenging of the orthodoxy and she was the object of intense derision and harassment. In an open letter to *Quaternary Research*, Steen-McIntyre wrote:

"Not being an anthropologist, I didn't realize how deeply woven into our thought the current theory of human evolution has become. Our work at Hueyatlaco has been rejected by most archaeologists because it contradicts that theory. Period."

Critics who were not just attacking Steen-McIntyre's character criticized the findings as being contaminated, or that the sedimentary and rock strata were disturbed by animals or floods. Of course, many others alleged that the artifacts were planted or that the dating results were simply faked.

What we may have here is a process of knowledge filtration that occurs in most scientific fields. You have people with egos and reputations and lifetimes of work based on the orthodoxy. Things that conform to accepted ideas will pass through the knowledge filter with no problem. If something comes along to challenge the existing belief in a radical way, it is rejected, even if facts and data are there to support the radical claim. The idea of science with testable hypotheses and data examination is a great thing when applied in its purest form, but most scientists do not admit to themselves and others that there is an "old guard" mentality at work in most scientific fields that seeks to preserve the status quo. Most of the work at Hueyatlaco has not been accepted because it never gets past this knowledge filtration process. The guardians of the textbooks and mainstream science publications will not let this story go to print.

There has been recent work at Hueyatlaco and at other sites in Mexico that challenge the scientific orthodoxy and push back the idea of human habitation in that country to the Pleistocene Epoch, and well past the 12,000 BC date that has been generally accepted. The carved bone and hearths at the El Cedral site in the Mexican state of San Luís Potosí have been dated as being 30,000 years old. The Babisuri Rock shelter on the Island of Espiritu Santo off the coast of Baja California has been dated as having been inhabited 40,000 years ago. There are 4 other sites with older dates including what's been called the Xalnene Tuff formation where human footprints have been found alongside tracks of extinct animal species. These footprints and tracks were made in the fresh field of ash from an active volcano and the site is located in the same valley as Hueyatlaco near a small ranch called Rancho Xalnene. These footprints have been dismissed as indentations made by pickaxes from an old mining operation. The tuff formation has been dated by one researcher as going back 40,000 years. Another researcher using the argon form of dating claims that the ash fell and the footprints were made over 1.3 million years ago.

So, given these "anomalous" dates at various sites across Mexico – the Hueyatlaco excavation the most famous among them – what are we to make of the early human history of Mexico and the peopling of the Americas in general? Are these seemingly exaggerated dates pieces of an elaborate hoax, are they well-intentioned errors, or do they give us pause and make us reconsider the pre-existing theories of human evolution and migration? Perhaps with more sophisticated dating methods we can finally solve the mystery at Hueyatlaco. Until then, scientists are left to argue amongst each other about the true history of the first people in Mexico.

THE PALENQUE ASTRONAUT: EVIDENCE OF ANCIENT ALIEN CONTACT?

In 683 AD near the end of Classical Maya civilization in the middle of the jungle we find a great city ruled by a great king, a man named Pacal, who lived to the ripe old age of 80. Under his rule Pacal's city kingdom flourished and great monuments were built. One of these monuments was a pyramid structure called the Temple of the Inscriptions. Inside the temple would be Pacal's final resting place. Archaeologists penetrated the building for the first time in the 1950s. What they found would astound the professional and armchair archaeologists alike: A gigantic stone slab weighing over a ton, placed on top of Pacal's tomb. On the surface of this slab they find a curious illustration, a man in a seated position with lots of activity below him, above him and on either side of him.

Ever since its discovery the carving has been the center of controversy and has been interpreted in two very distinct ways. One camp believes that this carved relief is proof of alien visitation because it shows a man in a spacecraft. The other group believes that this is an ordinary funerary illustration and that there is nothing to see here, besides the beauty of such a marvelously handcrafted work of art from so many centuries ago. The image has been one of the most celebrated and recognizable illustrations coming from the Maya civilization. An internet image search of "Palenque Astronaut" will yield tens of thousands of responses

Palenque, whose Maya name was Ba-ak Lakamha, is a UNESCO World Heritage site located in the eastern part of the Mexican state of Chiapas, near the present-day border with Guatemala. The city was part of the Maya civilization, which is not to be confused with the Maya Empire, which did not exist. Maya civilization was a loosely connected group of city states sharing the same cultural elements much like the ancient Greeks. So, Palenque was an independent city-kingdom ruled by a powerful dynasty. To this day the city is somewhat shrouded in mystery. No one knows how old Palenque really is. Its first recorded ruler is supposed to have reigned in 2325 BC, but many archaeologists regard this as a mythological king. During its heyday, between about 400 AD and its mysterious collapse around 800 AD, Palenque was home to tens of thousands of people and a powerful aristocracy. A great deal of work needs to be done on this "lost city" as only less than 10% of Palenque has been excavated. There are still well over a thousand buildings that have been identified but have not been cleared of the dense overgrowth of jungle comprised mostly of cedar, mahogany and sapodilla trees. Some may argue that Pacal's tomb is the first of many depictions of astronauts yet to be uncovered.

The "ancient astronaut" theory became popular in the 1960s and 1970s with books like "*Chariots of the Gods?*" and "*Gods from Outer Space*" by Erich von Däniken and "*The Outer Space Connection*" by Alan Landsburg. Those were the main ones. There was a lot in the tabloid press at the time and in movies and TV documentaries, usually with profound-sounding narration in a foreign accent. In recent times the ancient astronaut theories have been revived by TV shows like "Ancient Aliens." The Pacal-as-astronaut thesis has possibly tens of millions of adherents.

The opposing side bases its conclusions on years of academic research. The Mayanist or professional archaeologist looks at the Palenque Astronaut in context. The carved slab was found on a tomb and many of the symbols and motifs are found in other parts of the Maya world in other forms of art. Yes, the scene depicts a long journey, but not to Alpha Centauri or the Andromeda Galaxy. It depicts King Pacal at the moment of his death in his transition to the underworld, the land of the dead. This would be appropriate for a coffin lid. The overpowering element of this work of art is the world tree, found throughout Mesoamerica and the rest of the Maya world. It's in the shape of a cross and symbolizes the bridge between the underworld, the heavens and the earth. The tree's roots plunge into the underworld, giving the appearance of flames from a rocket exhaust. We see a double-headed vision serpent on the sides of the cross, which is also common in other works of art. On the top of the tree is a celestial bird, which represents the heavens. The king is seated, that is clear, but to the archaeologists it is not in the seat of an Apollo capsule. He is seated on the sun. To the ancient Maya, the sun made its journey across the sky, taking the dead with it to the underworld. So, Pacal is riding the sun to his new resting place. The sun is depicted here as being half skull. This indicates the transition to death and again, it is seen in other funerary-related carvings in Mayaland.   The astronaut theorists claim that Pacal's foot is on a pedal to somehow maneuver the spacecraft. The archaeologist claim that this is just a foot rest. According to the academic side in the dichotomy, Pacal's hands are in delicate positions, and not on controls. Delicate hand gestures are seen in Maya art throughout the region. It's a stylistic thing and may have some sort of fashionable significance. The final thing to look at on this slab is the supposed astronaut's breathing apparatus. Mayanists will argue that this is a nose plug, a form of adornment and if you look at it, it isn't attached to anything, so there are no tubes.

Some people may say that academics are too bogged down in what is perceived as practical explanations and may miss things. Careers may be on the line if the formal academic researcher proposes too wacky a theory. Some say that academia suffers from confirmation bias and peer pressure so that anything outside the accepted "norm" is discarded as rubbish and the status quo is preserved. The mainstream archaeologists have been working on the Maya for years – as it is a fascinating civilization to study – and a clearer picture emerges almost on a daily basis of this ancient people. The academics, however, have not been able to figure out what happened to the Maya. The last dated carving at Palenque was 799 AD and soon after the city was abandoned. Where did they go? Perhaps they all hitched rides on rockets and the ancient astronaut people are on to something here… or maybe they're not.

THE GREAT PYRAMID OF CHOLULA

As the bells to the church dedicated to the Virgin of the Remedies rang, a young Swiss-American stood at the base of the broad hill on which the church sat. Old women wearing *mantillas* made of cactus fibers ascended the hill along with well-dressed men and children anxious to receive the word of God. The year was 1881. The Swiss explorer's name was Adolph Bandelier and his many years roaming the American Southwest, Mexico and South America had made his eyes keen to spotting artificial formations out of natural ones. The massive hill which had been the home to La Virgen de los Remedios for nearly 300 years was really not a hill at all. Centuries of overgrowth combined with centuries of cultural memory loss had preserved a massive structure undisturbed at the time of Bandelier's arrival. Little did he know when the first shovel hit the dirt in this rural part of the state of Puebla that he was excavating the largest pyramid ever built by man.

Although not as tall as the Great Pyramid at Giza, the Great Pyramid of Cholula is larger by volume and area, thus making it the largest known pyramid ever built and one of the largest buildings in the entire world. While the Great Pyramid in Egypt rises to a height of 455 feet, this Mexican pyramid rises to only 217 feet. However, Cholula's volume is 4.45 million cubic meters versus Egypt's 2.5 million cubic meters.

Since Bandelier's time there have been two periods of intense excavations at the pyramid and much has been learned about the site from old Spanish documents, non-local native sources and the archaeological record. The name Cholula comes from the Aztec name Acholollan which derives from the Nahuatl word, cholollan, meaning, "place of refuge." The site on which the Great Pyramid stands was first inhabited long before the formation of the Aztec Empire. Built in 4 stages across almost eight hundred years, the first human occupation at the site dates to the Preclassic Period at around 300 BC. The ceremonial site, according to legend, was built by a giant named Xelhua who escaped the Valley of Mexico after a flood. There is a central Mexican connection as there is a definite influence from Teotihuacan, the gigantic city northeast of Lake Texcoco near modern-day Mexico City and was contemporaneous with Cholula. Archaeologists often call Cholula and Teotihuacan "sister cities" although we do not know the relationship they had with each other 2,000 years ago at the height of both sites. At this time there was also great influence coming from the Gulf Coast of Mexico with ceramic types uncovered at Cholula closely resembling those of El Tajín in Veracruz. Through this ceramic classification most archaeologists agree that the original inhabitants of Cholula were the Olmeca-Xicalanca with origins to the immediate east. According to the Toltec-

Chichimec History, a codex from the Cholula area, a king with the name Aquiyach Amapane lived at the Great Pyramid. The city surrounding the pyramid complex was once the second largest in all of Mexico at its height with an estimated 100,000 people living there. By the 8th Century, the population of Cholula dropped off and no one knows why. The Great Pyramid was abandoned at that time, although it still retained its religious importance. In the Twelfth Century the area was conquered by the Toltecs who let the remaining Olmeca-Xicalancas stay, but only on the southern fringes of the city. The Great Pyramid was still important, but the main religious focus shifted to a new temple that the Toltecs built at the site near the pyramid. Later Toltec burials were found around the base of the pyramid, showing that the structure was still revered, although the Toltecs did not clear the pyramid of growth nor did they build on it. In fact, they named the pyramid Tlachihualtepetl which means "artificial hill." Under the rule of the Toltecs, the ancient city of Cholula flourished and the population increased. In the 13th Century, feeling the pressure from the ever-expanding Aztec Empire, the Toltecs yielded to their overlords and Cholula became a client state of the Aztecs. By the time the Aztecs arrived, the Great Pyramid was so covered in vegetation that they did not use it nor did they try to clear it. Knowing that the hill was sacred to the natives, the Spanish constructed a church on top of it and dedicated the area to Our Lady of the Remedies, supplanting the shrine to the local Aztec rain goddess named Chiconauhquiahuitl whose feast day was September 8th. The Spanish made the feast day to Our Lady of the Remedies the same day, to ease the local population into Catholicism and so as not to create too much religious upset. In the 1960s, with the rise of a new indigenous consciousness in Mexico, the former Great Pyramid of Cholula became a place for a revived spring equinox celebration, which is closer in line with the original function of the pyramid, which, for most of its life was dedicated to the Mesoamerican god Quetzalcoatl. The equinox celebration is replete with Aztec dancers, poetry, fireworks, and the usual Mexican carnival fare, with the *paleta* man there alongside many other vendors.

Besides early incursions to the Great Pyramid made by the Swiss-American Bandelier, Cholula is one of the only major archaeological sites excavated and studied completely by the Mexicans themselves. There were no Yale University or BYU expeditions to this site. The study of the pyramid, which remains mostly covered to this day, came in two phases: one from 1931 to the early 1950s, and the second one from 1966 to 1970. Buildings around the Great Pyramid have been cleared and studied throughout the 20th Century and into the 21st, but all explorations of the pyramid itself ceased over 50 years ago. Under the direction of Mexican architect Ignacio Marquina, tunnels were constructed into the body of the pyramid which uncovered the successive layers that were applied to the original structure over the course of the monument's history. Marquina was hired by the Mexican government because of his restorative work in the 1920s at Teotihuacan. However, after his appointment to Cholula, he almost never made it down to Puebla from Mexico City. Great credit goes to the archaeological site's caretaker, a local indigenous man named Mariano Gómez, who planned and oversaw the digging of the tunnels. An archaeologist on site, Eduardo Noguera, gathered ceramic materials from the tunnels and began constructing a timeline for the pyramid. They named the first pyramid Building A or "La Conejera". It was built in about 300 BC, mostly out of simple adobe bricks built around a mound of earth with a stone core. The original building was painted black with white squares outlining the bricks. The second layer from the bottom, made sometime between 200 and 350 AD was called Building B or "The Pyramid of the Painted Skulls". This pyramid was also made mostly of adobe, with rock mixed in, and the surface was smoothed out with earth and lime. It is during this phase when the ceramics match most closely with those of Teotihuacan to the north. The smoothed surface of the pyramid during this phase allowed it to be painted. Once can only imagine the 4 faces of this pyramid covered with murals during the height of the city's power and prestige. After 350 AD, the pyramid was given another makeover and more layers were added to build up the structure. This building period lasted about a hundred years. This phase is labeled by archaeologists as Building C or "The Pyramid of the Nine Stories." The Cholulans also used adobe bricks for this phase, but finished off the pyramid's faces in rocks and stucco. The painting on the sides of the pyramid was less elaborate than that of the previous phase. This time, red, black and ochre paint was applied to the stucco, with red line patterns and some depictions of jaguars, serpents and other mythical creatures from the Mesoamerican cosmology.

Surrounding the Great Pyramid, there are many things of archaeological importance that continue to be excavated and studied. On the south side of the pyramid is a complex of buildings called The Courtyard of the Altars. Curiously, in one of the four rooms of one of the larger buildings there exists a representation of the Great Pyramid in miniature, much like one would find in a museum. The whole complex bears a close architectural resemblance to Teotihuacan with its talud-tablero building form and types of materials used. The massive altars in the courtyard have low-relief carvings on them. Other stone sculptures were found in the vicinity, notably, a gigantic human head, which may be a cultural relic from Olmec times, when that civilization carved massive human heads out of stone.

One of the most curious finds at Cholula to date is what has been called the largest mural in all of Mexico and is named "The Mural of the Drinkers." It was discovered accidentally in 1969 when an archaeologist named Ponciano Salazar Ortegón was digging and part of a building collapsed. The mural was discovered 25 feet below the surface and dates to about 200 AD. The mural's subject is an elaborate banquet, with the people depicted therein engaging in what some have called the first depiction of ritual pulque drinking. The mural measures 187 feet long and is masterfully done with hundreds of revelers engaged in a variety of activities, illustrated in lively colors. There are other smaller murals throughout the site, but there is a lot yet to be uncovered at Cholula.

One does not have to go to Egypt to marvel at monumental architecture and amazing ancient public buildings. The largest pyramid in the world is right in our own backyard. Few people know of the Great Pyramid of Cholula, partly because it hasn't been completely excavated – unlike many of the other major archaeological sites in Mexico – and it isn't much of a tourist draw. The fact that the site has been under complete control of the Mexicans also has something to do with it. As stewards of their own cultural heritage, the Mexican archaeologists appreciate the need to keep the tourists away and to preserve the past for future Mexicans.

VIKINGS IN ANCIENT MEXICO? THE STORY OF VOTAN

Ancient contact between the Old World and the New World — Eurasia and Africa with the Americas — has always been a difficult road to go down. As soon as Europeans made contact with the peoples in the Western Hemisphere, questions arose not only about the nature of the people the Europeans encountered, as in, whether or not they had a soul or were really completely human, questions arose as to the origins of these people. As ruins were uncovered of civilizations more ancient than the ones initially contacted, the questions about Native American origins intensified. People began looking for similarities between the Old World and the New, theories arose, and confirmation bias set in. According to Wikipedia, confirmation bias is defined as "the tendency to search for, interpret, favor, and recall information in a way that confirms one's preexisting beliefs or hypotheses, while giving disproportionately less consideration to alternative possibilities. It is a type of cognitive bias and a systematic error of inductive reasoning. People display this bias when they gather or remember information selectively, or when they interpret it in a biased way. The effect is stronger for emotionally charged issues and for deeply entrenched beliefs. People also tend to interpret ambiguous evidence as supporting their existing position." Cognitive bias plays an important role in the research of the mysterious and oft-maligned character from ancient Mexican myths and legends called Votan. He has been plugged in to many different researchers' theories and speculations about what happened in the New World during times before the European conquest. So, who was Votan?

Within the first decade of the Spanish conquest of the New World, members of the clergy and royal officials began the task of writing down everything they could about the newly conquered populations. This served several purposes. The main reason why there was such a push to document everything Native — especially ruling structures and religion — was so that the Spanish could better understand how to subjugate completely their newly conquered populations. Many of the early Spanish chroniclers had a very poor understanding of local languages and customs, and some interpretations of local histories and local belief systems are "off" as a result. The Spanish, who encountered living civilizations, some of which had formal written languages and complex social structures, are often the best sources from which to base further research. However, since the Conquest these often fragmented and incomplete writings have been augmented by modern scientific research, with specific emphasis on the science of archaeology to help piece together an accurate picture of life in the Americas before the Europeans. We will look at firsthand chronicles of the Votan story, examine any archaeological or scientific evidence for Votan and look at some modern interpretations.

The first documented account of the Votan legend comes from the Bishop of Chiapas, a man named Francisco Nuñez de la Vega. Bishop Nuñez' 1702 work titled *Constituciones diocesanas del obispado de Chiappa,* Votan was based on information taken from original indigenous written texts and calendars from the area of the modern Mexican state of Chiapas. We find that the person of Votan lived in a great stone structure, which he had been ordered to build by his uncle. The building was near the banks of the Usumacinta River in the kingdom of Na Chan, which was founded by Votan. The kingdom's territory eventually extended across the mountains and jungles of Chiapas and to the Pacific Ocean. The gods commanded Votan to divide up the lands among the people. Votan is also noted in the 1702 Nuñez work as to have been the one to give the ancient civilizations of Mexico written language. Further, Nuñez states that Votan, as the founder of the royal house of Cham or Snake, had many descendants in Chiapas and some still living at the time of his writing. Votan here also sounds more like a real historical person instead of a supernatural being. The bishop also made mention that the current Chiapans were now all faithful Christians and after having studied the Gospels for many years had claimed to be the sons of Noah of the biblical flood story. The Nuñez chronicle does not mention any physical characteristics of Votan or where he supposedly came from. Those and other pieces of information would be fleshed out by future researchers and those putting forth alternative hypotheses.

Votan next makes his appearance in the Spanish written record in a 1786 publication by a man named Antonio del Río. He took Bishop

Nuñez' writings and added to them, throwing in his own speculations and theories. Del Río wrote about Votan's travels in the Old World and his possible connection to the ancient Middle East. He speculated that Votan had come to Mexico after the destruction of the Tower of Babel and had also connected Votan to Noah, much as the native Chiapans themselves did 80 years before. Del Río's speculations may have come from hazy reports from local Indians who had by then been many generations removed from the Conquest and out of touch with their own pre-Hispanic legends and histories, or they may have been part of a fanciful embellishment on the part of del Río. During del Río's time, a few decades before Mexican independence, the ancient cultures of Mexico still had been poorly understood and there were many theories of the origins of the Native cultures at that time. During del Río's era similar information about Votan was coming from a Spanish priest named Ramón de Ordoñez y Aguilar, who was assigned to the Maya villages around the ruins of Palenque in Chiapas near the border with Guatemala. He wrote a book titled *Probanza de Votan* based on accounts of the locals, with some information supposedly coming from actual descendants of Votan. In the book it details Votan's 4 voyages back and forth between the Old World and the New World.

In modern archaeology, Votan has been associated with the Maya "God D" also known as Itzamná – "Reptile House" – among certain Maya groups. He looks like an old man with sunken cheeks and flowing robes as a scribe would wear. He is tall sometimes he is associated with wings on his head along with a flat obsidian disk in the middle of his forehead. The ancient Maya prayed to him as a granter of *k'uhul*, a sacred life force energy used for healing. Votan is seen as a god of kings and a patron of noble houses and is associated with the third day of the week on the Maya calendar. In the Maya creation story he also placed the 3rd stone on the Cosmic Hearth from whence all warmth generates. In newly translated Classical Maya writings this hearth stone is also called the Waterlily Throne Stone.

It was the Berlin-born Alexander von Humboldt who first made the connection between Votan and the northern European myths and legends in the early 19th Century. Von Humboldt was first struck by the similarities between the name Votan and Woden, the Anglo-

Saxon/Germanic version of the Viking god Odin. Name coincidences happen throughout the world and across many languages, but looking at the Odin/Woden connection to Votan, we see some similarities that may go beyond coincidence. Votan is credited with giving writing to the Mesoamericans. Odin gave runic writing to the Norse. Odin is pictured with wings on his head and wearing robes. Woden or Odin as one of the main gods of the ancient European legends was also known as a patron and helper of the ruling elite, much like the Mexican Votan. The proto-Germanic word, from which Woden originates is *wodaz* which means "prophet." One of Odin's other names in the Norse sagas is Valtam, which means "The Warrior." Perhaps the most curious coincidence, which even links the Votan/Woden story to the modern age is that the Mayan Votan was associated with the third day on the Maya calendar. Our third day of the week, Wednesday, in Old English, Wodensday, was named for the old European god Woden. Is our modern "hump day" named for the same person as this mysterious Maya god, or is it all just a coincidence?

When serious scholarly researchers attached to universities began exploring the connections between the Old World and the New, the various theories and apparent connections between the two areas of the world were slowly discounted, overturned, ignored by the establishment or dismissed as racism. The racist shut-down of much of the scholarly interest in the Old and New World connections picked up intensity in the 1960s and almost became a kind of dogma by the 1970s. The view was that it was racist to assume that the civilizations of the Americas were seeded or even influenced by outside forces because it negated Native genius and assumed that the ancient Americas could not have possibly given rise to complex civilizations independently. It was in the late 1960s and early 1970s when alternative or "fringe" theories began to emerge and the pulp press was full of books on explanations for the ancient civilizations of the Americas as products of Old World contact, the lost continent of Atlantis or even extraterrestrials. The prolific British writer, Graham Hancock, who has written on a variety of topics including the mysteries of the Great Sphinx, the connection of Mars to primitive earth and the lost continent of Atlantis, mentions Votan in his 1995 work *The Fingerprints of the Gods.* According to Hancock, Votan came to Mexico from the East on a ship with an entourage. Votan is described as a bearded Nordic-looking man dressed in flowing robes, remarkably resembling the Viking god Odin. Many people have discredited this work and the dozen or so other books by Hancock as "pseudoarchaeology" and severely lacking in any sort of scientific merit even though his books have sold well into the millions.

As the pendulum swings, more academic publications are opening up to more scholarly research about Old World and New World contact. Where this topic was completely off limits a mere 20 years ago, investigators are making some headway in the major journals and other "publications of merit." Perhaps one day researchers will be able to come to conclusions about whether or not Votan was a real Viking who made his way to ancient Mexico or maybe this story will be relegated to the heap of pulp paperbacks touting pseudoscience and wishful thinking.

PART SEVEN: UNCLASSIFIED

THE 2012 DOOMSDAY AND THE MAYA CALENDAR

In the Royal Library of Dresden, in the south-central part of newly formed German Empire, a 72-year-old man began writing down his thoughts about the colorful painted bark book before him. The year was 1894 and the man was Ernst Wilhelm Förstemann. Förstemann had been director of the Royal Library since 1865 and had a special affinity for what was called "The Mexican Book." As a mathematician and historian, the director had begun to see patterns in this lime-covered, ancient, bark book. His insights were based on 14 years of "eureka" moments which had culminated in the first ever explanation of the calendar systems used by the ancient Maya. The bark book is known as the Dresden Codex, the oldest known manuscript from the Americas. The book, one of only a handful still in existence, was written by the ancient Mesoamerican scribes themselves and describes astronomical observations and ritual cycles. Parts of it also serve as an almanac. As the first person to crack the Maya calendar, Förstemann was also the first person to come up with an apocalyptic scenario tied to the calendar. He interpreted the last page of the Dresden Codex to be the end of the Maya calendar and destruction of the world, although he did not tie this in to the year 2012.

A few decades after Förstemann came to understand the Maya calendar system, American archaeologist Sylvanus Morley added to what Förstemann was saying by writing that the Maya had predicted the end of the world in a great flood. Morley's book, *The Ancient Maya*, first published in 1946, was the first time the general public heard anything about a "Maya Apocalypse."

Scholars began to decipher the writing system of the Maya in the mid-20th Century and with the reading of the glyphs came a better understanding of the world of the ancient Maya. Because dates were so important in their association with major events and the lives of the Maya elites, calendar references were everywhere in the Maya world. Archaeologists, epigraphers and other researchers came to a complete understanding of Maya calendrics by the 1950s.

So, where did the 2012 connection come in? Before we look at the connection to our own times, we need to go over a general explanation of what the Maya calendar system is and how it functions. The ancient Maya had two types of calendars. One, called the Calendar Round, combined *Tzolkin*, a period of 260 days, and intersected with the *Haab'*, a period roughly corresponding to the solar year. Imagine two wheels turning next to each other and touching one another at one point to produce a date. The Calendar Round cycle repeated every 52 solar years. The Calendar Round primarily measures shorter periods of time. The Maya Long Count calendar was used independently of the Calendar Round to measure huge spans of time. The smallest measurement on this calendar was a *k'in*, or day. There were 8 other, much larger, measurements of time going from there. 1 w*inal* equals 20 *k'in*, or 20 days, for example. One *katun* equals 7,200 days or approximately 20 years. The highest measure on the Maya Long Count Calendar was 1 *alautun*, which corresponded with 23.04 billion days or a little over 63 million years. Many people who have studied the Maya calendar have questioned the need for measuring time in such vast quantities.

While this was all being figured out, researchers realized that in the 20th Century we were nearing the end of one of the larger measured time periods of the calendar, the 13th *baktun*. Most Maya scholars agree that the 13th *baktun* began on August 11, 3114 BC. This is the mythical "beginning point" of the Maya. Researchers took a while to figure out the day on which the time period called the 13th *baktun* would end and even now some learned people in the field of Maya studies are unsure of the exact day. For example, Maud Worcester Makemson, a professor specializing in archaeoastronomy at Vassar, noted in her 1957 publication, "The Miscellaneous Dates of the Dresden Codex," how important the end of the 13th baktun would be to the ancient Maya but using her complex methods used in decades of studying ancient astronomy Worcester Makemson came up with an exact date of June 13, 1752 for the ending of the 13th baktun cycle which is nowhere near the 2012 date. For the purposes of our own culture's 2012 intersection with the Maya "end date," respected Maya researcher Michael D. Coe came up with the date of December 24, 2011 in the first printing of his book *The Maya* in 1966.

Not only did he come up with this date, he also stated "there is a suggestion that Armageddon would overtake the degenerate peoples of the world and all creation on the final day of the 13th *baktun*." In 1980, in the 2nd edition of his book, Coe himself revised the date to January 11, 2013. Coe finally settled on the date of December 23, 2012 in the third edition of *The Maya* published in 1984. The first correlation we see in the popular literature to December 21, 2012 as the end of the Maya calendar cycle is found in a 1983 version of Sylvanus Morley's 1946 book *The Ancient Maya*. Some believe that Coe's date of Christmas Eve, 2012 was conveniently moved to the 21st so as to correspond to the winter solstice, thus making it more astronomically relevant, but we can never know for certain why there was a change made. We only know that it was repeated countless times as interest in the Maya Apocalypse grew.

In the late 1960s and early 1970s with the rise of the "Ancient Astronauts" phenomenon tied to lost civilizations, we see an increasing interest in the end of the 13th *baktun*. In books with names like *The Outer Space Connection*, pulp paperback authors conjectured that on the day of the end of the Maya calendar cycle the aliens would return to colonize earth. The Mesoamerican feathered serpent god Quetzalcoatl – called Kukulcán by the Maya – who had promised to return to ancient Mexico at some point in the future, was also linked to the 2012 phenomenon. Who, exactly, would be coming back in the form of the feathered serpent god? Many publications pondered this question.

By the 1980s we saw the coming of the New Age Movement, a philosophy that looked for spiritual meaning outside the traditional religious, philosophical and scientific beliefs of the West. "Mayanism" became popular at this time. As defined by Wikipedia, Mayanism is "a non-codified eclectic collection of New Age beliefs, influenced in part by Pre-Columbian Maya mythology and some folk beliefs of the modern Maya peoples. Adherents of this belief system are not to be confused with Mayanists, scholars who research the historical Maya civilization." The Maya were seen as a peaceful people comprised of astronomer priests who were either descended from extraterrestrials or who had contact with them. Because the New Age movement is a kind of philosophical globalism and draws from many cultures across the world, past and present, it sought to validate the 2012 apocalypse by tying it in with other belief systems which some critics would claim as a form of cherry-picking. Thus the so-called Maya end date became tied to such disparate works and ideas as the *I Ching*, the prophecies of the Hopi Indians and the legend of Atlantis.

During the 1980s many argued that the end of the Maya *baktun* cycle was not representative of the physical end of the world, rather, it marked an upcoming shift in human consciousness. The 25-year countdown to the end of the current *baktun* officially began in August of 1987 with the Harmonic Convergence, the world's first synchronized meditation event. The chief promoter of the event was José Argüelles who released the book *The Mayan Factor: Path Beyond Technology* to coincide with the event. The idea of something big happening on December 21, 2012 was now taken out of the New Age context and propelled into the mainstream as many people not connected with the Harmonic Convergence or the New Age Movement became curious about the Maya calendar and its implications.

The 1980s and 1990s saw the tying in of the end of the Maya *baktun* cycle with astronomical events. In the 2012 literature we start seeing the mentioning of the "galactic alignment." According to John Major Jenkins in his 1998 book, *Maya Cosmogenesis 2012: The True Meaning of the Maya Calendar End-Date*, "The Galactic Alignment is the alignment of the December solstice sun with the Galactic equator. This alignment occurs as a result of the precession of the equinoxes. Precession is caused by the earth wobbling very slowly on its axis and shifts the position of the equinoxes and solstices one degree every 71.5 years. Because the sun is one-half of a degree wide, it will take the December solstice sun 36 years to precess through the Galactic equator." This galactic alignment coincidentally occurred on December 21, 2012 and the adherents to the belief in this astronomical theory claim that the *baktun* cycle ended on that day because the Maya predicted it. This alignment was not associated with any sort of planet-wide catastrophe, but some people believed that in addition to being aligned with the galactic center, the sun would also be aligned with a supermassive black hole located in the center of the galaxy called Sagittarius A. This alignment would cause destruction on a global scale. Others tying the end of the *baktun* cycle to astronomical events also claimed December 21, 2012 would see the return of Planet X – also called Niburu – as per the old Mesopotamian legends, that the red giant star Betelgeuse would go super nova and that the main star in the Pleiades would emit a series of photons that would form a belt around earth thus altering life as we know it.

As the year 2012 came closer, books and disaster movies of impending catastrophe ramped up. Preppers stocked up on the basics: non-perishable food, water and ammunition. By New Year's Eve of 2012 most people in the United States had heard something about the end of the world being in 2012 but were unsure of the details. There was a measurable amount of hysteria in parts of the world, as earth ramped up for yet another doomsday. There were now hundreds of theories as to what was going to happen and why, and many interconnected and overlapping ideas. The whole 2012 phenomenon became a dizzying mess. There was a huge backlash from traditional Maya scholars as we got closer and closer to the fateful date. As already mentioned, even the archaeologists could not agree as to when the *baktun* cycle would end, so many were baffled as to what seemed to be an out-of-control apocalypse prophesy. As December 21, 2012 came and went, humanity sighed a collective sigh. While nothing physically noticeable happened on that date, many believe that something unseen did happen and we have yet to see the results of what started in motion on that day.

Since the middle of the 20th Century when the Maya calendar was sorted out for the first time, there have been discoveries of the end of the *baktun* cycle written on Maya monuments. One is at the site of Tortuguero in the Mexican state of Tabasco. On a partially-defaced inscription there, a series of glyphs have been interpreted to mean that when the 13th *baktun* ends there will be a display of "investiture" of the god B'olon Yokte' who has been associated with sacrifices to ends of cycles of years at other Maya sites. The other reference is found at the Guatemalan site of La Corona, in a series of inscriptions on a staircase, and compares the then-recent completion of 13 *katuns* with the future completion of the 13th *baktun*. To this day, these two references to 2012 are the only ones we have and they say nothing of prophesy or have anything to do with the end of the world. It is not surprising, though, because the Maya were not known for predicting future events or recording what they thought might happen in the future. It is no wonder that a civilization that was unable to predict its own demise was not able to predict the end of the world.

TABLE OF LONG COUNT UNITS

1 k'in = 1 day
1 winal = 20 k'in = 20 days
1 tun = 18 winal = 360 days = 1 year (approx.)
1 katun = 20 tun = 7,200 days = 20 years
1 baktun = 20 katun = 144,000 days = 394 years
1 piktun = 20 baktun = 2,880,000 days = 7,885 years
1 kalabtun = 20 piktun = 57,600,000 days = 157,704 years
1 kinchiltun = 20 kalabtun = 1,152,000,000 days = 3,154,071 years
1 alautun = 20 kinchiltun = 23,040,000,000 days = 63,081,429 years

THE MUMMIES OF GUANAJUATO IN FACT AND FICTION

Yes, Mexico has its mummies, but unlike mummies from Egypt and other parts of the world, these mummies are accidental and are of common people. They date from the post-Conquest era, specifically the 19th and early 20th Centuries. So, how did Mexico come to have mummies? What's their story, and how have they captured the imagination of a country in its pop culture?

The mummies we speak of come from the city of Guanajuato and its surroundings. Guanajuato was declared a UNESCO World Heritage Site by the United Nations in 1988. The city is truly enchanting and deserves this designation. One can get lost marveling at its colonial architecture and wandering its numerous narrow side streets and alleys called *callejones*.

The name Guanajuato comes from the Tarascans or Purepecha and was originally called "Quanax huato," which means "hilly place of frogs." In pre-Hispanic times the Aztecs were here and called the area Paxtitlán, "the place of straw." Before that, it was known as Mo-o-ti, which means "the place of minerals." The Aztecs mined precious metals here mostly for ornamental purposes and to feed the market for elite items hand crafted out of metal. When the Spanish arrived in the early 1500s they heard of the Aztec mines and discovered gold for themselves in the 1540s. Soon a garrison was sent to protect the mines, a town was set up and the city became formalized as Santa Fé Real de Minas de Guanajuato in 1548. The largest mine in the area, La Valenciana, at one point was producing one third of the world's silver and helped contribute to a bottoming out of the silver market and overall economic downturn in the 1600s. The vast wealth created by the mines helped fuel the artistic building frenzy in Guanajuato. Some of the finest examples of baroque architecture in all of Latin America can be found in the religious buildings of this place. The city also played an important role in the Mexican War of Independence from Spain. The first battle of the war between the royalist forces and the insurgents led by Father Hidalgo occurred at a granary inside the city. Mining lessened in importance throughout most of the 1800s but became important again in the 1870s when Porfirio Díaz, the long-lasting ruler of Mexico, encouraged foreign investment to develop more mines.

It was during this time when the government instituted a perpetual burial tax. If survivors of the buried person could not pay the tax, the body of the relative would be exhumed. It was during this time when the mummies were discovered, much to the surprise of the people responsible for enforcing the penalties of not paying the tax. The mineral-rich soils and the dryness of the climate are two conditions generally thought to have aided in the preservation of the bodies, but according to experts the soils have very little to do with this phenomenon, if anything. 100% of the bodies were recovered from above-ground crypts and only 1 in 10 have been found mummified. Although some mummies were previously embalmed, most of them, according to scientists, were preserved by the utter dryness of the air, which caused the bodies to mummify quickly. This phenomenon only occurs in one other place in Mexico, in a small region in the state of Jalisco to the west. The majority of the mummies came from exhumations done in the late 19th Century. The burial tax ended in 1958 and so no new mummies were unearthed after that time.

Soon after the discovery of the mummies, the naturally preserved bodies drew attention from the curious. In the late 1800s people began paying to see the mummies which were stored somewhat haphazardly in a building near the cemetery. Now considered to be the largest collection of mummies in the Western Hemisphere, the Guanajuato Mummy Museum opened in 1970 to showcase the remains behind glass for all the curiosity-seekers to see. The collection has 111 total mummies, many of them women and children. Most of the mummies have their original clothes. Many of the children are dressed up as angels or little saints for an easier entrance into the afterlife. The museum claims to have the smallest mummy in the world, that of a fetus. There are many legends surrounding why some of the mummies have contorted and twisted faces including a famous story that people were mistakenly buried alive and tried to escape their fate but died in the attempt. In 2007 a team led by a Texas State University at San Marcos professor, Jerry Melbye, examined 22 of the mummies in the Guanajuato Mummy Museum collection. The purpose of the study was to increase overall scientific and historical knowledge of the mummies. Dr. Melbye has studied mummies in Egypt's Sahara desert, those in Mesa Verde National park in the Southwest US and specimens from Vancouver Island, British Columbia. The team's examinations have revealed evidence of such diseases as rheumatoid arthritis, extreme anemia, and tuberculosis, sometimes severe enough to cause death. They have also found evidence of smoke inhalation, either from smoking tobacco or from working in the local mines. A number of babies in the mummy study died at a very early age, possibly from a common bacterial infection that infants in pre-industrial societies often contract when adults begin to feed them solid food that they have softened by chewing.

The mummy museum engenders mixed feelings among its patrons. These are real people on display and the exhibit is not for the faint of heart. Many people consider the museum too morbid and skip it on their tour of the beautiful colonial city of Guanajuato. As is typical in Mexico at such tourist destinations, one can purchase most anything mummy-related outside the museum including keychains, mummy replicas, coffee mugs and barely edible mummy candy.

Beyond the museum the mummies of Guanajuato have entered the pop culture psyche of Mexico. The first person to write about the mummies, however, may have been the American author Ray Bradbury. Known for his science fiction writing, Bradbury published a book of short stories in 1947 written in the horror genre called *The October Country*. In that book is a story called "The Next in Line" about an American tourist couple visiting Guanajuato for Day of the Dead. The wife dies in the story and this very brief piece examines themes like the fear of death and the need to belong. Author Bradbury wrote the story to get the whole experience of the mummy museum out of his head, to release the demons that had haunted him after a brief visit to the attraction with his own wife. Bradbury writes:

"Jaws down, tongues out like jeering children, eyes pale brown-irised in upclenched sockets. Hairs, waxed and prickled by sunlight, each sharps as quills embedded on the lips, the cheeks, the eyelids, the brows. Little beards on chins and bosoms and loins. Flesh like drumheads and manuscripts and crisp bread dough. The women, huge ill-shaped tallow things, death-melted. The insane hair of them, like nests made and remade..."

Mummy movies with an Egyptian twist were popular in the United States in the 1930s and 1940s. At the same time, during the "Golden Age" of Mexican cinema an Aztec mummy would pop up here and there but never the mummies of Guanajuato. The main movie that put the mummies we speak of on the map was the 1971 film called "Santo Contra las Momias de Guanajuato." Translated into English, this means "Santo Against the Mummies of Guanajuato." This was followed up a year later with a sequel, "The Theft of the Mummies of Guanajuato." The star of the films, Santo, was a famous Mexican wrestler, of *Lucha Libre* fame, and in the 1960s and 1970s he and other wrestlers such as El Mil Máscaras and Blue Demon would battle monsters and evil superheroes, among them Dracula, the Spiders from Hell, the Vampire Women, the Wolf Man, and of course, the Mummies of Guanajuato. In the first film about the mummies, one of the mummies comes back to life to seek revenge against Santo because when he was alive he was a wrestler, too, and battled one of

Santo's ancestors. The now-reanimated former wrestler is the 7-foot-tall Satán and he gets the help of several of the other mummies from the museum to go after Santo, killing and terrorizing the townsfolk along the way. The mummies, of course, can't be killed with bullets. Santo, however, knows how to kill them because of his family history.

Since the early '70s there have been a few low-budget knock-offs of the wrestler movies but nothing really has been made about the Mummies of Guanajuato in the pop culture arena until fairly recently, possibly as a reaction to the popularity of zombie movies in the United States. In 2014 an animated film came out of Mexico called "La Leyenda de las Momias de Guanajuato," starring children as the protagonists. As with the wrestler movies, in this movie the mummies come alive and cause havoc amongst the Guanajuato citizenry. A few years ago a children's book came out on this side of the border written by James Luna called, "A Mummy in Her Backpack," about a girl named Flor who visited the mummy museum and later finds that a small mummy from the Guanajuato museum hitched a ride in her backpack. Flor then must deal with it in the United States. As zombie movies continue to be popular in the United States we can be sure that the Mexicans will answer to this with their own home-grown equivalent. The fictionalization of the mummies of Guanajuato is not over.

DAY OF THE DEAD: AN OVERVIEW

In Mexico the holiday is called *Día de muertos* or *Día de difuntos*. The back translation in the United States is Día de los muertos. It is celebrated in the beginning of November but just because it's at that time of the year and involves happy skeletons, this holiday has nothing to do with zombie movies, devil worship or voodoo and it is NOT the "Mexican Halloween." The only thing in common that traditional Day of the Dead has in common with Halloween is that it is syncretic, that is, it blends older pagan beliefs with Christianity. There have been some Halloween elements that have crept into the holiday from the North, but that has only been recent, with the flow of returning migrants and the overpowering nature of American culture in the age of globalization.

The original basis of the holiday dates back possibly thousands of years and is rooted in the pre-Hispanic cultures of central and southern Mexico. The Aztecs were the most dominant civilization in central Mexico when the Spanish first arrived and throughout their vast empire they honored the goddess Mictecacihuatl, informally known as "Lady Death" at the beginning of the summer. The celebrations included human sacrifice and individuals constructed altars to honor the dead primarily by giving offerings of skulls made of a mixture of corn meal and animal blood. The Spanish knew they could not wipe out these traditions entirely, so they moved the Lady Death celebration so that it aligned better with the Catholic calendar and thus the new Day of the Dead was born on All Souls Day and All Saints Day. The more indigenous the community, the more of the older traditions were kept. The more European the community, the more traditionally Catholic the celebrations. This remains to this day throughout central and southern Mexico. It's important to note how regional this holiday is. The largest states in Mexico – Sonora and Chihuahua – have no history of this holiday because the Aztec Empire did not extend that far north.

Day of the Dead celebrations vary from place to place but there are some common threads and themes across Mexico. A few days before the holiday people start to build altars or *ofrendas* in their homes to honor those who have passed. There are a lot of books out now on Day of the Dead and the books usually show elaborate altars that take up most of an entire room that have cost a fortune to build. That's a little over the top for most Mexican people. The average *ofrenda* is pretty simple and includes some basic elements: a table cloth to make it nice, mementos of loved ones such as personal keepsakes and photos, religious iconography including statues and pictures of the saints or Virgin Mary, and flowers. Depending on availability, the flowers are usually a Mexican variety of marigold, in the vernacular called *cempasúchil,* or any other flowers that are in season or available. On the two days that make up the holiday incense is burned at the altar, usually from the copal tree, and the incense combined with the smell of the marigolds is supposed to produce a mild "high" in the inhaler. Also closer to the holiday, food is placed on the altar, usually the favorite foods of the person who has passed in addition to special foods prepared specifically for the holiday. All of this is done so that the deceased will feel welcome enough to return to earth on these few days to be with loved ones.

Day of the Dead is huge for crafts. Nowadays *muertos* crafts are plentiful online and are available year-round. Deep in the heart of Mexico, however, the best crafts are made in October, right before the holiday. The crafts are sold to people who are going to use them to decorate their altars or their homes and they come in various forms. Some are long-lasting and some are ephemeral, and only meant to last a few days, like the cut tissue paper strands called *papel picado*. Clay happy skeleton figures are meant to amuse the spirits, and entertain the living. These crafts take as many forms as the artist creating them can imagine. Another major craft whipped up right before the holiday is the sugar skull. In Mexico they are made of sugar and egg whites. Because of the fear of salmonella poisoning, in the United States people use meringue powder instead of raw eggs. The skulls made with egg whites always have a dull shine to them, unlike the meringue powder version which tend to look like just big blocks of sugar. Sugar skulls are not meant to be eaten. They are nice to look at and give off a sweet smell for the spirits. The whole tradition of sugar skulls was introduced to replace the Aztec skulls of cornmeal and blood. *Alfeñique* is the name of this kind of sugar craft and originated among a religious order in Sicily a few centuries before the Aztec conquest and was brought to Mexico by the Catholic clergy.

While sugar skulls are not to be eaten – they are as hard as a brick – there are special foods available in the marketplaces that one can actually eat. Chocolate skulls and lollipops are common and can range from plain to extra fancy. There is also *pan de muerto* "dead bread" that is served at this time. It's typical of Mexican *pan dulce* in that it really isn't that sweet and it's not really that distinctive.

Depending on the town, there may be religious processions that lead to the church and are followed by a mass. Many of these religious celebrations are followed by all-night vigils in the cemeteries that are often very festive with food, drink and music. Tourists are often surprised to see how the holiday is celebrated differently in different towns. Day of the Dead in Pátzcuaro, for example will be different from the same holiday celebrated in Oaxaca or Veracruz.

Day of the Dead celebrations are relatively new in the United States, in fact one would be hard pressed to find any celebration that dates back to before 1995 anywhere, even in the places like the Southwest with large Mexican immigrant or Mexican-American populations. As an example, Day of the Dead was a relatively new import to the Phoenix area in the late 1990s. At that time most of the Mexican-American population, over 90% had roots in the border state of Sonora which had no tradition of the holiday. So, a lot of the people who started celebrating the holiday had no family history of celebrating it, and in some cases that meant hundreds of years of their family being Mexican and having no history of celebrating Day of the Dead. The popularity of Day of the Dead seemed to rise with the popular Latino consciousness that was just taking off in the 1990s and a lot of Latinos were drawn to Day of the Dead as a sort of cultural expression. Most of the people of Hispanic origin who started celebrating the holiday in the 1990s got most of their information off the internet, like anyone else curious about it. In an age when cultural sensitivity has bred the term "cultural appropriation," it is quite ironic that Mexican-Americans themselves would be adopting a cultural tradition from Mexico that they had no experience with.   Part of the definition of culture, however, is that it is shared among people. Proof of this is the exponential growth of the interest in this holiday in the United States over the past decade or so. With increased immigration and more Latino cultural awareness in the US, the holiday is sure to grow over time.

DRUG USE IN ANCIENT MEXICO

The modern "Drug War" in Mexico is responsible for over a hundred thousand deaths, tens of thousands of people declared "missing" and countless individuals and families ruined beyond repair. It has had a deep impact on everyday life in Mexico and has strained relations with Mexico's neighbor to the north. While many people are very aware of aspects of the Drug War in Mexico today, many do not know that drug use in this country goes back thousands of years. As a sidebar, although the colloquial term for cannabis, marijuana, may sound Mexican, and the plant is currently cultivated in Mexico, it had its origins in Asia and not the ancient Americas. The ancient Mexicans had plenty of other substances that they were using before the arrival of the Spanish. Evidence of ancient drug use in Mexico can be found in the archaeological record, in the writings of the ancient Maya and from Spanish chroniclers who encountered intact and living indigenous civilizations.

According to the Spanish medical journal *Neurología*, "Pre-Columbian Mesoamerican cultures used hallucinogenic substances in magical, therapeutic, and religious rituals. These substances are considered entheogens since they were used to promote mysticism and communication with divine powers. The purpose of using these substances was to enter a trance and achieve greater enlightenment and open-mindedness. The altered state of consciousness the user aimed to reach was characterized by temporal and spatial disorientation, a sensation of ecstasy and inner peace, hallucinations of vivid colors, tendency towards introspection, and an impression of being one with nature and with the gods."

Drug use was often solely the domain of the shaman or priest who was an intermediary between our earthly existence and the supernatural. While it is unknown how widespread abuse of hallucinogenic substances was in ancient Mexico, it is generally assumed that the cactus, leafy plants and mushrooms harvested for their mind-altering properties were solely used for prophesy or in religious ceremonies. Complex rituals surrounding the use of these substances kept widespread use in check.

One of the oldest hallucinogens used in ancient Mexico was peyote, a type of cactus found throughout the country. Buttons of the cactus, which contain mescaline, may be chewed or brewed into a tea. The drug may induce hallucinations, altered perceptions of time and space and a feeling of weightlessness. Evidence of peyote use dates back over 5,000 years to the prehistoric period and can be found in the archaeological record, as traces of peyote have been found in ritual contexts along with ceremonial artifacts. At the time of the Spanish Conquest the survivors of the collapsed Maya civilization were still using peyote along with the indigenous people who lived in the Aztec Empire. In the 1550s, a Franciscan Friar named Bernardino de Sahagún, who was responsible for gathering native knowledge throughout the newly conquered Spanish territories in modern-day Mexico, wrote a book titled *Historia de las cosas de Nueva España*, or, in English*History of the Things of New Spain*. In this book he describes peyote and its use:

"There is another herb like mountain prickly pear, named *peiotl*, which is white and can be found in the north. Those who eat or drink of it see terrifying or absurd visions; this inebriation lasts two or three days and then subsides. It is a delicacy often enjoyed by the Chichimeca, for it is sustaining and spurs them to fight with no thought of fear, thirst, or hunger, and they say that it protects them from all danger."

Soon after peyote was chronicled it was the subject of derision by Spanish authorities. Throughout New Spain its use was prohibited and its users were subjected to the Inquisition as the effects of the drug were seen as encouraging communion with the Devil or demonic forces.

Along with peyote, the use of "sacred mushrooms" prevailed from central Mexico all the way through the Maya region of the Yucatán and dates back at least 3,500 years. We see mushrooms painted in murals at Teotihuacán, the largest urban center in Mexico 2,000 years ago. Mushrooms are depicted on various decorative items from the Maya area and in the illustrated bark books, called codices, of the ancient Maya. The ancient Mixtec people of Oaxaca had a god named Seven Flowers always shown with magic mushrooms in his hands. The most common mushroom used was called *k'aizalaj Okox* by the Maya and *teonanácatl* by the Aztecs. In Latin, the scientific name for this fungus is *Psilocybe cubensis*. This mushroom was consumed fresh or ground into a powder. The effects of *teonanácatl*, which may last days depending on how much is consumed in one sitting, include euphoria, detachment, feelings of introspection and visual field distortion. We go back to the Spanish chronicler Sahagún for the initial European reaction to the practice of using "magic mushrooms":

"The little mushrooms that grow in this land are named *teonanácatl*. They grow beneath the hay in the fields and plains. They are round, and their stems are tall and round and slender. Their taste is unpleasant; they cause sore throat and drunkenness. They are used as medicine for fever and gout. No more than two or three should be eaten. Those who eat them see visions and feel fluttering of the heart; the visions they see are sometimes frightening and sometimes humorous. Those few who eat them in excess are driven to lust. Silly and naughty boys are told that they have eaten *teonanácatl*."

In addition to the magic mushrooms and the peyote cactus, there existed a handful of different hallucinogenic plants used throughout Mexico. We will look at the three most popular ones here. From the modern-day state of Oaxaca, we find what the Mazatac people called *pipiltzintli*, which is a green leafy plant with white and violet-colored flowers, and a member of the sage family. It was originally confined to the shady areas of the cloud forests of the high sierras of Oaxaca and later its cultivation spread throughout Mexico. In Spanish this is called *María Pastora* or *yerba de la pastora* and its Latin scientific name is *Salvia divinorum*. When smoked it produces sensations of motion, uncontrollable laughter, re-living of past memories, speaking in tongues, and a feeling of overlapping realities, or bilocation, the sense of being in two places at the same time. The genus of Datura plants, called *Toloache* or *Toloatzin* by the ancient Mexicans, was once native to central Mexico and Central America but has since spread throughout the world and is cultivated primarily for its trumpeting white blossoms. The plant is highly poisonous and the seeds were used by the shamans of Mexican antiquity to induce a state of delirium, which is an inability to differentiate fantasy from reality, instead of introspective trance states or hallucinations. It produces severe pupil dilation, rapid heartrate and sometimes bizarre and violent behavior. As this plant produces highly volatile reactions, it was probably under tight shamanic control in ancient times. In the US we commonly call this plant Jimson Weed or Moonflower. It has many other names according to the regions in which it is found. More widespread than *pipiltzintli* or *toloache* in ancient Mexico was a type of morning glory called *ololiuhqui* whose Latin name is *Turbina corymbosa* and whose Spanish name is *Flor de la virgen*. This very common plant found throughout Mexico was cultivated for its round, coffee-colored seeds which contain alkaloids of the LSD family. The seeds are ground up and mixed with water. Immediately after drinking this mixture, the user experiences a psychic void and feelings of vertigo. A half hour later, the user experiences a heightened sense of euphoria and visual illusions along with changes in perceptions of reality. *Ololiuhqui* was used by the Maya and the Aztecs along with the Mixtecs and Zapotecs in the modern-day state of Oaxaca. Sometimes the ancient Maya would mix this plant with the bark of a tree and honey and called the drink *balché*. We see the recipe for this drink in the Maya holy book, the *Popol Vuh*. *Balché* was often administered as an enema. There have been several Spanish accounts of the use of *Ololiuhqui*. We can return to the words of the Franciscan Sahagún:

"There is an herb named *coatl xoxouhquij* (green serpent), and it grows a seed they call *ololiuqui*. This seed produces inebriation and madness. People mix it in potions to give to those they wish to harm; those who eat it appear to see visions and terrifying things. Sorcerers mix it with food and drink, and so do those who hate others and wish to do them ill."

Besides the hallucinogens already mentioned, there were many regional and lesser-known uses of plants and animals to achieve altered states. In some parts of the Maya world, for example, a certain water lily was used, in other parts of ancient Mesoamerica even the glands of certain toad species were harvested to use in potions to alter reality or to commune with the gods. It seemed that wherever the Spanish went in their newly conquered territories they were finding Indians using various substances to go into trances or states of delirium or hallucination. Not appreciating the cultural or medicinal significance of what they were seeing, the Spanish were generally shocked and appalled at what they witnessed and ascribed the byproduct of the use of these natural drugs to unseen demonic forces that had to be eliminated. In a 1591 book called *Problemas y secretos maravillosos de las Indias*, or *Problems and Marvelous Secrets of the Indies*, Spanish author Juan de Cárdenas writes this:

"In sooth they tell us that peyote, and *ololiuqui*, when taken by mouth, will cause the wretch who takes them to lose his wits so severely that he sees the devil among other terrible and fearsome apparitions; and he will be warned (so they say) of things to come, and all this must be tricks and lies of Satan, whose nature is to deceive, with divine permission, the wretch who on such occasions seeks him."

In spite of Spanish attempts to eliminate the use of "medicinal" plants in colonial times, natural, plant-based drug use continues to this day in Mexico, usually under the radar and outside the realms of the murderous drug cartels often associated with this topic.

FRIDA KAHLO'S POLITICS

The date was Thursday, May 12, 2016 and it was a beautiful spring day in New York City. As the temperatures cooled and the city settled into a quiet weekday evening, excitement abounded at Christie's auction house. The big event was Christie's Impressionist & Modern Art Evening Sale. Featured at the sale were some big names in the art world: Picasso, Monet, Matisse, and several other 20th Century giants. Of particular interest in this sale was a small painting made by Mexican artist Frida Kahlo in 1939 titled "*Dos desnudos en el bosque*," which translates to English "Two Nudes in the Forest," featuring a small monkey looking out from a jungle on two women in a tender embrace. By the end of the evening the painting had made history: It sold for a little over $8 million and became the highest-selling Mexican painting ever to sell at auction and one of the highest-selling paintings by a female artist of all time. One can only imagine what Frida herself would have thought of such an unbridled display of capitalism in motion. As an avowed Marxist-Leninist and a card-carrying member of the Mexican Communist Party for decades, how would such a sale have meshed with Frida's political sensibilities? It turns out that the story of Frida Kahlo's political activism is a long and convoluted tale.

Frida Kahlo was born in the Mexico City suburb of Coyoacán on July 7, 1907 in the waning days of the Porfiriato, the decades-long dictatorship of Porfirio Díaz. During her childhood she experienced the Mexican Revolution unfolding around her which interested her and played an important role in shaping her. In fact, later in her life she would publicly claim her birth year as 1910 so as to coincide with the beginning of the Mexican Revolution, one of the many instances of Frida's use of "artistic license" to redefine her life and make it fit her own agendas and whimsies. In Frida's early teen years the country of Mexico had come out of the Revolution with new ideas and it struggled to redefine itself. New social movements emerged and Mexico looked inward to discover what it really looked like. A growing awareness of Mexico's indigenous past, previously only relegated to the stuff of myths, emerged and fought for space alongside Mexico's desire to be more European and modern. The old order of the Porfiriato would be replaced with something else and in the days immediately after the Revolution Mexico was not quite sure what that would be. It was an exciting time to be young, and Frida was in the thick of things as a student at the National Preparatory School in Mexico City, one of the first females to be admitted to what was seen as the finest high school in Mexico. In her later activism as a communist, Frida would give little credit to the upper-middle class privilege that gave her the opportunity to study at that school and be exposed to all of the new socio-political ideas percolating at the time. While at the school Frida learned how to speak two foreign languages – English and French – and had profound and heated discussions with her peers - who hailed from some of the most elite families in the country - about such things as social justice, science and history. Here Kahlo received quite a political education both inside and outside the classroom and considered herself a "daughter of the Revolution." Her friends from that time period in her life would become successful members of the Mexican social and political upper class.

In her post-high-school years Frida reveled in the modernity of 1920s Mexico City. While most of the country of Mexico was still extremely poor, Frida had no connection or interest in what was happening in the countryside. The Mexico City of the 1920s was a permissive place full of free expression, much like Paris or Berlin of the same era. It was then when Frida became engrossed in the café scene and joined groups of other young people to explore such topics as feminism, communism and polyamory. It was then and there where Frida met the Marxists, communists and political exiles that would influence her. At a party held by the Italian-American photographer Tina Modotti in June of 1928, when Frida was almost 21 years old, Kahlo met her future husband, Diego Rivera, the avowed communist Mexican muralist who had returned to Mexico from France some 7 years before. Kahlo had met Rivera briefly a few years earlier, but it was at the party in 1928 when they initiated their love affair that would eventually lead to their tumultuous union. Some of Diego's politics would rub off on Frida, but during the early years of their marriage especially her political ideology seemed to be all over the place and she tended to focus more on individual personalities instead of movements, political theories or dogma.

By the early 1930s the pendulum in Mexico swung in a different direction and the political climate became hostile to leftists. Communists were either jailed, deported or killed. Diego Rivera had an "out." In September of 1930 he and Frida went to the United States on the request of architect Timothy L. Pfleuger to paint for him in San Francisco. While in the States, Rivera got many more commissions for paintings and an eventual show in New York City. While in the US Frida dabbled in painting and was more of a consort to Diego than anything else. While she enjoyed the lavish parties and attention, she was ultimately not satisfied with being away from home and had mixed feelings about the Americans. In November of 1931 she wrote: "I don't like the gringos at all. They are very boring and they all have faces like unbaked rolls." After 4 years in the States the pressure Frida was putting on Diego to leave had reached its height. Diego was riding a wave and his work was becoming more visible and more appreciated. This was particularly important for Rivera because most of his paintings had intense political messages and he was aware of the power of visual propaganda. Diego wanted to stay in the US because he was convinced that a true workers' revolution would happen in an industrialized country and he was working tirelessly to influence the minds of Americans through his art. Although she had joined the communist party in 1927, Frida was not on board. In the end, Diego eventually gave in to something as trite as Frida's homesickness. So much for "the cause." Later, a letter Frida wrote to a friend surfaced about her thoughts about what she experienced in the United States. She claimed that she was interested in the industrial and mechanical progress the US had made but felt, "a bit of a rage against all the rich guys here, since I have seen thousands of people in the most terrible misery without anything to eat and with no place to sleep, that is what has most impressed me here, it is terrifying to see the rich having parties day and night while thousands and thousands of people are dying of hunger." Besides going to lavish parties and events and appearing at Diego's side when needed, and in spite of having a lot of "down time" while spending 4 years in the United States, Frida did nothing to act on her feelings or supposed convictions as a communist the entire time she was in America.

In 1930s Mexico with the rise of Lázaro Cárdenas on the national stage, Mexico once again welcomed communists and other leftists into the political fold. In 1936, Diego Rivera brokered a deal with President Cárdenas to have Leon Trotsky spend his time in exile in Mexico. Frida admired Trotsky who was the former head of the Red Army in Soviet Russia and had been expelled from the communist Central Committee after an ideological break with Stalin whose faction gained control of the Soviet Union. Trotsky and his wife would stay at Kahlo's "Blue House" until his assassination a few years later, while Frida and Diego lived in their new residence in the wealthy upscale San Angel neighborhood. Even though it was well known that Kahlo had an affair with Trotsky during his Mexican exile, later in life Frida would claim that her alliance with him and the Trostskyite communists was an error and her real admiration was for strongman Josef Stalin, who ruled the Soviet Union with impunity and was responsible for a terrible oppression in that country that led to the deaths of tens of millions of people. One of Frida's last paintings was titled "Self Portrait with Stalin." It was during the 1930s and the rise of fascism in Europe that Frida started claiming that she was Jewish, seemingly to ride the wave of sympathy of oppression of Jews in Europe and to turn her back on her German heritage on her father's side. A 2006 investigation done by the *Jerusalem Post* set out to prove or disprove Frida Kahlo's Jewishness. The newspaper traced Kahlo's European lineage back to the 16th Century and while they found a long line of craftsmen, soldiers and gingerbread makers, they found no evidence at all that Frida was even remotely Jewish. In the *Jerusalem Post* article it was even mentioned that in 1949 Frida had written to her father asking about a possible Jewish background and he told her that there wasn't any and that they were from a long line of Lutherans. That did not stop Frida from using more "artistic license" in her life and she held on to the claim of Jewish heritage until she died. Frida's Jewishness went hand in hand with her emphasizing her indigenous heritage. While real, her Native roots was very remote from her. Frida's mother was a *mestiza*, or of mixed Native and European descent, but she had no connection to any sort of tribal culture and was generations and generations removed from anything authentically indigenous. It all fed into Frida's self-made brand of what leftists would today call, "intersectionality," and she used it for own ends and to fulfill a series of her own agendas.

An offshoot of Frida's politics often explored especially lately is the topic of Frida Kahlo's "Feminism." Indeed, in the decades since her death, Kahlo has been transformed into a sort of feminist icon. Scant information exists, however, as to what Frida actually did to advance the causes of women. In an online Google search of "Frida Kahlo" and "Feminism," the top article is, "6 Reasons Why Frida Kahlo is a Feminist Icon," by author/blogger Maddy Crehan. Crehan gives one of the reasons as, "She's just so damn fierce," along with, "She embraced weirdness."   While we might think that Frida was somewhat unconventional for her time, we must realize that the early permissive years spent in the bohemian scene of Roaring Twenties Mexico City had a definite influence on her. She was doing pretty much what everyone else was doing at the time and that included her share of "gender bending," and defying convention by following the trendies. The claims that Frida was "ahead of her time" fall flat when examining the context of her youth and are usually made by people who know nothing of Frida's "time." Kahlo's flamboyant indigenous-inspired mode of dress may not have even been her own creation. While married to Diego, Rivera had his opinions of women's dress which stemmed from his communist ideology. He was quoted as saying that Mexican women who do not wear Mexican clothing, "are mentally and emotionally dependent on a foreign class to which they wish to belong." Perhaps Frida's way of clothing herself was a kind of uniform of sorts to signal that she was rejecting the Old Order so shunned by the intellectual communist elite in Mexico at the time. Kahlo's very relationship with Rivera seems to destroy the notion that she was any sort of feminist, politically or otherwise. Major parts of her art and her life were defined by her relationship to a man, her husband. She wrote thousands of words of her heartache, her torment, and her joy as defined by her husband. The following is a quotation from her voluminous writings on the topic of her husband:

"Nothing compares to your hands, nothing like the green-gold of your eyes. My body is filled with you for days and days. You are the mirror of the night. The violent flash of lightning. The dampness of the earth. The hollow of your armpits is my shelter. My fingers touch your blood. All my joy is to feel life spring from your flower-fountain that mine keeps to fill all the paths of my nerves which are yours."

Quotes like these are numerous and dispel the myth that Frida was a strong feminist; she defined herself primarily by a relationship to a man, Diego Rivera, who often treated her unkindly, cheated on her, lied to her, and it made no difference to Frida as she always went back to him.

Frida professed communism with greater intensity the older she got and the more life became difficult for her. Because of childhood illnesses and a tragic bus accident as a young woman, Frida suffered through dozens of surgeries and medical treatments and in the last years of her life she ended up a bedridden morphine addict. There was a part of her that believed that "communism" equaled "community" and that this political ideology would protect her from being alone, which was one of her greatest fears. She ramped up her political writings from her bed and her paintings took on a more ideological bent. Although she had been a card-carrying communist for over a quarter century, for most of her life she had ignored Rivera's example of using art to further political causes and instead she spent most of her time as a painter painting portraits of herself. The later years, with her world closing in on her, Frida finally decided to take on more political themes and began to sound more "activistic" in her writings. By July 13, 1954, it was too late, however, and the physical and mental anguish had overtaken her.

Because Frida was somewhat ambiguous during her life and shifted a lot according to trends and fashions, many people decades after her death have ascribed things to Frida Kahlo that had very little to do with her. She is often described as being very political, but just a brief exploration of this topic shows she had little in the form of solid ideology and very seldom lived by her alleged convictions. This fact hasn't stopped people from venerating her in almost a religious fashion to this day. She is an icon for feminists, "People of Color," persons with disabilities, Mexican-Americans and the LGBT "community." She is everything to everyone. Since her death, Frida has become like water and takes the shape of whatever vessel a person brings to her to fill. The fact that the reality of Frida Kahlo is not what most people think does not seem to matter to her cultish followers, which are ever growing in numbers.

MEXICAN SIGHTINGS OF BLACK EYED CHILDREN

María Arteaga González opened her door after hearing incessant knocking. Her home was located in the modest Colonia el Bosque neighborhood of Tijuana, the largest city of the Mexican state of Baja California located right across the border from San Diego. It was the late afternoon in March of 2016 and María was getting ready to start dinner as she always did at that time.   The two children on her doorstep were about 10 years old, a boy and a girl, with their heads bowed slightly downward. They were wearing what appeared to be handmade clothing. From what María could tell, the children had very pale skin and very even features. Even though they spoke perfect Spanish, she knew that these kids were not from her neighborhood. María thought to call her three children to the door who were about the same age as the two standing before her, but something told her not to. She then asked if they were lost and where their parents were. The two strange children replied with their original request for water and permission to enter the house. María asked them again if they

were lost and the girl of the two repeated, "No, we want to come in."
María was at a loss as to what to do. It was when she grabbed her
phone to call her husband that the two children finally looked up.
What María saw filled her with terror. After making eye contact with
them, she screamed while instinctively slamming the door. The two
children had solid black eyes, something María had never experienced
before. The sight of them had so disturbed this Mexican housewife
that she couldn't speak of it for days. María's was not the only
sighting of what has been termed "Black Eyed Children" in Tijuana that
year. In fact, the same sort of thing had been happening throughout
Mexico, from northern Baja to the Yucatán, since about the year 2002.

Initial reports of what has been termed Black Eyed Children or
Black Eyed Kids, have been popping up since the mid-1990s. It seems
like the phenomenon started in the United States and the UK and has
spread to other parts of the world. The scenario is rather similar
wherever it is experienced. One to three elementary-school-age
children will show up at the potential victim's door, lost, hungry,
wanting to use the phone or the bathroom. They tend to speak in a
monotone voice. It could be a boy or girl or combinations of boys and
girls who show up.   They are never accompanied by adults or animals
of any kind. These mysterious visitors never physically force
themselves into a home, but always ask permission to enter. They
always knock, even if there is a doorbell. Their primary objective, it
seems, is to get into the house. It is unknown what they do if they are
granted entry because there have been no reports across Mexico or
throughout the world of anyone letting them in. They are pale-
skinned and their hair color may vary but their facial structures are
always even and their complexions flawless. Their features are
Caucasian and never appear in the forms of other races. Often, these
strange kids are wearing handmade clothing or clothes from another
time period. They initiate their contact looking down or looking away.
When they first make eye contact, the person they are facing is often
filled with an intense feeling of horror, as if their appearance is
accompanied by a potent form of malevolence. The eyes of these
children are completely black with not a single sliver of white or color
from the iris. Soon after revealing their black eyes the kids usually
disappear, leaving no trace that they were there. This phenomenon

seemed to have spread slowly out of the US and England and now can be found in other parts of the world. In Mexico, the children have been called *"Los niños con ojos completamente negros."* Sometimes Mexican paranormal researchers use the term *"Los Beks"* a Spanglish twist of the English abbreviation for "Black Eyed Kids" – B E K – "bek."

In early March of 2015 in the opposite end of the Mexican Republic from Tijuana a spate of sightings of Los Beks occurred in Mérida, the centuries-old capital of the state of Yucatán. According to an article found in *Milenio Novedades*, the sightings began with two appearances of the children in two different areas in the city, in the México and Xibalbá neighborhoods. In each case, the mysterious kids appeared on the doorsteps of private homes asking for water and if they could come in the houses. The children in both cases fit the standard black eyed kids description and caused great distress in those who experienced them. On Sunday, March 7th, two separate instances involving these children occurred in Merida's Xoclán Cemetery. Juana Solís was at the graveyard with her three daughters leaving flowers at the tomb of a relative who had recently passed. A small boy with *ojos completamente negros* approached them asking for water. When they turned around, the boy had disappeared. Later that day, a man identified as Pedro saw two children fitting the appropriate description in the same cemetery but he had no interaction with them and they vanished as quickly as they had appeared.

There are dozens of theories as to what the Black Eyed Children actually are. As this phenomenon has cropped up and spread in the mid-1990s, some allege that it is an early version of what is called "creepypasta." The word creepypasta comes from the combination of two words, "creepy" and "copypasta," the latter term first coined on 4chan to denote a doubtful story that is copy and pasted all over the internet. So, one of the biggest theories about the black eyed children alleges that it is just an urban legend that has gone wild because of the internet. Urban legends aside, there have been many real people who have actually claimed to have seen these kids. An online article stated that in one year in Mexico alone there were two sightings in Tijuana, 4 sightings in Monterrey, 3 sightings in the state of Tamaulipas and 11 sightings in the state Sinaloa. If we are to believe these people who have come face to face with these mysterious beings, what could they

be? Are they physical or something more paranormal, like ghosts?
Are they interdimensional beings? If they are really flesh-and-blood
children, what explains their appearance, their actions and their
motives? Some claim that *los beks* are alien-human hybrids sent to
earth to mingle with humans. Their awkward mannerisms may
indicate beings who are not entirely familiar with human civilization.
Are they normal human children – possibly kidnapped - subject to
some sort of medical experiment or mind control? That theory would
not explain the uniformity in skin color and features, however. Also,
the total blackening of the eyes would not allow light to enter the eye
and would thus make vision impossible. Are they related to the alien
race better known as The Greys? With big black eyes and pale skin,
the black eyed kids vaguely resemble the legendary race of spindly,
big-headed, ashen-skinned, nefarious abductors. Their sightings are
not connected with UFOs or anything else, so it seems. Most of the
black-eyed children sightings happen randomly to random people. As
this phenomenon has been studied intensively in the past few years,
researchers have been looking for patterns but have been unable to
find any. Many believe that the kids represent a type of psychic
vampire, in that they inspire fear in those who see them, and
somehow inspiring fear is their nourishment. There is a similarity
between the black eyed kids and the vampire legends in that the kids
ask to be let into the house and seem like they can't do anything
without an invitation. The ease with which the children appear or
disappear, combined with the terror they strike in the people they
choose to victimize have led some to believe that the black eyed kids
are demons or manifestations of occult rituals. There is even a theory
floating around the internet stating that the black eyed kids are the
product of a CIA experiment gone wrong. So the story goes, the CIA
during the Cold War wanted to weaponize the occult and recruited a
Catholic priest from Nebraska to summon demons to be used by
military intelligence against America's enemies abroad. As with many
"genie out of the bottle" stories, the demons could not be controlled
and so they slowly spread among the earth. This would serve to
explain why these mysterious children started showing up first in the
United States in the 1990s and then in Mexico about ten years later.
There is no physical evidence of the visitations of the black-eyed kids

and one has never been detained for questioning or study. All that we have are eyewitness accounts, rumors and stories of stories in a "friend of a friend" sort of way. The growth of this phenomenon seems to have been going hand in hand with the growth of the internet.

No theories or claims of legends would have been of any comfort to a woman identified as Valeria who had an encounter with a black eyed child back in February of 2012. A resident of a small town in the Mexican state of Colima, Valeria was very tired one day after spending hours in class and the rest of her day at her part-time job at a factory. In the early evening she heard a knock on her door, a very persistent knock. She opened her door to see standing before her a boy of about 4 or 5 years old looking down and muttering the words, "mama, mama." Valeria asked the child questions. Was he lost? Where were his parents? Thinking the boy's caretakers must have been somewhere close by, Valeria took the boy by the hand and started to walk away from the house toward the road. She was surprised how cold the boy's hand was, but it was February and they were higher up in elevation and it was cold at that time of day. After about 8 steps toward the road, the child let go of Valeria's hand and then looked at her with his completely black eyes. When her eyes met his, Valeria let out a scream and started to run. The kid ran in the other direction. It took her days for her life to feel normal. She never saw the child again.

There are dozens of stories like this coming from Mexico and the rest of the world. Whether or not this phenomenon is real, there exists a foolproof and sound piece of advice to all who may cross paths with the Black Eyed Children on this side of the border or the other: Don't let them in!

BIBLIOGRAPHY

Argüelles, José. *The Mayan Factor: Path Beyond Technology.* Rochester, VT: Bear & Company, 1987.

Bierhorst, John. *Latin American Folktales: Stories from Hispanic and Indian Traditions.* New York: Pantheon, 2003.

Blanton, Richard E., et al. *Ancient Mesoamerica: A Comparison of Change in Three Regions.* Cambridge: Cambridge University Press, 1986.

Bradbury, Ray. *The October Country.* New York: Del Rey, 1985.

Brinton, Daniel G. *Nagualism. A Study in Native American Folk-lore and History.* Fairford, UK: Echo Library, 2009.

Carod-Artal, F.J. "Alucinógenos en las culturas precolombinas mesoamericanas," in *Neurología*, January-February 2015, vol. 30: 42-49.

Carriveau, G. W. and M. C. Han. "Thermoluminescent Dating and the Monsters of Acámbaro" in *American Antiquity,* vol 41, *1976.*

Castillo, Ana. *Goddess of the Americas: Writings on the Virgin of Guadalupe.* New York: Riverhead Books, 1993.

Cedillo, Juan Alberto. *Los Nazis en México: La Operación Pastorius y nuevas revelaciones de la infiltración al sistema político mexicano.* New York: Penguin Random House, 2013.

Chesnut, R. Andrew. *Devoted to Death: Santa Muerte, the Skeleton Saint.* Oxford: Oxford University Press, 2012.

Chouinard, Patrick and Paul Von Ward. *Lost Race of the Giants.* Rochester, VT: Bear & Company, 2013.

Clissold, Stephen. *The Seven Cities of Cibola.* New York: C. N. Potter, 1962.

Coe, Michael D. *Breaking the Maya Code*. New York: Thames and Hudson, 1992.

Coe, Michael D. *The Maya*. New York: Thames and Hudson, 1993.

Corbeaux, Lazarus. *Santa Muerte Rituals*. CreateSpace, 2015.

Corral, Ramón. "Biografía de José María Leyva Cajeme" In *Obras históricas: Reseña histórica del Estado de Sonora*. Hermosillo: Biblioteca Sonorense De Geografia e Historia, 1959.

Corrales, Scott. *Chupacabras and Other Mysteries. New York: Greenleaf Publications, 1997.*

Cremo, Michael and Richard L. Thompson. *Forbidden Archeology: The Hidden History of the Human Race*. Alachua, FL: Bhaktivedanta Book Publishing, 1998.

Crosby, Harry. *The Cave Paintings of Baja California*. Tucson: Sunbelt Publications, 1998.

De Aragon, Ray John. *The Legend of La Llorona*. Santa Fe: Sunstone Press, 2006.

Díaz del Castillo. *The Discovery and Conquest of Mexico*. New York: Farrar, Straus and Giroux, 1972.

Di Peso, Charles C. "The Clay Figurines of Acámbaro, Guanajuato, Mexico" in *American Antiquity,* vol 18, *1953.*

Egan, Martha. *Milagros: Votive Offerings from the Americas*. Santa Fe: Museum of New Mexico Press, 1991.

Fuentes, Carlos. *The Diary of Frida Kahlo: An Intimate Self-Portrait. New York: Abrams Books, 2005.*

Gallenkamp, Charles. *Maya: The Riddle and Rediscovery of a Lost Civilization*. New York: Viking Penguin, 1985.

Gardner, Erle Stanley. *The Host with the Big Hat*. New York: William Morrow, 1969.

Gonzalez Avelar, Miguel. *Clipperton, Isla Mexicana.* San Diego: Fondo de Cultura Económica, 2004.

Grabman, Richard. "The Blond Who Came in From the Cold." *The Mex Files.* 1 January 2010.

Griffith, James S. *Folk Saints of the Borderlands: Victims, Bandits, and Healers.* Tucson: Rio Nuevo Publishers, 2003.

Guinn, James Miller. *A History of California: Extended History of its Southern Coast Counties.* Los Angeles Historic Record Company, 1907.

Hancock, Graham. *Fingerprints of the Gods.* New York: Three Rivers Press, 1996.

Hapgood, Charles H. *Mystery at Acámbaro: Did Dinosaurs Survive until Recently?* Chicago: Adventures Unlimited Press, 2015.

Herren, Ricardo. *Doña Marina, La Malinche.* Mexico City: Planeta, 1992.

Herrera, Hayden. *Frida: A Biography of Frida Kahlo.* New York: Harper Perennial, 2002.

Hu-DeHart, Evelyn. *YaquiResistance and Survival: The Struggle for Land and Autonomy, 1821-1910.* Madison: University of Wisconsin Press, 1984.

Hunter, C. Bruce. *A Guide to Ancient Maya Ruins.* Oklahoma City: University of Oklahoma Press, 1986.

Irwin, Constance. *Fair Gods and Stone Faces: Ancient Seafarers and the New World's Most Intriguing Riddle.* New York: St. Martin's Press, 1963.

Jenkins, John Major. *Maya Cosmogenesis 2012: The True Meaning of the Maya Calendar End-Date.* Rochester, VT: Bear & Company, 1998.

Kurillo, Max and Erline Tuttle. *The Old Missions of Baja and Alta California, 1697-1834.* New York: M&E Books, 2014.

Landsburg, Alan and Sally Landsburg. *The Outer Space Connection.* *New York:* Bantam Books, 1975.

León-Portilla, Miguel. *Time and Reality in the Thought of the Maya.* *Oklahoma City:* University of Oklahoma Press, 1990.

Lynn, Kimberly. *Between Court and Confessional: The Politics of Spanish Inquisitors. Cambridge: Cambridge University Press, 2013.*

Marten, James, ed. *Children in Colonial America.* New York: NYU Press, 2006.

"Mass Exorcism Performed at Mexican Church." BBC: 26 Nov. 2013

"Mexico Pilots Release UFO Film." *BBC News:* 17 May 2004.

Milbrath, Susan. *Star Gods of the Maya: Astronomy in Art, Folklore, and Calendars.* Austin: University of Texas Press, 1999.

Morley, Jefferson. *Our Man in Mexico: Winston Scott and the Hidden History of the CIA.* Kansas City: University Press of Kansas, 2008.

Museo de Panteón de Belén. On-site Brochure. 2014.

Newman, John. *Oswald and the CIA.* New York: Skyhorse Publishing, 2008.

Niemann, Greg. *Baja Legends.* San Diego: Sunbelt Publications, 2014.

Paredes, Américo, ed. *Folktales of Mexico.* Chicago: The University of Chicago Press, 1970.

Porter Weaver, Muriel. *The Aztecs, May and Their Predecessors.* New York: Academic Press, 1985.

Preston, Douglas. *Cities of Gold: A Journey across the American Southwest.* Albuquerque: University of New Mexico Press, 1999.

Putnam, Robert B. "Bowling Alone: America's Declining Social Capital," in *Journal of Democracy,* vol. 6, no. 1, pp. 65-78.

Radford, Benjamin. *Tracking the Chupacabra.* Albuquerque: University of New Mexico Press, 2011.

Riva Palacio, Vicente. *Memorias de un impostor: Don Guillén de Lampart, Rey de México.* Mexico City: Libreria de Porrúa, 2000.

Ronan, Gerard. *The Irish Zorro: The Extraordinary Adventures of William Lamport.* Dublin: Brandon Books, 2004.

Ronnin, Meier. "Frida Kahlo's Father Wasn't Jewish After All." *Jerusalem Post,* 20 April 2006.

Santo Toribio Romo: del sueño a la gloria. Dir. Moisés Cruz Jáuregui. Cuevas de Arena Films, 2012. Film.

Schele, Linda and David Freidel. *A Forest of Kings: The Untold Story of the Ancient Maya.* New York: William Morrow, 1990.

Skaggs, Jimmy M. *Clipperton: A History of the Island the World Forgot.* New York: Walker & Company, 1989.

Soulié, Maurice. *The Wolf Cub: The Great Adventure of Count Gaston de Raousset-Boulbon in California and Sonora, 1850-1854.* Indianapolis: The Bobbs-Merrill Company, 1927.

Steen-McIntyre, Virginia. "Suppressed Evidence for Ancient Man in Mexico." *Nexus,* August-September 1998.

Thomas, Hugh. *Conquest: Montezuma, Cortés, and the Fall of Old Mexico.* New York: Simon and Schuster, 1993.

Tompson, J. Eric S. *The Rise and Fall of Maya Civilization.* Oklahoma City: University of Oklahoma Press, 1973.

Torres, Noe and Ruben Uriarte. *The Coyame Incident: UFO Crash Near Presidio, Texas. CreateSpace: 2013.*

Vaillant, George C. *Aztecs of Mexico.* Garden City, NY: Doubleday, Doran & Company, 1941.

Villanueva, Alma Luz. *Weeping Woman: La Llorona and Other Stories.* Tempe: Bilingual Review Press, 1994.

Villanueva Medina, Salvador. *Estuve en Venus.* Bogotá: Instituto Cultural Quetzalcoatl de Antropología Psicoanalítica, 1973.

Von Däniken, Erich. *Chariots of the Gods? Unsolved Mysteries of the Past.* New York: Putnam, 1969.

Von Hagen, Victor W. *The World of the Maya.* New York: Mentor Books, 1960.

Von Wuthenau, Alexander. *Unexpected Faces in Ancient America.* New York: Crown Publishers, 1975

Wauchope, Robert, ed. *Handbook of Middle American Indians.* Austin: University of Texas Press, 1976.

Winters, Clyde. *Atlantis in Mexico.* Lulu.com: 2005.

Yturría, Santiago. "Exclusive: Mexican DOD Acknowledges UFOs in Mexico." Rense.com: 14 May 2004.

Zavaleta, Antonio Noé. *El Niño Fidencio and the Fidencistas: Folk Religion in the US-Mexican Borderland.* Authorhouse, 2016.

WEBSITES
Atraviesa lo desconocido
Campo de Cahuenga Historical Site
Catholic Forum
El Heraldo de Chihuahua
Inexplicata – The Journal of Hispanic UFOlogy
Santi e Beati
Tercer Milenio
Texas State University Guanajuato Mummy Project
Wikipedia
YouTube

Mexican War, 106, 115, 118, 120, 213

Mexican-Americans, 219, 230

Mexico City, 2, 3, 4, 15, 19, 20, 21, 24, 28, 29, 34, 38, 40, 42, 46, 55, 58, 59, 66, 73, 76, 92, 99, 101, 102, 105, 106, 107, 111, 114, 116, 117, 123, 124, 125, 129, 131, 149, 164, 166, 175, 177, 181, 186, 190, 192, 198, 200, 225, 228

Michoacán, 38

Mictecacehuatl, 33, 34

Mídanos. *See* Clipperton Island

milagros, 31, 32

Milky Way, 175

mission, 5, 21, 22, 23, 42, 48, 67, 71, 92, 115

Mixtecs, 133, 167, 221, 223

Modotti, Tina, 226

Moebius, Otto Guido, 101

Monterrey, 101, 102, 142, 143, 232

Montezuma, 6, 7, 8, 9, 10, 47, 85, 86, 87, 88, 166, 176, 177, 179, 180

Morrow, Dwight Whitney, 39

Mothman, 146

mummies, 212, 213, 214, 215, 216

Mussolini, Benito, 101

Na Chan (Kingdom of), 203

Nachito, 11, 14

nagual, 151

Nahua, 47, 50, 167

Nahuatl, 16, 24, 28, 47, 70, 84, 85, 86, 133, 138, 151, 161, 167, 181, 198

Nahui Ollin, 70, 71, 72

narcotraficantes, 98

Narváez, Pánfilo de, 1, 2

NASA, 63

National Geographic, 76

National Institute of Anthropology and History, 73, 176

Navarro, Cayetano, 106

Nayarit, 106

Nechiporenko, Oleg, 126

New Chronology (theory), 185

New Mexico, 4

New Orleans, 125, 128

New Spain, 48, 49, 91, 111, 112, 115, 135

New York City, 103, 224, 226

Niburu, 211

Nicolaus, Georg, 101

Niño Fidencio, 40, 41, 42, 43, 44, 45, 240

Nordics, 63

Nueva Galicia, 3

Nuevo Leon, 40, 41, 143, 145, 156, 180

Nuñez de la Vega, Francisco, 203

Oaxaca, 138, 151, 219, 221, 222

Ocotelulco, 46

Odin, 205, 206

ofrenda, 217

Ojuelos de Jalisco, 69, 70, 71, 72, 73

Olmecs, 138, 151, 159, 201

Oñate, 5

orbs, 58, 61, 74

Ordaz, Diego de, 134

Ordoñez y Aguilar, Ramón de, 204

Orozco y Berra, 151

Orozco, José Clemente, 103

OSS, 100

Oswald, Lee Harvey, 121, 122, 123, 124, 126, 127, 129, 130, 131

Otomi, 15, 16, 47, 167